T0083632

IBERIAN AND LATIN AMERICAN STUDIES

Killing Carmens

Killing Carmens

Women's Crime Fiction from Spain

SHELLEY GODSLAND

UNIVERSITY OF WALES PRESS
CARDIFF
2007

www.uwp.co.uk

British Library Cataloguing-in-Publication Data
A catalogue record for this book is available from the British Library.

ISBN 978–0–7083–2016–7

Typeset by Columns Design Ltd, Reading
Printed and bound in Great Britain by Antony Rowe Ltd, Chippenham, Wilts

Contents

Series Editors' Foreword

Over recent decades, the traditional 'languages and literatures' model in Spanish departments in universities in the United Kingdom has been superceded by a contextual, interdisciplinary and 'area studies' approach to the study of the culture, history, society and politics of the Hispanic and Lusophone worlds – categories which extend far beyond the confines of the Iberian Peninsula, not only to Latin America but also to Spanish-speaking and Lusophone Africa.

In response to these dynamic trends in research priorities and curriculum development, this series is designed to present both disciplinary and interdisciplinary research within the general field of Iberian and Latin American Studies, particularly studies which explore all aspects of **Cultural Production** (*inter alia* literature, film, music, dance, sport) in Spanish, Portuguese, Basque, Catalan, Galician and the indigenous languages of Latin America. The series also aims to publish research on the **History and Politics** of Hispanic and Lusophone worlds, both at the level of region and that of the nation-state, as well as on **Cultural Studies** which explore the shifting terrains of gender, sexual, racial and postcolonial identities in those same regions.

Acknowledgements

The Introduction and a significant part of Chapter 1 of this work were researched and written during a Visiting Research Fellowship to the School of Languages, Cultures and Linguistics at Monash University which I held between April and June 2005. I wish to express my profound thanks to Professor Brian Nelson, Head of School, and to Dr Margaret Florey, Chair of the Research Committee, for generously granting me the Fellowship. I was able to take up the award in Melbourne as my home institution, Manchester Metropolitan University, provided me with a grant of £400 to cover my invigilation and some administrative duties during that period. Thanks are due to the Department of Languages and the Manchester European Research Institute for contributing half each of that sum, and also for a grant of £401 to cover the cost of the services of a professional proof-reader to review the manuscript.

Chapters 2 and 3 of the book were researched and written while I was the Jubilee Research Fellow in the Department of Hispanic Studies at Royal Holloway, University of London. My very special thanks to Professor Abigail Lee Six for appointing me to that position, and for her unfailing personal and professional support both during my fellowship and since.

Particular thanks are due to a number of individuals who have supported and assisted me during the completion of this project. First, I wish to thank the novelists Maria-Antònia Oliver and Alicia Giménez-Bartlett for generously agreeing to attend conferences I organized in Prato (Florence), Porto, and London, and for sharing with delegates their fascinating and valuable insights into their craft. I also wish to offer very special thanks to my dear colleague Dr Anne M. White of Bradford University. During the early days of this project Dr White encouraged and supported me and we co-authored two papers on Spanish women's crime fiction. Her research expertise, extensive knowledge of the fields of crime fiction and Hispanic Studies, and her personal support (including several delicious lunches in Bradford) were vital to assisting me with this major project. Particular thanks are also due to my colleague Dr Stewart B. King of Monash University who, during his sabbatical in Spain in 2004, collected and sent to me every news item he could find on violence against women and the new legislation. During my Visiting Research Fellowship at Monash Dr King also assisted me by borrowing vast amounts of library material on my behalf, lending me his own books, and reading my entire manuscript. His support has been unfailing.

Thanks, too, to Professor Anny Brooksbank Jones of the University of Sheffield for her comments and information on post-feminism. These pointed me in the right direction when seeking further material. I also want to express my gratitude to Mrs Sheila Candeland, Humanities subject librarian at Manchester Metropolitan University Library, for locating and requesting books and articles that were often almost impossible to find. Many thanks, too, to all of the people who supported me throughout the research and writing of this project: good friends, colleagues from institutions across the globe, and especially my mother and multitudinous aunts and Professor W. I. Glet.

Some small parts of Chapter 1 first appeared in an article entitled 'From Feminism to Postfeminism in Spanish Women's Crime Fiction: The Case of Maria-Antònia Oliver and Alicia Giménez-Bartlett' which was published in *Letras Femeninas* in 2002. I am very grateful to *Letras Femeninas* and its current editor, Professor Carmen de Urioste, for the very kind permission to reproduce here some of the material from the original paper. Some work in Chapter 3 originally formed part of a chapter co-authored with Anne M. White which appears in *Investigating Identities: Questions of Identity in Contemporary International Crime Fiction* (Rodopi 2007), edited by Marieke Krajenbrink and Kate M. Quinn. I wish to express my thanks to Marieke and Kate, and also to Rodopi, for their generous permission to use parts of that chapter in this volume. Other parts of Chapter 3 also appear in a single-authored paper on Catalan women's crime fiction published in number XVIII of *Antípodas* (2007). I am grateful to Professor Roy Boland, the journal's Editor, for kind permission to reproduce some small sections of that article.

Shelley Godsland
2007

Introduction

The crime novel has been one of the key genres used by writers in
Spain to articulate and analyse national socio-political concerns
during the past thirty years, and many texts of this sort have
achieved best-seller status. The female contribution to this type of
literature has been extensive, particularly in the last decade and a
half. But while fiction by male authors has warranted innumerable studies both within and outside the academe, women's
narratives have largely been overlooked in both national and
international studies of the Spanish *novela negra* (the post-
dictatorship hard-boiled novel) and its more recent derivatives – a
situation which replicates an acknowledged and generalized
absence of serious scholarly scrutiny of Spanish women's writing
across the board until very recently.[1]

For example, early critical volumes such as Juan Paredes
Núñez's edited collection *La novela policiaca española* [The Spanish
Crime Novel] (1989) make no mention of female authors, while
monographic works like Salvador Vázquez de Parga's *La novela
policiaca en España* [The Crime Novel in Spain] (1993) and the
excellent *El cadáver en la cocina* [The Body in the Kitchen] (1997)
by Joan Ramon Resina refer only tangentially to a couple of
women writers. Similarly, *Monographic Review/Revista Monográfica*
for 1987, a special number on 'the thriller' in Spain, contains only
one essay on a woman – the Galician Marina Mayoral (Zatlin
1987), and Juan Tébar's 1985 review article in *Ínsula* lists a mere
three female novelists in an inventory of 68. More recently,
women who publish in the genre have been afforded a little more
critical attention. In *Ortodoxia y heterodoxia de la novela policíaca
hispana* [Orthodoxy and Heterodoxy in the Hispanic Crime
Novel] (2002) the Texas-based scholar Genaro Pérez included
one chapter which analysed female practitioners of detective
fiction and another on the Chicana novelist Lucha Corpi, while
papers devoted to specific authors are also becoming more

numerous in journals and edited collections. It still remains the case, however, that any sustained critical engagement with women's crime writing from Spain is a result of publications devoted specifically to female authors, such as the special number of *Letras Femeninas* I edited in 2002, or the more recent volume I co-edited with Jacky Collins (Collins and Godsland 2005).

The increased academic interest afforded women's crime fiction in Castilian, Catalan, Galician and, much more recently, Basque,[2] may be a product of the greater visibility of women authors in Spain (a point to which I want to return later), and also of the endeavours of Anglophone feminist critics working in British and North American universities in particular whose scholarly project often focuses specifically on female writers. The generalized critical lacunae surrounding their work, however, should not be read as symptomatic of any long-term absence of their engagement with the genre, for women have been penning crime narratives for a century. Spain's *grande dame* of late nineteenth- and early twentieth-century letters, Emilia Pardo Bazán, published a novella entitled *La gota de sangre* [The Drop of Blood] in 1911, as well as a considerable number of short stories in the style of the Sherlock Holmes' ratiocinative mysteries which, nonetheless, were also eminently Naturalist in their concerns, thus reflecting the author's positioning within a particular literary generation in Spain.[3] As I shall discuss in Chapter 2 of this work, in the 1930s Mercè Rodoreda, the most acclaimed twentieth-century Catalan novelist, wrote a whodunit which parodied the 'cosy' enigma style popularized by Agatha Christie and her British contemporaries. Even during, and immediately after, the brutally tumultuous years of the Spanish Civil War (1936–39) women were producing crime fiction. Josefina de la Torre, writing under the pseudonym Laura de Cominges, published *El enigma de los ojos grises* [The Mystery of the Grey Eyes] in 1938, and Mercedes Ballesteros Gaibrois, using the pen-name Rocq Morris, published *City Hotel* (1938) and *París–Niza* [Paris–Nice] (1939), all with the printing press of the *Diario de Las Palmas* [Las Palmas Daily News] in the Canary Islands in a series called *La novela ideal* [The Ideal Novel].

During the 1950s, and following the dark years of starvation and horror that marked the previous decade, the crime genre came to enjoy great popularity among readers in Spain. Penned by a significant number of writers – many of whom used anglicized versions of their own name or other pseudonyms – works tended to emulate wholesale the British 'country house' template and were usually set in England and featured stereotypes drawn (supposedly) from British aristocratic or upper middle-class society. While some were of dismal literary quality, many others were finely crafted narratives by eminent names. In keeping with the tendencies noted above, critical overviews of the detective fiction of this period – all of which are by Spanish scholars working in their country of origin – tend to ignore completely women's contribution to sustaining a genre that sold like proverbial hot cakes (Vázquez de Parga 2000*a* and 2000*b*), even if in very poor quality paperback format, printed on rough paper encased in luridly illustrated, shiny paper covers.

Although they often concealed their identity behind a male pen-name, during this first boom of the crime novel in Spain female authors were actively writing and publishing, with some prolific women novelists putting out vast quantities of work. Their numbers were never as great as those working with the *novela rosa*, Spain's particular brand of saccharine sweet Catholic romance novel, but much of their work warrants being rescued from the (gendered) oblivion into which it has undeservedly fallen. One writer of particular note from this period, but who has merited no critical attention beyond a brief entry in the *Antología biográfica de cuentistas españolas* [Biographical Anthology of Female Spanish Short Story Writers] (1954) which she herself edited, is Isabel Calvo de Aguilar. In the 1950s she published a number of fascinating crime novels including *Doce sarcófagos de oro* [Twelve Golden Sarcophagi] (1951), *El misterio del palacio chino* [The Mystery of the Chinese Palace] (1951), *La isla de los siete pecados* [The Island of the Seven Sins] (1952), and *La danzarina inmóvil* [The Immobile Dancer] (1954). These fictions can be read as fundamentally feminist texts that articulate the concerns of their author about the straitjacketing of women, their intellects, and aspirations, under the Franco regime. It is therefore perhaps unsurprising that Calvo de Aguilar should have been the organizer of the *Primer Congreso de Cultura Femenina* [First Conference on Women's Culture] that took place in Madrid in 1953, bringing together women from all over the Spanish-speaking world, and that she should have promoted initiatives such as the aforementioned biographical anthology of women writers. Despite the quality of her work and her apparent public profile, scholars both inside and outside Spain have ignored her *œuvre*, as noted above, while her contemporary, Francisco García Pavón, originator of a series featuring Plinio, a rural Civil Guard, has been the subject of exhaustive articles, theses, and other commentary. The gender bias of critical endeavour, then, is clearly apparent, and the result of this strategy has been to erase from the annals of Spain's literary history the names of the many women who worked in the crime genre during – and even before – the dictatorship.

Throughout the latter years of the Franco regime, female authors continued to publish crime fictions, although at the time the genre was lacking both the quantity of output that had characterized it during the 1950s and early 1960s and the quality 'literary' commitment to renovating it that would see the emergence of the *novela negra* following the death of the dictator and as a response to democratization. As I discuss in Chapter 1, 1979 saw the appearance of Spain's first female-authored woman sleuth – in Lourdes Ortiz's *Picadura mortal* [Deadly Sting] – an innovation within Spanish letters that has since been replicated in any number of texts written in both Castilian and Catalan. Indeed, from the 1980s large numbers of women began to publish novels and short stories within the genre. In Catalonia the name of Núria Mínguez merits mention. During a career spanning more than three and a half decades, Mínguez has published a considerable corpus of gentle, enigma-style novels written in her native Catalan, earning her the soubriquet of the region's Agatha Christie according to the jacket blurb of many of her books. Other Catalan women writing this type of literature include Margarida Aritzeta and Assumpta Margenat – also authors of numerous texts, a selection of which are analysed in this study – and Teresa Pàmies, whose many fictional and autobiographical texts contain elements of crime sub-genres (Pérez 1998). Olga Xirinacs, Isabel-Clara Simó, Anna Grau, and Maria-Antònia Oliver have also contributed to the evolution of this type of writing in Catalan. In Galicia, Marina Mayoral has published four novels based around the investigation of a crime or featuring a detective: *Cándida, otra vez* [Cándida, Again] (1979), *Al otro lado* [On the Other Side] (1980), *La única libertad* [The Only Freedom] (1982), and *Contra muerte y amor* [In the Face of Death and Love] (1985). Crime fiction by women publishing in Castilian has also witnessed an increase since the 1980s, and female authors now engage with a very wide

variety of sub-genres ranging from children's and juvenile literature, to the postmodern experimental detective text, by way of the
police procedural, the psychological crime novel that aims to
uncover the reasons for a murder, drama, and short stories that
replicate many of the themes of earlier Spanish literary realism.
More recently, women crime novelists in Spain have also jumped
on the bandwagon of the religious mystery thriller made interna-
tionally popular by Dan Brown's *The Da Vinci Code* (2003). Julia
Navarro has to date sold almost half a million copies of her first
novel, *La hermandad de la Sábana Santa* [The Brotherhood of the
Holy Shroud] (2004), and her *La Biblia de barro* [The Bible of
Clay] appeared in 2005 (Piña 62). Writing in a slightly different
sub-genre Núria Masot has been successful with *La sombra del
templario* [The Shadow of the Templar] (2004), *El laberinto de la
serpiente* [The Serpent's Labyrinth] (2005), and *La llave de oro*
[The Golden Key] (2006), a series of medieval mysteries featuring
Guillem de Montclar which appeared in both the Catalan and
Castilian versions almost simultaneously.

This 'boom' in the number of crime narratives by Spanish
women is in part due to a generalized increase in the publication
of female literature within the country and an expanding female
readership. Observers note, however, that despite media reports
of women writers taking the publishing world by storm, life for
Spain's 'ladies of letters', whatever their chosen genre, is certainly
not the walk through the roses that popular or media perception
would have it to be (Freixas 38; Henseler 10). Laura Freixas
points out that a mere 20 percent of published authors in Spain
are women (34: 192–3), and that, with reference to her country,
'La idea de que la escritura se está feminizando es, cifras en
mano, pura y simplemente falsa' [The idea that women are taking
over the literary world is quite simply false if we bear in mind the
statistics] (192). Akiko Tsuchiya says, furthermore, that Spanish
women writers must struggle to achieve visibility for themselves
and their work, and labour hard to overcome the commodifica-
tion of their fictions (239–40). For a female author, achieving
media noticeability can be a double-edged sword, for as Christine
Henseler observes, in Spain it is alleged that women sell more
books because of their 'celebrity status', rather than as a result of
the literary quality of their work (3). Added to this is the often
negative critical bias against female writers noted by Henseler
(11) and also highlighted in this Introduction. Combining both

concepts, then, Freixas asserts that in her country there prevails the notion that 'las mujeres triunfan en lo comercial y mediático, y fracasan en la calidad y el prestigio' [women writers succeed as far as sales and the media go, but fail when it comes to literary quality and prestige] (41). And what is more, despite the fact that in Spain more women than men read fiction (Freixas 39 and 193; Tsuchiya 239), Henseler points out that editors and critics in fact significantly overstate the power of female readers (10), while Freixas says that although women read more, they do not necessarily read – and therefore buy – books by or about women (193–4).

Despite these very real obstacles to publishing, to achieving critical appreciation, and to reaching a readership, the generalized increase in the number of women writing and getting into print in Spain has undoubtedly functioned to promote their genre literature, too. It should also be remembered that the period since the end of the dictatorship has been *the* epoch of the Spanish crime narrative. The death of Franco, the move towards democracy, and the inevitable *desencanto* [disillusionment] experienced nation-wide as a result of the failures of the democratic system on which so many Spaniards had pinned so many hopes, functioned to give impetus to a genre which had hitherto consciously avoided the North American hard-boiled model as the type of realism on which it was founded would not have been well received by the regime's censors. The literary form spawned during this period and by its attendant political changes was the *novela negra*, a direct translation from the French *roman noir*, a sub-genre very like its US precursors in the hard-boiled mode in that it featured a lone private eye very much at odds with the social environment within which he operated, investigating crimes that uncovered high-level corruption and law-breaking as well as other ills that plagued society.[4] Other types of crime narrative also flourished, including the parodic, postmodern texts of authors such as Antonio Muñoz Molina and Eduardo Mendoza, while some authors revised the norms of the earlier enigma-style novel. The police procedural – a sub-genre hitherto largely absent from Spain – also came in from the cold, not least because, with the advent of democracy, the police's reputation as the Franco regime's bully boys began to wane.

Given the origins of the *novela negra*, as well as of other sub-genres, within Spain's Transition to democracy and the *desencanto*, crime fiction became the nation's pre-eminent literary vehicle for the articulation of wider political concerns. Issues that generated particular unease and disquiet were those pertaining to government and institutional corruption and the identification of the people of Spain as victims of these 'fat cats'. Key, too, were the failure of the democratic process to deliver on its promises, and the enforced amnesia about the questionable past of any number of leading players on the Spanish political stage, many of whom had links to repression, torture, or atrocities perpetrated during the Civil War and the Franco period. In view of this politicization of the genre following the many years of dictatorship (during which it was often studiously de-politicized by many writers – although there were important exceptions, one of which is considered in Chapter 3 of this work), it is equally unsurprising that considerable numbers of female writers in Spain should have chosen to use the form to interrogate *gendered* politics.

Indeed, Anglophone critical endeavour has identified the crime novel as a principal forum for the literary exposition of a feminist and female-centred problematics – in spite of the assertions of some observers who posit crime or detective fiction as inimical to the feminist project, as discussed in Chapter 1. Kathlyn Ann Fritz and Natalie Kaufman Hevener (107) and Barbara Lawrence (38) all argue, for example, that it is the genre that facilitates *par excellence* the portrayal of the rational, thinking female (who often focuses on woman-centred crimes and thus solves dilemmas relating directly to her sex). Carolyn Heilbrun celebrates the detective text's capacity for making 'androgyny' possible – which she reads as 'the opposite of sexual stereotyping' in the most positive way – and which reveals women's capacity for coping with whatever is thrown at them (1–2). The feminist critic Maggie Humm remarks that when written and protagonised by women, this type of literature shows how they can 'have power' (237), while Lyn Pykett explores the ways it permits this when the usual dichotomy of male = hunter / female = hunted is inverted (65), perhaps in the figure of the female sleuth or criminal. In more general terms, scholars working with narratives in English have indicated the limitless possibilities for a feminist re-evaluation, through the medium of the crime novel, of topics such as violence against women, 'sisterhood', women's siting in the wider socio-political hierarchy, female occupation of the urban space, or the family (see e.g. Bird and Walker 1993; Cole 2004; Craig and Cadogan 1981; Klein 1995b; Mizejewski 2004; Munt 1994; Reddy 1988; Walton and Jones 1999). Such concerns are central, too, to the crime fictions of women writing in contemporary Spain in one of the nation's four major languages, and I would assert that this type of literature is in fact a primary one for the articulation of such matters.

This book, then, will explore the ways in which Spanish female authors deploy the genre to examine issues central to their existence as women in contemporary Spain. It is my contention that female novelists and short story writers of crime fiction raise many of the gendered concerns broached by their counterparts who publish in English, but I would also maintain that they in fact engage in a far more complex assessment of a very significant number of themes than do even the most highly regarded Anglophone writers publishing within the genre. Furthermore, given the aforementioned absence of critical responses to this type of writing by women in Spain, I want to redress the existing imbalance and, in the three chapters that follow, show that women have been major contributors to what has arguably been an extremely popular genre among Spanish readers for half a century at least, and that they have often innovatively reformulated the paradigms for this sort of literature.

In the first chapter I analyse the novels and short stories of Maria-Antònia Oliver and Alicia Giménez-Bartlett, two of Spain's most critically acclaimed crime writers, both of whom feature a female investigator who works with a male subordinate. My basic premise is that Oliver's works – written between the mid-1980s and the mid-1990s – can be read as overtly feminist narratives which textualize an often somewhat didactic second wave equality feminism. On the other hand, Giménez-Bartlett's crime fictions (published from the mid-1990s on) articulate a far more ambiguous view of women's status in contemporary Spain, and many of the notions to which her detective subscribes can be read as reflecting the current post-feminist reality which, I argue, is underpinned by theories expounded by Spanish difference 'feminists' whose work reflects that of the Italian promulgators of this line of thought.

I offer a reading of a number of themes recurrent in the works of both writers and support my analysis of them as, respectively, a producer of a feminist ideology and an analyst of the contemporary post-feminist economy, with a parallel evaluation of a body of theoretical material in both Spanish and English and with contrastive reference to fictions in English. Secondary material used as a framework for the study of Oliver's fiction is drawn largely from literary criticism focusing on feminist crime fiction in English, and I also refer to Spanish feminist theory. The examination of Giménez-Bartlett's novels and stories is founded theoretically in the work of an extensive body of Anglophone observers of the post-feminist environment, and of Spanish scholars who have developed a national corpus of difference 'feminist' theory. I assess the possibilities for presenting differing woman-centred ideologies inherent in the figure of the lone private eye (Oliver) or the police inspector (Giménez-Bartlett), and study how generic revisions are used by each author to flag up their personal vision of issues such as women's socialization, motherhood, sexual liberation, and female victimhood.

Chapter 2 focuses specifically on the gendering of victimization and of the criminal. The tendency towards increased violence against women in Spain and other national arenas is overviewed through a reading of recent criminological and sociological texts written in Spanish and English, and novelists' strategies for portraying and discussing the problem are then analysed. I also consider how the writers studied take issue with the portrayal of the male victimizer of women as somehow pathological or socially marginalized. Through a combined reading of fiction and recent Spanish criminological material I show how female crime writers revise the literary and social norm of portraying as a social aberration male murderers, rapists, and other criminals who target women. Within the chapter I also use key critical works on crime narrative to analyse how and why Spanish women writers reformulate traditional notions of the female criminal and the *femme fatale* to show how they justify female law-breaking as a response to gendered victimization or social marginalization, and thus provide their largely female readership with fictions of empowerment and agency that in many cases draw heavily on late twentieth- and early twenty-first-century 'girl power'. It is my contention that they achieve this end through the positive characterization of criminal female protagonists, an assertion supported with reference to recent work by Spanish criminologists.

The third and final chapter focuses on texts written in Catalan. Catalonia was the first area of Spain to witness writerly interest in detective fiction and the genre has long been used to articulate and discuss the issues of nationalism and political autonomy as they pertain to the region. Consideration is given to how women who write in Catalan deploy the crime novel to draw a parallel between the subjugation of their region's women and the historical oppression of Catalonia as a political and cultural entity separate from the Spanish nation. I analyse woman-authored Catalan fiction from the 1930s that parodies the British 'enigma' style detective story in order to comment on Catalonia's role within Europe, and I study novels from the 1950s which use the US hard-boiled model to portray the violence to which Catalan culture was subjected under the Franco regime.[5] With reference to more recent fiction published since the 1980s, I discuss how women writers reformulate the thriller to foreground female characters who challenge the validity of the traditional male hero. This part of the book also reflects on how the chosen authors use genre literature to articulate questions of women's access to citizenship and to national politics. I suggest that many figures such as the female criminal, female sleuth, and female thriller heroine, are in fact portrayed as the depositories of a national Catalan culture, and that the crime and detective genres provide unique opportunities for this characterization which also draws in part on nineteenth-century female symbolism in Catalonia.

In each part of this work, the novels and stories selected for analysis have been chosen for a number of reasons. The first chapter focuses on the two most acclaimed women writers of detective fiction in contemporary Spain. The volume of their published output, as well as the scope of the theorization of women's social siting that underpins them, then, was essential when identifying a coherent, extensive body of fictional material to conduct a sustained reading in conjunction with Spanish (and other) feminist theories. Narratives identified for study in Chapter 2 all share the common theme of violence against women or the protagonization of a female criminal, and those analysed are indicative works by key female contributors to the genre who produce material in both Castilian and Catalan. Most of the writers studied have either been acknowledged critically for their non-genre literature or are crime novelists whose works have sold well in Spain, although I also survey texts by some lesser-known names as they furnish equally important insights into the issues to hand. Finally, fictions studied in the last chapter of this work were all published in Catalan, and were selected because they foreground the issues of nation, language, and citizenship that seem so central to the concerns of many Catalan writers. Moreover, most of them are structured around the interrogation of the parallelism between gendered aggression and crimes against the nation that constitutes the two-pronged engagement with violence essayed by the chosen authors.

On a final note I want to briefly clarify the genre terminology deployed in this study. Thus far – and, indeed, throughout this book – I use the terms 'crime genre', 'crime narrative', or 'crime novel' as well as 'detective novel' or 'detective genre' to describe the fictions under analysis. According to Alison Young a crime fiction is one that emphasizes the characterization or psychology of a criminal whose identity is usually known to the reader from the very beginning, and within which textual suspense is generated as a result of the uncertain future awaiting the lawbreaker (82–3). The detective tale, as Todorov identified in his now classic essay 'The Typology of Detective Fiction', must perforce protagonize an investigator. It 'contains not one but two stories: the story of the crime and the story of the investigation' (44). '[T]he first – the story of the crime – tells "what really happened", whereas the second – the story of the investigation – explains "how the reader (or the narrator) has come to know about it"' (45). This book, then, is not simply about detective texts, although many of the fictions analysed within it do indeed portray a sleuth of one sort or another. Rather, as the title suggests, it is about fictions by Spanish women which feature a crime, a crime that is always an essential, integral, and central part of the text, a crime around which the entire narrative is structured. And the crimes that Spanish women are writing about are not only those that women investigate, but also those that women perpetrate, and of which women are victims, thus echoing the multiple gendered relationship to crime inherent in the figure of Carmen, the 'archetypal' Spanish female.

Female Spanish authors of crime fictions also write within many different and clearly identifiable sub-genres. These include the 'cosy' or 'country house' type of mystery popularized in the UK by the likes of Agatha Christie and Margery Allingham,

particularly in the years prior to World War II; the police procedural, perhaps the best-known exponent of which is Ed McBain in
the USA; the spy thriller or espionage novel in the vein of John Le
Carré's Smiley tales or Ian Fleming's rather more excitingly
popular Bond series; the *noir* thriller, which first appeared in the
USA in the 1930s; and a number of other narrative forms that use
elements from one or more of the crime sub-genres. Where
necessary within this study, I outline very briefly some of the
essential characteristics of the particular sub-genre(s) within
which the authors studied are working. What I have avoided,
however, are lengthy – and tedious – descriptions of each sub-
genre as most readers will have a clear notion of what these entail
in terms of narrative, characterization, and ideology, and those
who do not can access the myriad studies, encyclopaedias, and
'companions' that focus on crime and detective literature.

Within this study, all quotes originally in Spanish or Catalan are
accompanied by a translation into English to ensure that students
and scholars with no knowledge of these languages can access all
the material. Where published translations of works of fiction exist
these have been cited alongside the original, and the title of the
source in English noted. Otherwise, all translations are my own,
and, in the case of novels and short stories in particular, I have
aimed to convey the tone and vocabulary of the crime narrative, as
well as retaining as much detail as possible from the source text.

NOTES

1   This absence of serious scholarly appreciation of Spain's female
    writers of fiction has been noted by any number of concerned critics
    (see, for example, Brown 1991; Davies 1994; López 1995; Nichols
    1995; Pérez 1988).
2   I am aware of only one Basque woman who writes detective fiction
    and she is in fact French. Between 1994 and 2000 Itxaro Borda
    published a series of novels and short stories featuring a Basque
    lesbian detective called Amaia Ezpeldoi.
3   For a complete anthology of Pardo Bazán's crime narratives accom-
    panied by a critical commentary, see her *Cuentos policiacos* [Police
    Tales] (2001).
4   For a thorough overview of this topic and of the wider socio-political
    engagement of the *novela negra*, see Colmeiro, ch. 6.
5   It should be noted, however, that the number of such fictions was
    never extensive.

Chapter 1

From Feminism to Post-Feminism: The Strange Case of the Female Detective

Introduction

The fictional female sleuth in Spain is a product of the same process of democratization of the nation as Spanish feminism, and it is therefore unsurprising that, as with other forms of women's writing, the detective novel should demonstrate an engagement with, and awareness and articulation of, that particular woman-centred ideology. In this chapter I want to analyse women's crime fiction from Spain that protagonizes a female investigator, focusing specifically on two authors: the Majorcan Maria-Antònia Oliver who writes in Catalan, and Alicia Giménez-Bartlett, originally from Almansa, who lives in Barcelona and publishes in Castilian. I have selected Oliver and Giménez-Bartlett as the focus of this section of my study in part because they are the two best known and most prolific Spanish female novelists to have produced a series of detective texts featuring the same sleuth,[1] a strategy that permits the sustained articulation of a coherent gendered line of thought, but also because their work has already excited some scholarly enquiry which furnishes a preliminary critical springboard from which to operate and to which to respond. It is my contention that both Oliver and Giménez-Bartlett consciously deploy the woman sleuth to propound their particular – and very different – perspectives on the significance to women in Spain of schools of feminist thought, and to comment on the positioning of their countrywomen within contemporary Spanish society. In this section, then, I propose to outline the development of the essential tenets of Spanish feminism from the later years of the dictatorship onwards in order to situate theoretically the general thrust of the works to be studied. I would note, however, that in each of the following sections of this chapter devoted to the selected writers, when focusing on specific issues as essayed in their fiction I will substantially develop the notions outlined here.

Juana María Gil Ruiz observes that feminism emerged in Spain 'con un retraso de décadas' [with a delay of decades] (149) in comparison to other feminist movements in the West,[2] and also notes that in the absence of a discursive mode of its own, bound itself up with other political groupings such as established (but illegal) left-wing parties (149–50). However, in her study of the role of women during the dictatorship, Pilar Folguera insists that by the mid-1960s women were politically engaged in pro-democracy movements within which they began to verbalize a distinct and specifically gendered discourse of a clearly proto-feminist type (1997: 547).[3] Similarly, Anny Brooksbank Jones has signalled the 'dual activism' (i.e. feminist and pro-democratic change) that characterized early feminism across the country (7), thus confirming the existence of woman-centred groups and ideologies before the end of the Franco regime. A cohesive set of feminist demands therefore clearly begins to be heard in Spain at the same time as the position of women underwent rapid and monumental change within what had hitherto been a society structured around strongly traditional gendered roles and expectations. In Geraldine Scanlon's opinion, however, this shift was due more to the exigencies of the Spanish economy (which needed women to participate in the paid workforce) than to any incipient women's liberation movement (342).

The demands of Spanish feminists on behalf of the nation's women were multiple, and were in part a reflection of claims articulated by other Western (predominantly Anglophone) feminisms, although some aspects of their ideology stemmed from the particular political circumstances that had prevailed in Spain for several decades. The battle for democracy was initially a key concern as it underpinned the notion of a return to individual civil liberties. Spanish feminists also denounced laws that discriminated against women, calling for urgent legal change, and also proposed the construction and dissemination of a positive image of the female in an attempt to foment an altered social perception of women. Full parity was also sought, not least in the workplace, with women fighting for equal pay for performing the same jobs as men. Other key areas of activity included campaigning for the legalization of contraception, abortion, and divorce, while an end to the entrenched discrimination against prostitutes and lesbians was also demanded. Feminists also exerted pressure on legislators to afford illegitimate children legal recognition, to decriminalize adultery, to pardon female political prisoners incarcerated during the dictatorship, and to provide free childcare for working mothers. Vociferous calls were also heard for the abolition of what was known as the law of *patria potestad* [supreme legal authority of the husband or father over the female] which institutionalized and legalized the marginalization of women both in the home and outside it (see, inter alia, Brooksbank Jones 9–10; Larumbe 2004: 79; Levine 60–1).

It is important to point out, however, that these demands were not articulated by one single group that was a feminist voice for all women in Spain. Although multiple feminist organisations did exist, a vast number of other groupings of women operated alongside them, often working towards raising awareness of their own specific agenda which might be founded on one or more – or none – of the issues outlined above.[4] Given this diversity of activisms it is unsurprising that Spanish feminism should never constitute a single, coherent school of thought. Indeed, observers have noted that quite the opposite was the case, and that feminist ideologies within the country have been – and still are – significantly divergent in their foundational principles (see, e.g. Amorós 1986; Folguera 1988: 119; Gil Ruiz 150). Scholars generally concur that the *Jornadas Feministas* [Feminist Conference] that took place in Granada in 1979 marked the parting of the ways for what had already become widely differing lines of feminist debate (Garrido 569; de Grado 28–9). The primary conceptual difference existed between the equality feminists on the one hand, who worked towards ensuring the kinds of gains for women in the legal, professional, sexual, and social ambits already noted, and the difference 'feminists', on the other hand, who based their philosophy on notions of 'difference' as theorized by French scholars such as Irigaray: it denied the possibility or validity of any sort of equality with men, positing, instead, the need for women to establish alternative networks to the prevailing patriarchal political ones.[5] In Spain, this difference 'feminism' also has clear origins in the philosophies propounded by the Italian difference 'feminists', and indeed, many scholars working in this particular area acknowledge a profound debt primarily to their Italian precursors, rather than to French philosophers and theorists of this sort. As I discuss in the third section of this chapter, difference 'feminism' was expounded and elaborated by Spanish thinkers from the 1980s onwards, and they often posited notions that overlapped with the theorization of the post-feminist environment in which such women were working.[6]

It was in the context of this multi-faceted debate and divergence of opinion and thought that the female detective appeared for the first time in a text by a Spanish woman author. In 1979, Lourdes Ortiz, hitherto a major contributor to a female-centred non-genre literature in Spain, published her first detective novel, *Picadura mortal* [Deadly Sting]. Protagonized by Bárbara Arenas, an attractive, sexy PI, it investigates the disappearance in the Canary Islands of a wealthy industrialist among whose family members Bárbara must conduct her enquiries. Significantly, the tale elicited widely divergent critical responses. On the one hand Patricia Hart (1987) opined – quite correctly – that Bárbara Arenas was a clothes-obsessed dimwit, and Robert C. Spires claims that the detective is simply a negative copy of the male hard-boiled sleuth (204). A considerable group of other critics, however, have signalled what they perceive to be the positive character traits inherent in Ortiz's character which permit her to function as a means of articulating important notions about gender issues in Spain and even the nation's history (see McGovern 1993; Talbot 1994), while more recently Alison Maginn (2002) and Alicia Giralt (ch. II) have argued very coherently for the case of Bárbara Arenas as an eminently contradictory character who, because of her ambiguities, is well placed to comment ironically or parodically on the status of women in the Spain she inhabits.

The two detectives analysed in this chapter – Maria-Antònia Oliver's Lònia Guiu and Alicia Giménez-Bartlett's Petra Delicado – can also both be considered ambiguous personalities, not least, as I argue in the next two sections, because they occupy the role of detective, a function which, for some critics, is in itself inherently skewed towards the masculine. Guiu and Delicado also demonstrate responses to violence or gender, for example, that are often ambiguous and sometimes inconsistent. Ideological difficulties of this sort are not the sole preserve of the Spanish woman-authored detective novel featuring a female sleuth, however, for in the Anglophone context very many critics have observed similar narrative conflicts. A major concern for many feminist scholars is the apparent difficulty of coherently or credibly textualizing the female investigator because she might be a replica of the male hard-boiled 'dick' – but evidently without the dick (Walton and Jones 99; Cole 137). Indeed, Rosalind Coward and Linda Semple say of the genre, 'it is hard to imagine a form less susceptible to a feminist interpretation' (46), a view with which Anne Cranny-Francis concurs, alleging that the female detective is predicated on an ideology 'inimical' to that of any feminist author (1990: 161). Other problematical issues that the woman novelist must negotiate within her crime text are the essential belief in a return to bourgeois (patriarchal) order with the resolution of a case (Cranny-Francis 1990: 172); the assumption that criminal acts are perpetrated by the individual, rather than being a product of the wider (patriarchal) society (Godard 50); and the questioning of discourses of legitimacy/illegitimacy and legality/illegality (Cranny-Francis 1990: 172; Godard 56). As I shall discuss in the next two sections of this chapter, many of these notions are central to the female-centred detective narratives of Oliver and Giménez-Bartlett, as are more inherently 'female' themes such as violence against women, the siting of the female within political hierarchies, female links to authority and power, the ownership of the female body, and the rights and freedoms of women in the Spain in which their texts were written.

The Feminist Private Eye: Maria-Antònia Oliver's Lònia Guiu

The Majorcan author, Maria-Antònia Oliver, had published an extensive corpus of non-genre fiction before penning her first detective novel, *Estudi en lila* (1985) [*Study in Lilac* (1987)]. This early full-length foray into the genre was followed just two years later by *Antípodes* (1987) [*Antipodes* (1989)],[7] but readers had to

wait some seven years for the next and – to date – last novel in the
series: *El sol que fa l'ànec* (1994) [*Blue Roses for a Dead . . . Lady?*
(1998)].[8] Written in Catalan, the texts were made available in
Castilian translation, and then in English thanks to the endeavours of the North American academic Kathleen McNerncy,[9] and
are protagonized by Lònia Guiu, whom Nancy Vosburg has characterized as 'A hard-hitting, hard-talking, and bullheaded crime
buster' (57). Lònia, a feisty, fearless, feminist PI, also collects
lipsticks – demonstrating a marked preference for those in exotic
containers – and is aided in her sleuthing exploits by Quim, her
gay sidekick. That the detective agency is Lònia's property, and
that, despite their friendship Quim is very much under her
orders, is made apparent from very early on in the first novel in
the series: 'jo era qui tenia el carnet, jo era qui havia posat el
despatx, jo era qui pagava la llicència fiscal; a ell li deia soci
perquè em feia gràcia, però en realitat era un llogat. Per tant, jo
era qui triava la feina i qui la distribuïa' (*Estudi en lila* 16) ['it was
me who had the license, the office, and who paid the yearly fees; I
called him a partner because I wanted to, but in reality he was
hired help. So I was the one who chose which job to do, and
distributed the others' (*Study in Lilac* 11)]. In this very preliminary manner, then, Oliver's sleuth makes it clear that it is she who
'wears the trousers' in this particular partnership, thus flagging
up the way she upsets the more usual hard-boiled paradigm of the
male investigator who works with a male side-kick or sometimes
with a female assistant. With this device Oliver draws readerly
attention to the way Lònia inverts traditional gendered roles
within patriarchal society, a strategy that also highlights her
fundamental feminist beliefs founded in contesting gendered
hierarchies skewed against women.

Lònia Guiu's feminism is made very apparent within the texts
she protagonizes, and Oliver uses the first-person narrative as an
obvious textual ploy that permits her character to articulate a set
of feminist convictions.[10] The detective's feminist beliefs exactly
replicate those of her author,[11] and – perhaps like the feminist
movement in Spain at the time the first two novels were written –
are in a process of rapid evolution, developing as she has
increased contact with other women who are more politically
aware (usually women from Barcelona, the 'centre' to Lònia's
'peripheral' place of origin in rural Majorca).[12] Her discourse,
like her actions, aims primarily to raise awareness of the relentless

discrimination and victimization of women in Spain and elsewhere, and to proffer strategies for protecting other females, and
Quim becomes used to what he calls Lònia's 'perorates feministes'
(*El sol que fa l'ànec* (67)) ['feminist disquisitions' (*Blue Roses for a
Dead . . . Lady?* 34)]. One particular discourse that is repeated in the
two later novels in the series is that questioning alleged female
freedom of choice, and the detective can only conclude that
women's lives are a slavery of one sort or another whatever they do,
whether they be wives, prostitutes, or unmarried hotel employees
like the girls she is interviewing:

> Creus que hi ha cap puta que ho sigui per gust?, m'havia dit na
> Lida. Bé, el que és jo, abans m'estimaria més llogar el cony com les
> putes que no les mans com aquestes noies. En definitiva, perquè el
> cony ha de ser més sagrat que qualsevol altra part del cos? Si una
> dona volia llogar el seu cos a un home per boixar, no hi tenia el
> mateix dret que si el volia llogar per escriure-li les cartes i els
> informes a màquina? O per rentar-li els plats i els calçotets i, en
> aquest cas, ni tan sols cobrar? El mal era que sempre fossin les
> dones que haguessin de llogar qualque cosa, la cotorra, les mans,
> l'esquena o el cap . . . (*Antípodes* 137 [ellipsis in original])

> [Do you think there are any whores who do it for pleasure? Lida
> had said to me. I myself would prefer to rent my cunt like the
> whores than my hands like these girls. In the end, how come the
> cunt is always considered more sacred than any other part of the
> body? If a woman wanted to rent her body to a man for fucking,
> didn't she have as much right to do that as she had to rent herself
> to him to write his letters or do his typing? Or for washing his
> dishes and underwear and not even get paid for it? The problem is
> that it's always women who have to rent something, her box, her
> hands, her back or her head . . . (*Antípodes* 116 [ellipsis in
> original])]

The lack of choice with which women have to contend is also
referenced in *El sol que fa l'ànec*, as Lònia ruminates: 'vaig pensar
que hi ha dones que venen el cos i el cap i són considerades
esposes i mares de família. Què té més, vendre el cony d'una
manera o d'una altra?' (23) ['I thought, there are women who sell
their bodies and their brains too, and they're considered wives
and mothers. What difference does it make which way you sell
your cunt?' (*Blue Roses for a Dead . . . Lady?* 7)]. Although Lònia
herself *has* been able to make her own professional and lifestyle
choices in the face of social and familial opposition, she is

nevertheless more than aware of the realities underpinning the existence of her countrywomen, an understanding that signals her feminist quest for greater gendered equality in Spain.

Unsurprisingly, then, Oliver's tales investigate crimes that highlight the relentless multiplicity of aggressions to which women are subjected by men, and function as a sounding board for the author's commitment to second wave or equality feminism. In *Estudi en lila*, Lònia is asked by an antique dealer to find three men who allegedly paid her for a piece of art with a false cheque. Oliver's detective investigates the case, which runs in tandem with her search for a Majorcan teenager who is believed to have disappeared in Barcelona. The 'answer' to both cases lies in the prevalence of rape in the Spain which forms the backdrop to the fiction, for Sebastiana, the runaway girl, left her home in fear and shame after being raped, while Elena Gaudí, the middle-aged, middle-class antique dealer, had been raped by the three men she had asked Lònia to locate for her. A related theme is explored in *Antípodes*, as Lònia exchanges Majorca for Australia where she uncovers a huge prostitution racket stretching right across the world, which forces girls into sexual slavery and dependence on drugs. In her last novel to date, Oliver's intrepid investigator follows clues that lead her to Germany and then back to her island home where she uncovers a horrific paedophile prostitution set-up, run mostly for German tourists and protected by some members of the Majorcan police.

In this section, then, I want to discuss how Oliver deploys the detective genre protagonizing a female sleuth to propound her feminist ideology. While in the next part of this chapter that focuses on the police procedurals of Alicia Giménez-Bartlett, I use Spanish and Anglophone post-feminist and difference 'feminist' theories as a framework for textual analysis, here I want to adopt a rather different approach. I propose to read Oliver's narratives rather more in conjunction with the extant criticism on Anglophone feminist crime fiction than strictly with reference to feminist theory, for two reasons. First of all, because Oliver's feminism is one that adheres largely to the central tenets of Spanish equality feminism which I overviewed in the introductory part of this chapter and on which I will draw throughout this section and, secondly, because reference to Anglophone critics who analyse literature that is very similar to Oliver's genre fiction will also elucidate the essential tenets of this type of feminism as it is articulated within this particular gendered sub-genre.

The sort of feminism expressed by Maria-Antònia Oliver's character is largely convergent with the Spanish feminist thought of the 1970s and 1980s that emerged alongside democracy. It is also the ideology that underpinned Anglophone woman-authored and woman-centred crime fiction of roughly the same period, particularly texts by novelists such as Sara Paretsky, Marcia Muller, or Sue Grafton, for example. Writing at the time, Maureen Reddy in her now classic study of the gendering of the genre, *Sisters in Crime. Feminism and the Crime Novel* (1988), clarified how she defined 'feminism' in the context of the female detective text:

> I am using *feminism* to mean a way of looking at the world that places women's experiences at the center. It sees women as capable of intelligence, moral reasoning, and independent action, while also giving attention to the multivarious social, legal, and psychological limitations placed on women by the patriarchal society in which most live. Feminism is always aware of the complexity and diversity of women's lives, especially those dissimilarities arising from differences of class, race, and nationality; however, it also insists that within this pluralism is a shared core of experience that is overlooked only at peril. (9) [italics in original]

What Reddy calls simply 'feminism', Joke Hermes identifies as 'everyday feminism' for the woman reader of this sort of fiction (216), and for Sally Munt it is the 'mainstream' current within feminist thinking. With reference to best-selling women's crime fiction in English Munt says: 'feminism is still foregrounded – in its liberal form – as a central narrative structure, self-consciously articulated in the character of the detective hero herself' (31) – a pattern replicated in Oliver's Lònia Guiu novels. And although Munt's stance on this particular type of feminism seems to posit it as twee, bourgeois, and outmoded, at the time Oliver was writing her first two detective novels it was a discourse of immense importance to the women of post-dictatorship Spain in their quest for gendered equal participation in the democratic process, and its significance should not be overlooked.

Although it is my contention that the way in which Oliver operates on the detective genre was crucial to defining it within Spain as a possible vehicle for expression of a contemporary feminist ethos, some critics have contended that this particular form of literature and feminist ideology are impossible bedfellows. In her now re-issued *The Woman Detective* (1995*b* [1988]), Kathleen Gregory Klein lists the concerns of feminism which can be central to the woman-authored crime narrative: 'feminism rejects the glorification of violence, the objectification of sex, and the patronization of the oppressed. It values female bonding, awareness of women without continual reference to or affiliation with men, and the self-knowledge which prompts women to independent judgement on both public and personal issues'. She then goes on to claim, however, that these are all issues that 'keep [. . .] feminism and the detective formula from meshing' (1995*b*: 201). Alison Littler takes a similar tack:

> How the term 'feminist' is defined, of course, will be crucial to the kind of answers that are offered. If, for example, 'feminist' is used in a liberal-humanist-independent-career-woman-in-control-of-her-own-life sense, then most certainly the recent series of women private eyes are feminist. If, however, 'feminist' refers to a woman deconstructing phallocentric ideologies wherever they are naturalized and structured into social, cultural, and political practices, then a feminist private eye is a contradiction in terms. (133)

Despite the concerns of Anglophone critics such as Klein and Littler, and in spite of the very real ideological problems inherent in simply transmuting the male hard-boiled PI into a female version, Oliver does manage to overcome the apparent contradiction of the 'feminist investigator', and her character questions coherently and very audibly the kind of 'phallocentric ideologies' Littler mentions, while functioning as a credible investigative figure. If, as Anne Cranny-Francis observes, the feminist sleuth is 'sexually autonomous, economically independent, intelligent and courageous' (1990: 165), the 'new creature' that according to Kathlyn Ann Fritz and Natalie Kaufman Hevener combines the best of what has traditionally been posited as 'feminine' and 'masculine' (122), then Lònia Guiu undoubtedly fits the bill.

The Spanish scholar, Pilar Folguera, entitles her study of women's history in Spain between 1939 and 1975 'El retorno a la esfera privada' [The Return to the Domestic Space] (1997), thus clearly highlighting the Francoist policy of promoting family and home as the primary reserves of female activity. Despite the rosy portraits of happy mummies surrounded by smiling kiddies that prevailed in images conceived and disseminated by the regime, Anny Brooksbank Jones reminds us that the dictatorship's model for the family was a particularly oppressive one (74), and women were subjected to the authority of their fathers or husbands even in such matters as opening a bank account, obtaining a passport, or applying for paid employment.[13] It was against the drudgery of domestic toil and large families, and the power afforded men within the domestic unit (as elsewhere) that Spanish feminists would clamour as part of a wider set of demands articulated during the 1970s and beyond.[14] It is therefore unsurprising that Oliver's Lònia Guiu should reject the relevance of the domestic space and the traditional family to her existence as a Spanish woman of the 1980s. In contrast to Giménez-Bartlett's Petra Delicado who, as I discuss in the next section, is frequently portrayed in her home, Lònia appears to spend very little time in her apartment, preferring to engage in maniacal car chases along the highways and byways of pre-Olympic Barcelona. Similarly, while Petra is often sited in her kitchen, Lònia appears to enter this particular room only to eat what others have prepared for her, and even this she does only on the rarest of occasions – perhaps in ironic gendered counterpoint to Manuel Vázquez Montalbán's sleuth, Pepe Carvalho who, in the early novels, at least, spends much of his time creating culinary delicacies and who relishes the delights of his home.

It is interesting that it should be the detective novel, the 'masculine' genre *par excellence*, that should make possible the rejection of the domestic for its female protagonist. On the one hand, of course, this particular textual politics is facilitated by the male sleuth's rejection of hearth and home, but it is also made possible because he is usually sited in environments that emblematize the male public domain: male investigators trad-itionally move freely and fluidly through the 'mean streets' of the city in which they operate, visiting other public spaces such as bars or businesses or bordellos. This figure, however, like the nineteenth-century *flâneur* in whom he almost certainly partly has his roots, was always male – both in US hard-boiled texts and in the Spanish *novela negra*. The woman who pounded the pavement could never simply be a *flâneuse* in the nineteenth-century con-text, nor, in more recent texts, could she be just a female equivalent of the tough male sleuth; rather, she was always perceived as a 'public' woman who occupied public spaces. The advent of the feminist investigator in Anglophone fiction radically revised this paradigm, of course, and it is also fundamentally re-written by Oliver. Lònia refuses to be relegated to the periphery – to the suburbs, to the margins of the urban environment – but operates at the centre of the cities in which she conducts investigations. She names their constituent parts, thus making them her own and 'feminizing' them, as Helena Buffery and Deborah Parsons (2002) suggest occurs with the Catalan capital in some contemporary cultural products. Lònia's project is not always a simple one, however, for the 'masculinity' of the city is emphasized even in its naming policies. In *Antípodes*, as she careens madly through the streets of Palma in her car and describes her route, with the single exception of the Plaça de Santa Catalina Tomàs [St Catherine's Square], all the other streets and avenues carry the names of male figures from the island's or the nation's history, thus confirming the perception of the urban space as one designed by, built by, named for, and traditionally occupied by men (*Antípodes* 139–45; *Antipodes* 120–4). Furthermore, as Concepción Bados Ciria (1995) points out, for Oliver's detective, Barcelona can sometimes be an adverse, hostile, and overwhelming place. Nonetheless, Lònia walks along and drives through the streets of Barcelona, Palma, and Melbourne, reclaiming the space not only for herself but for other women too, thus re-gendering the ownership of the urban landscape.

Just as Lònia rejects the validity of the domestic environment as a suitable space for a woman, similarly she is no supporter of the family, avoiding contact wherever possible with her mother and her brother, a small-minded bigot. In this regard, Kathleen Thompson-Casado notes that in Oliver's detective series 'the father figure has been eliminated, and the relationship with his authoritative substitute, the brother, is extremely strained due to the latter's disapproval of the protagonist's personal and professional choices' (2004: 143). Lònia's mother is also unhappy with her daughter's choice of career, preferring to tell neighbours that she is a teacher. The detective and her parent appear to profess not the least affection for each other, and Lònia confesses to Quim that she feels 'un odi obscur per mumare' (*El sol que fa l'ànec* 62) ['I always held a deep grudge for mother' (*Blue Roses for a Dead . . . Lady?* 31)].[15] Earlier, in *Antípodes*, she ponders on her bond with her mother as she flies into Palma airport: 'M'atacava els nervis, mumare. Em treia de solc' (*Antípodes* 126) ['She drove me nuts, my mom. Pushed me to the limit' (*Antipodes* 106–7)]. It should be noted, however, that although the mother is portrayed as a whinging, old-fashioned hypochondriac, she is far from being the monstrous maternal figure responsible for the criminal pathologization of her offspring that is apparent from some of Giménez-Bartlett's novels, or the mother who merits death at her child's hands of the sort studied in Chapter 2.

Rejection of the family as a workable model of social organization is also a norm of Anglophone women's detective narratives (Cole 144; Reddy 105; Vanacker 71) and, in keeping with the hard-boiled notion of the investigator as a loner, Oliver's protagonist does not have a stable life partner, enjoying, rather, a series of sexually very gratifying affairs, a pattern also observed in this type of novel in English (Cole 144–5; Dilley 27–9). Indeed, Lònia makes no bones about her demands and expectations in this regard, asserting: 'Jo volia una relació temporal, una relació agradable, superficial i sense entrebancs, sobretot sense implicacions sentimentals tret de la simpatía mutual' (*Antípodes* 75) ['I wanted a temporary relationship, an agreeable, superficial relationship without difficulties, especially no sentimental implications beyond mutual sympathy' (*Antipodes* 57)]. She does, however, benefit from the support and love of her aunt, Antònia, who acts as confidante, carer, and surrogate mother in the apparent absence of any parental love, and who also supports her niece's choice of profession.

Just as Antònia is a 'replacement' for the parent, so Lònia constructs around herself alternatives to the traditional family unit, another feature of women's feminist detective tales in English (Godard 50; Humm 249; Vanacker 73). This strategy is most apparent in *Estudi en lila* and *El sol que fa l'ànec.* In the first novel in the series Lònia is part of an extensive network of women friends, all of whom support each other personally and professionally wherever possible. In her search for the men who raped Elena Gaudí, the antique dealer, Lònia calls upon the assistance of Neus the photographer, Mercè the gynaecologist, Berta the medic, and Pepa who works in the offices of the port of Barcelona, and numerous other female acquaintances are mentioned by the detective. That Mercè and her colleagues in particular collaborate to form a group founded in a strongly feminist ethos is made clear from Lònia's observations on their activities:

Ella [Mercè] i unes quantes més de la seva especialitat es dedicavan a controlar casos de violacions no denunciades, d'avortaments desesperats i coses per l'estil [. . .] També tenien muntada una xarxa diguem-ne clandestina – perquè no era gens oficial – contra actuacions professionals irresponsables. 'Hi ha massa dones sense ovaris, pel mon', m'havia dit. (21)

[She (Mercè) and a few other women in her field dedicated themselves to dealing with cases of unreported rapes, desperate abortions, and things like that [. . .] They also had a more or less clandestine network – not at all official in any case – against irresponsible professional behavior. 'There are too many women in the world without ovaries', she had told me. (15)]

Similarly, in the most recent of Oliver's genre novels, Lònia works with Madame Tasi, a clairvoyant, Mrs Cros – the mother of Júlia Corriol, a young woman who has disappeared in mysterious circumstances – as well as with other women who will help her to eventually uncover the child prostitution racket upon which Júlia had stumbled, a discovery that led to her murder. Indeed, within *El sol que fa l'ànec* the significance of the all-female environment in providing a personal support network and in resolving a case – a staple, too, of Anglophone woman-authored, woman-centred detective fiction (Coward and Semple 52–3) – is made very clear in the siting of Madame Tasi. This exceptional woman, apparently blessed with special powers, inhabits an apartment decorated with exotic items, fabrics, and colours that aim to emphasize her particular 'wisdom'. The only males who enter her domain – Quim, who is gay, and a deformed dwarf who is Tasi's servant – are so far removed from the 'norm' of the male in the hard-boiled genre as to constitute almost a negation of that type of masculinity.

The importance to the female investigator of support networks of this sort is made contrastively clear in *Antípodes*. In that text Lònia decides to hire a male PI to carry out some of her sleuthing as she realizes that in Australia she is operating outside the scope of her usual cultural parameters. Henry Dhul, the man she contracts, soon becomes her lover, but he is ultimately revealed to be an untrustworthy misogynist – thus showing that relying on a man for professional or emotional support can prove to be disastrous for the woman detective, and that the female groupings of which she is a member are therefore far more valuable and reliable. Indeed, it is within *Antípodes* that what Patricia Hart sees as one of the principal themes of the Lònia Guiu series is made very apparent, 'namely that men and women rarely manage better than an uneasy coexistence spiced by sex' (1998: ix). When Henry Dhul evinces his belief that working as a detective really is 'an unsuitable job for a woman', our intrepid heroine is rendered silent because of the love she professes for him:

—És que . . . mira, la veritat, *darling*, trobo que aquesta no és una feina per dones.

Ai cony!

—Què vols dir? —vaig fer, com una idiota.

—Això que he dit, exactament. Hi ha feines per homes i feines per dones. I la d'investigador privat no és una feina per dones. No m'agradaria que t'hi volguessis tornar a dedicar.

Vaig quedar tan de pedra que no vaig tenir esma de reaccionar. Si la Mercè hagués sentit allò l'hauria esgarrapat, segur. Però jo estava enamorada d'ell i només em vaig sentir desconcertada. (100 [italics in original])

['It's just that, look, darling, the truth is that I don't think it's a job for a woman'.

Oh, fuck!

'What do you mean?' I said like an idiot.

'Just what I said. There are jobs for men and jobs for women. And private investigator is not a job for a woman. I wouldn't like you to go back to it'.

I froze, completely unable to react. If Mercè had heard that, she would have scratched his eyes out for sure. But I was in love with him and my only feeling was bewilderment. (81)]

Lònia's response is indeed unexpected, not least because she has heard this particular line of argument previously – from both her mother and from the wife of a policeman friend who is concerned for her welfare in her 'dangerous' profession. On the other hand, however, the stance of all the characters replicates very closely that of Spanish employers when first faced with a large female workforce from the late 1970s on, and who failed to comprehend the motivations or needs of their women employees (Larumbe 2004: 28–9).

Another key tenet of the type of feminism espoused by Lònia Guiu is its articulation of the victimization to which women are unceasingly subjected within patriarchy. As Helen Carr has asserted, 'Second wave feminism was perhaps the last of the radical movements that could emerge self-consciously modelled on the idea of a clear oppressor and oppressed' (12). Most Spanish women authors who write in the crime genre (with the possible exception of Alicia Giménez-Bartlett, whose fiction I analyse in the next section of this chapter) ensure that violence against women is foregrounded in their texts, to the extent that this has been a literary preoccupation in any number of novels and short stories, as I shall discuss in Chapter 2. Widespread gendered aggression is also central to the Lònia Guiu series, but where Oliver's texts differ from those studied in detail in the next chapter is in the highly sexualized nature of the violence perpetrated against women, and also in the targeting of the detective herself.

From the mid-1970s, and in line with similar campaigns organized in Britain, France, and Italy, Spanish feminists – pre-eminent among them Lidia Falcón – began to raise awareness of the violence, and specifically the sexual aggression, to which their countrywomen were subjected, and to demand action to end such abuse (Larumbe 2004: 154–5). Between 1977 and 1978 in particular, women's groups throughout Spain, and especially at the University of Barcelona, organized demonstrations and marches to highlight their situation as victims of male violence and to petition for changes to legislation in a bid for heightened protection (ibid. 156 *et seq.*). It was also around this time that the slogan 'Contra violació, castració' [Against rape, castration] began to appear in lilac paint daubed on walls across Barcelona in particular (Larumbe 2002: 181). It is this context, then, that informs the cases that Lònia Guiu must investigate in *Estudi en lila* – the title of which alludes to the graffiti slogan mentioned above – and in *Antípodes.*[16]

In her extremely valuable study of rape in the works of Oliver and Giménez-Bartlett, Nina Molinaro points out that the textual treatment the authors afford the theme of sexual violence against women reveals several shortcomings, particularly when assessed from a feminist stance.[17] What I do consider to be of primary importance, however, is the fact that Oliver unquestionably signals to her reader the unfailing pervasiveness of the sexual assault of women by the individual male and by groups of men, thus confirming her belief in a central notion of second wave feminist theory, in opposition to the denial of universal female victimhood proposed by the kind of post-feminists and difference 'feminists' I overview in the next section with reference to Giménez-Bartlett's tales. The prevalence of this type of gendered crime on a world-wide scale, as made evident particularly in *Antípodes* in which Lònia uncovers an international sex slave ring trading in women, also serves to underscore notions posited by feminist scholars – particularly in the USA – who asserted that raping women is an activity inextricably enmeshed with the prevailing patriarchal social structure which sponsors and promotes sex crime because it is an action founded on the subjugation of the female by the male. In her now classic essay, 'Rape: The All-American Crime' (1971), Susan Griffin asserted that within the patriarchy the male learns to rape – a synonym for other forms of violence, too – because the system is predicated on male aggressivity and female passivity. Susan Brownmiller's *Against our Will: Men, Women and Rape* (1975) echoed many of Griffin's assertions, observing that rape is a foundation stone of patriarchal society and functions to effectively control women's social participation.

It is this reality, then, that Oliver uncovers in her novels, and she also deploys the genre to assess social responses to rape. The Spain in which the first two novels of the Lònia Guiu series were penned was one still largely governed by an 'honour code' inherited from the dictatorship years and much earlier, and within which, as Anny Brooksbank Jones notes, 'women tended to see rape as a source of humiliation and shame. Especially for girls with little education or confidence, reporting a rape to often unsupportive authorities was complicated and traumatic' (95). It is in just such a situation that Sebastiana, the young runaway whom Lònia shelters in her apartment within *Estudi en lila*, finds herself. Unable to return home because her father has threatened her with physical violence for 'allowing' herself to be raped (as a consequence of which she had become pregnant), and unsure whether to undergo an abortion, the girl commits suicide in Lònia's bath, much to the detective's profound distress. Nor does the sleuth herself avoid the threat of sexual violence. Within the same novel she is attacked by two heavies employed by the evil mafioso Gòmara, and they make a point of ripping off her shirt and bra to leave her breasts exposed, before one of them subsequently tries to rape her. This particular narrative strategy replicates that identified by the critic Siv Jansson in Sara Paretsky's detective novels, in which her female supersleuth, Warshawski, is threatened with rape specifically because of her *sex*; she is not a victim of violence because of her profession, as a male PI would be (160).

Rape is not the only form of aggression to which Lònia is subjected, however, for Oliver's novels – and *Estudi en lila* in particular – seem to contain barely a narrative sequence in which she or other women are not the victim of some form of violence: rape or attempted rape, beatings and assault, verbal aggression, demands of sexual favours by men in return for assistance or information, being sacked from a job for no reason, denigration of female intellect or activity . . . In *Antípodes* a young female member of a Majorcan ecological group with which Lònia has contact is mugged as a warning to her associates to keep from investigating planned land racketeering, and in Melbourne Lònia witnesses the murder of two entirely innocent women – also to silence them.[18] The detective novel, with its focus on crime, can thus be revised to foreground the gendering of violence, a point I develop in the next chapter. More specifically, it can function to deny the hard-boiled myth that the female somehow 'deserves' to be the focus of such aggression. It is important to note, however, that despite often being a victim herself, Lònia – unlike Giménez-Bartlett's Petra Delicado – refrains from engaging in gratuitous violence, and, when Quim suggests she arm herself she affirms her avowed refusal to carry a gun: '—Jo? Jo, agafar una pistola? Mai de la vida' (*El sol que fa l'ànec* 96) ['Me? A gun? Not on your life' (*Blue Roses for a Dead . . . Lady?* 78)].[19] She rejects such a possibility not only because she knows that this most potent of phallic signs is in and of itself symbolic of male-authored violence (some of which, at least, is directed against women), but also because if she were armed with a pistol she would not hesitate to use it against those who, like the paedophiles she discovers in *El sol que fa l'ànec*, abuse those weaker than themselves: 'Per això jo no en vull, d'armes. Perquè si aquell dia n'hagués duita una, no hauria fet només el que va fer el subcomissari Maiol. Amb la ira que duia, no hauria tingut compassió' (208) ['That's why I refuse to carry arms. Because if I'd had one that day, I'd have done more than subcommissioner Maiol did. With the fury I had inside, I'd have had no mercy' (113)].

Such a perspective can again be read as symptomatic of Oliver's entrenched feminist stance, because as Cranny-Francis remarks, 'In feminist texts violence must be carefully negotiated' – not least because the type of aggression that prevails in hard-boiled literature is 'largely an expression of misogyny' (1990: 168). Rejecting gratuitous violent behaviour, then, functions to signal the disavowal of male behaviours forged in patriarchy, and for this reason Oliver's feminist investigator uses violence only to protect herself or other women – again a norm in similar Anglophone texts (Shuker-Haines and Umphrey 77). Indeed, all of the cases Lònia investigates are linked in some way to defending members of the female collective, with the sleuth taking direct action in the opening pages of *El sol que fa l'ànec*, beating up a sleazy pimp who had been threatening a group of street prostitutes in a poor part of town (15; *Blue Roses for a Dead . . . Lady?* 5). On this occasion she subdues the man with a series of punches, arm twists, and a knee in the groin, not least because surprise is on her side. But the detective's strategy in this text – as in the others – is a risky one, for Lònia often seems unaware that her stature and strength are not equal to those of her male assailants (Hart 1998: ix–x; Vosburg 58–9). Indeed, Lònia is frequently the victim of thumpings and beatings, and in *Antípodes* and *El sol que fa l'ànec* is horribly attacked. As a result of the assault to which she is subjected in the latter text she becomes permanently deaf in one ear, suffers several broken ribs, extensive bruising and cuts, and is hospitalized. In both novels she is saved in the nick of time by her trusty sidekick Quim, accompanied by his 'band of merry men'. Oliver thus once again highlights the all-pervasive nature of violence against women, and, equally importantly, reminds her reader that most females are *not* physically able to fight back against male brutality.

Some discussion of women victims' responses to violent assault does permeate *Estudi en lila*, however, for towards the end of the narrative Lònia discovers that her client Elena Gaudí had castrated one by one the men who had raped her, in a fitting tribute to the type of graffiti mentioned earlier in this section and from which the novel draws its title. Upon realizing what the older woman is doing, Lònia is initially horrified, but ultimately condones the other's scalpel-wielding exploits, leaving her alone with her intended final victim in full knowledge of the fate that awaits him. If Elena Gaudí were to figure in a male-authored Spanish *novela negra*, it is likely that she would meet the unhappy end meted out to female lawbreakers in so many crime texts by men, for as Walton and Jones observe, 'the malicious and resourceful woman seems to be associated in the hard-boiled genre with the degenerative forces at work in the social system. She is not just a criminal; she poses a larger danger, outside of, and threatening to, the social order itself. Therefore, according to the conventions of the hard-boiled story, she must be killed, imprisoned, or otherwise punished by the detective in order for the plot to be resolved' (192–3). However, Oliver portrays the castrator as a woman whom only her attackers need fear, and who poses a threat to certain members of the patriarchy as a specific response to their victimization of her, not because they are male *per se*. She also allows her character to escape from Barcelona.

Permitting a female character to engage in this form of aggression and get away with it does, however, raise the thorny ideological issue of inverting the more usual gendering of violence (i.e. male aggression directed against women); as Lònia's fellow (fictional) detective Lluís Arquer remarks at the end of *Estudi en lila* in response to the tale of Gaudí's exploits: '—Val a dir que també hi ha dones bèsties . . .' (195; [ellipsis in original]) ['Which means women can be beasts too' (159)].[20] I discuss in greater detail revenge as an option for the aggressed female in the next chapter, but would suggest that Gaudí's tactics function to highlight a very real situation in which women victims do not have open to them many avenues for responding to, or dealing with, the men who assault them. Certainly brute force would rarely, if ever, be a match for a man's strength, and so Gaudí devises an alternative, and even more devastating, violent response to violence – and the ethics of this sort of retaliation are also considered in Chapter 2 of this work.

Another key issue that the theme of gendered violence also introduces is the gendering of justice. Despite uncovering police corruption and identifying police stupidity throughout all of the novels she protagonizes, at the end of *Estudi en lila* Lònia enquires of Gaudí why she did not report the rape to the police: '—I per què no va fer una denúncia? —De què hauria servit? De res, naturalment. I molt menos tractant-se d'uns aligots poderosos com ells' (181) ['Why didn't you go to the police?' 'What good would that have done? None, of course. Much less with powerful vultures like those' (150)]. This fictional case nonetheless echoes slogans painted across Barcelona by women's groups during the late 1970s which, among other things, warned other females: 'Mujer, si eres violada no acudas a comisaría, allí puedes encontrar al violador' [Women: if you are raped don't go to the police station; you might find your rapist there] (Larumbe 2004: 157). Such stances were the product of a reality in which 'policías y jueces mostraban una clara indiferencia y nunca había una respuesta contundente frente a los agresores' [the police and the judiciary displayed a palpable indifference and never offered a firm response when faced with the attackers] (ibid. 156). It is therefore perhaps unsurprising that Lònia the feminist should shift the meaning of 'justice' from signifying official 'law and order' to 'fair play', just as Dilley reminds us is the case with feminist crime fiction in English. Similarly, much as Dilley observes, this new form of 'justice' includes some component of vigilantism (50).[21]

While this consideration of the significance of the gendering of justice is specific to the detective novel, many other issues central to the Majorcan author's crime narrative are more generally articulated in feminist fiction, both in Spain and elsewhere. Indeed, I would posit that for Oliver the genre text functions as what in the Anglophone context Lisa Maria Hogeland has called 'the consciousness-raising (CR) novel', a form of feminist fiction that 'was important and influential in introducing feminist ideas to a broader reading public, and particularly in circulating feminist ideas beyond the small-group networks that made up radical feminism' (ix). Hogeland observes that 'the CR novel' crossed established literary boundaries to include popular fictions (x), and whereas it emerged in Britain or North America during the 1970s, I would suggest that the later development of second wave feminism in Spain produced an equivalent there from the 1980s on. While I assert that Oliver's crime fictions can be read as part of a corpus of Spanish feminist fiction, I would point out that, as Biruté Ciplijauskaité (1988) has made clear, there exist numerous feminist tendencies within peninsular (and other European) female literatures, of which the Lònia Guiu series is just one sort. Earlier in this section I reviewed at length the classification of detective narratives as feminist texts. To conclude, I want to consider a more general comment offered by Catherine Davies in her study of two Spanish women writers who are contemporaries of Maria-Antònia Oliver. With reference to the case of Spain she proffers the observation that:

> if the writer supports the general objectives of the Women's Movement, that is, she critiques patriarchy and sexism and questions the ideological underpinnings of femininity, if she is engaged in the transformation of dominant gender relations in society and considers the practice of writing a means of doing this, then she is perforce a feminist writer. (5)

Oliver's detective tales, then, can be read as symptomatic of a wider culture of feminist writing prevailing in Spain – particularly at the time the first two novels were published.[22] In their engagement with, and forceful articulation of, essential tenets of equality feminism they differ very significantly from the post-feminist environment that informs Giménez-Bartlett's police procedurals, as I shall discuss in the next section.

The Post-Feminist *Policía*: Alicia Giménez-Bartlett's Inspector Petra Delicado

During the 1990s and the early years of the twenty-first century, women writers from Spain have been publishing crime and detective fiction in a variety of formats in ever increasing numbers. Many texts focus on the female victim of crime or on the woman criminal and, as I shall analyse in detail in Chapter 2 of this study, authors use these figures to articulate cogent concerns about the increased visibility of gendered violence within their country and the enhanced response to this issue on a national level. Their strategy is a strongly feminist one and their narratives reflect many of the issues highlighted by Maria-Antònia Oliver in her Lònia Guiu series. By the late 1990s, however, and in spite of the continued interest on the part of very many woman writers in the feminist possibilities of the gendered victim and criminal, a very different female investigator had appeared on the Spanish literary scene: the police detective.

With the exception of Margarida Aritzeta's Coia Moreno (to whom I shall return in the next chapter), the character of the female police officer had hitherto been absent from woman-authored Spanish fiction. As discussed previously, positive narrative portrayals of the nation's police really only began to emerge in Spain with the entrenchment of democracy and the normalization of an institution that had for a very long time quite literally been the strong arm of the regime.[23] However, 1996 saw the publication of the first of an on-going series of police procedurals penned by Alicia Giménez-Barlett which protagonize Petra Delicado, a woman police inspector.[24] This section analyses the six genre novels and three short stories Giménez-Bartlett has written to date. This new figure of the female law enforcement agent is used by the author to articulate a very different vision of the siting and function of women in contemporary Spanish society from that proffered by Oliver in her Lònia Guiu novels or by those authors who focus on female victims. I therefore propose to read Giménez-Bartlett's fiction in conjunction with Spanish and international theories of difference 'feminism', as well as with some of the overarching notions of what constitutes the current post-feminist environment, as it is my contention that the author reflects on elements of both schools of thought through the figure of her woman Inspector with the ultimate aim of uncovering and commenting on her countrywomen's lot.

Born in 1951, Alicia Giménez-Bartlett is thus roughly the same age as Maria-Antònia Oliver (born 1947).[25] She achieved some considerable recognition as a writer of 'literary' fiction during the 1980s and 1990s, and in 1997 won the prestigious Premio Femenino Lumen [The Lumen Women's Literary Prize] for *Una habitación ajena* [A Room Not of One's Own]. She decided to create the figure of Inspector Petra Delicado of her own volition, rather than at a publisher's behest, as she considered such a character could function as a useful mouthpiece for commentary on the situation of women in contemporary Spain.[26] Her first genre novel, *Ritos de muerte* [Death Rites] (1996) introduces Petra Delicado and her male sidekick, Deputy Inspector Fermín Garzón. While Petra is relatively new to the Cuerpo Nacional de Policía [Spanish National Police Force][27] and has been sidelined from active service to work as the force's librarian and archivist – possibly in deference to her former employment as a lawyer and because she is a woman – Fermín is an old hand. He has recently moved to Barcelona – where this, and all subsequent novels are largely set – from Salamanca, in provincial Castile, following the death of his wife, a bereavement he seems not to lament. In the absence of any other officers to carry out the investigation, Petra and Fermín are given the case of the rape of a young girl from an economically disadvantaged background whose assailant marked her with a flower-shaped metal object after the attack. As other girls are assaulted and 'branded' it becomes clear that the detectives must identify and locate a serial rapist.

The second novel in the series appeared a year later, in 1997. Entitled *Día de perros* [Dog Days], it again opens with Petra and Fermín – still very much the 'odd couple' or the 'new kids on the block' at their particular police station – being assigned what appears to be yet another case of minor importance: the apparent murder of a clearly very marginalized individual. As in all of the Petra Delicado novels, the intrepid detectives trawl the sordid Barcelona underworld and the poverty-stricken areas of the city that were hitherto unknown to the 'lady' inspector, revealing a world of illegal dog fighting, murder, and corruption. In 1999, Giménez-Bartlett published *Mensajeros de la oscuridad* [Messengers of Darkness]. By now Petra is such a well-known member of the force that she has appeared as its representative on a television chat show, a media foray that results in her receiving vast amounts of fan mail, among which is a packet containing a severed human penis. The repulsive contents of the parcel set Petra and Fermín off on an investigation that leads them to Russia and finally to the discovery of a bizarre sect whose members cut off their own penises in a bid to deny sexual desire.

In the next tale in the series, *Muertos de papel* [The Paper Murders] (2000*b*), the dynamic duo also spend some time outside Barcelona in the course of their enquiries, this time in Madrid. The murder of an unpleasant journalist develops into a frenetic race through all strata of the capital's multifaceted society and, as in *Día de perros*, the case turns out to have its roots in individual human greed. This theme carries through into the two most recent volumes in the Petra Delicado series. In *Serpientes en el paraíso* [Serpents in Paradise] (2002) Petra and Fermín are called out to look into the murder of a young, wealthy man whose corpse is found floating in the swimming pool of his very expensive residential complex. A lengthy investigation, based largely among the extremely privileged *haute-bourgeois* residents of the luxury housing scheme, reveals the killing to have been a crime of passion prompted by jealousy, although tangentially the police uncover wholesale crime and corruption which show that Barcelona's elite is rotten to the core. The latest novel, the enigmatically titled *Un barco cargado de arroz* [A Ship Full of Rice] (2004), also opens with a dead body, but this time of an old man believed to be a member of the city's ever growing homeless population. In a series of disturbing investigative scenes, Petra visits psychiatric hospitals, homeless encampments, derelict buildings, and social welfare centres in a bid to solve this puzzling case, one she finally discovers is motivated by financial concerns. Petra Delicado also features in three short stories. 'Muerte en el gimnasio' [Death in the Gymnasium] (1998) relates the tale of a brutish bodybuilder 'cooked' in the sauna of his gym by the lover he spurned. 'Modelados en barro' [Moulded from Clay] (1998) and 'La voz de la sangre' [Blood is Thicker than Water] (2002) detail, respectively, murder cases in the world of Barcelona fashion houses and the city's thriving sex 'industry'.[28]

Given Giménez-Bartlett's solid formation as a fiction writer of renown, as well as her critical awareness forged while researching a doctorate on Spanish literature from the University of Salamanca, and her role as a critic and journalistic contributor on contemporary debates, it is unsurprising that the Petra Delicado novels should be of very considerable 'literary' quality and are strongly plot-driven, as the genre demands. Furthermore, the author demonstrates within her detective texts an intimate and sympathetic understanding of the Barcelona of the marginalized, the delinquent, and the dispossessed – among whom Petra Delicado has, inevitably, to carry out her investigations – and a keen familiarity with the language deployed by both the police and the criminal fraternity. To this happy interplay of knowledge and expertise is added the novelist's dry sense of humour, made manifest in Petra's ponderings on the meaning of her existence as a policewoman, and her exchanges with Fermín, during which each often functions as a foil for the other's witticisms. Indeed, it is this interaction between the two characters that Sara Martín Alegre has identified as central to the narratives, asserting: 'la serie Delicado se basa en dos ejes básicos: la personalidad de la Inspectora y su relación con su compañero [. . .] el Subinspector Fermín Garzón' [the Delicado series is based on two central ideas: the Inspector's personality and her relationship with her colleague [. . .] Deputy Inspector Fermín Garzón] (417). Later in her article, Martín Alegre develops her notion further, alleging that Giménez-Bartlett's novels owe their popularity to the unusual coupling of the 'lady' police officer and her portly subordinate who is nearing retirement, rather than to the feminist awareness apparent in so many Anglophone woman-authored crime novels (420). The Spanish critic dwells at some length on the issue of feminism, and in her opening observations signals to her reader that Petra does not attempt to articulate a feminist ideology within her workplace, and that in any case both Petra and her creator, Giménez-Bartlett, have severe reservations about the value of feminist discourse (415), an assertion that, as I shall show throughout this chapter, succinctly summarizes the author's ideology in this regard.

Martín Alegre also makes the point that the National Police is an inherently conservative body and thus resistant to gendered ideologies other than its own, traditional one (415). What is also key to understanding the narrative analysed here, of course, is that the very genre of the police procedural is of itself also intrinsically conventional in the gender and other patterns it replicates, what Georges Tyras, in the context of Giménez-Bartlett's detective novels, calls 'una forma por esencia condenada al conservadurismo' [a literary form condemned to conservatism by its very nature] (101). With reference to the Anglophone literary world – from which Giménez-Bartlett and other Spanish writers have 'imported' this particular sub-genre – Lorraine Gamman has highlighted the incompatibility of the police novel and feminist thought: 'With all its patriarchal and authoritarian associations, law enforcement seems an unlikely site for "feminist intervention"' (19). Although Gamman's study dates from 1988, her stance is replicated in a more recent article by the Canadian scholar Sandra Tomc. Tomc points out that a perceptual shift became apparent in women's detective fiction in English from the 1980s to the 1990s as the female-authored police procedural gained ascendance over texts featuring a lone operator PI or other independent woman investigator. She summarizes this move by pointing out that one of the more recent cultural products she analyses – *Prime Suspect*, a popular British television series protagonizing a woman police officer – 'is different from detective fiction modeled after Marcia Muller because it features the woman detective not as a renegade but as an aspiring member of the very institution responsible for her victimisation' (47), a characteristic of a number of novels she studies.

What Tomc is signalling, then, is the move from a sub-genre that was intrinsically eminently suited to the foregrounding of feminist issues – despite the concerns of critics reviewed in the previous section and in the introduction to this text – to the use of one that offers up a very different woman-centred discourse. And although she works with material written in English, the pattern she identifies is clearly discernible in Spain, too, as exemplified in the ideological disparity between the works of Maria-Antònia Oliver on the one hand, and the fiction of Alicia Giménez-Bartlett on the other. While Oliver's liberal, bourgeois feminist ethos is 'personified', so to speak, in the figure of her feisty, intrepid investigator, Giménez-Bartlett's stance with regard to female activism is very different, as summarized in my earlier overview of Martín Alegre's work on her narrative. Indeed, it is my contention that the inherent generic – and gendered – limitations of the police procedural (and the police force, of course) in fact function to facilitate Giménez-Bartlett's project: the uncovering and portrayal of the siting of contemporary Spanish women within a largely post-feminist environment, by which I mean one to which earlier forms of feminism have little relevance and, I shall argue, one which has been informed, however informally, by discourses such as difference 'feminism'. In fact, I think it is possible that an author of Giménez-Bartlett's erudition and awareness of contemporary political debate, both within the academe and in a wider context, purposefully selected the police procedural as the ideal format for revealing several key realities: that women in her country are living a post-feminist moment; that feminist activism of the sort discussed by Oliver in her genre texts has not resulted in equality; and that within contemporary Spain women continue to be constrained by all manner of patriarchal impositions. It is precisely because of the implications of siting a female officer within a rigidly hierarchical and patriarchal environment such as the Cuerpo Nacional de Policía, then, that Giménez-Bartlett's chosen sub-genre functions so well to her specific ends. The police force, an overtly ordered environment overseen by men, is simply the author's metaphor for the wider social milieu in which women's behaviours and bodies must be rigorously restrained. And even though Petra is one of those charged with policing that society, the constraints and checks to which she herself is subjected by her male superiors, and even colleagues, clearly suggests

that the control mechanisms exercised against the female population exist even when women are afforded a space for professional
and personal expression or some – apparent – degree of 'equality'.

What I want to do in this section, then, is to discuss the
strategies Giménez-Bartlett deploys to demonstrate that her protagonist, Inspector Petra Delicado – like other Spanish women –
exists within a post-feminist economy, and that this siting proves
eminently problematic because many concerns of earlier feminist
movements have not been resolved even though post-feminism
has evolved as the contemporary *modus operandi* and *modus vivendi*, so to speak. Petra is undoubtedly an ambiguous figure – a
woman who appears to enjoy social, sexual, financial, and some
professional autonomy, but whose positioning within the police
force and whose own perspective on many gender issues appear to
render many of those autonomies of questionable authenticity. I
will therefore read the character's attitudes and gender philosophy in conjunction with the central tenets of two key woman-
centred discourses: post-feminism and difference 'feminism' –
particularly as the latter has been formulated by key thinkers in
Spain. Post-feminism as an attitude to gender issues has been
developed by a number of – particularly younger – women in the
USA, while in Spain this has not occurred, but the contemporary
post-feminist environment has been examined and theorized
within the country by some well-known female scholars and
observers. On the other hand, difference 'feminism' as an area of
allegedly feminist thought has been expounded by two pre-
eminent women thinkers who work in the line of the Italian
difference 'feminists'. I want to make clear that in this section I do
not intend to equate post-feminism with difference 'feminism',
but would assert that they share many common notions (such as
their energetic denunciation of earlier equality feminists), and
would suggest that the prevailing contemporary post-feminist
ethos has been very much informed – even if such an influence is
not generally acknowledged – by difference 'feminism' as well as
by other discourses like that of 'backlash' politics. It is this wider
culture, then, that I contend underpins Giménez-Bartlett's genre
fiction and with which her character, Petra Delicado, has to deal,
and within which the investigator has to negotiate her identity as a
woman.

It is not incorrect to affirm that within Spain – in keeping with most Western nations, where a feminist discourse had countered the hegemony of patriarchy during some of the twentieth century – feminism as a viable, coherent, and sustained set of principles has allegedly ceased to be of any transcendence whatsoever. In their introduction to a recent volume on the status of women in contemporary Spain, Jacqueline Cruz and Barbara Zecchi acknowledge that 'El feminismo ha dejado prácticamente de existir en cuanto discurso y práctica política' [feminism has practically ceased to exist as political discourse and practice] (9–10), while Juana María Gil Ruiz observes that 'Ni siquiera las propias organizaciones de mujeres se auto-definen como "feministas"' [Not even the women's organizations define themselves as 'feminist'] (278). This resistance to naming is also apparent at an individual level, and Cruz and Zecchi observe that 'La palabra *feminismo* se considera casi una palabrota, de tal modo que es escandalosamente habitual oír comentarios del tipo 'No me considero feminista', 'No me gustan las etiquetas', etc., incluso por parte de mujeres cuyas opiniones en defensa de la igualdad de la mujer podrían considerarse feministas' [the very term 'feminism' is considered almost a swear word, to the degree that it is quite normal to hear scandalous comments along the lines of 'I don't consider myself a feminist', 'I don't like to be labelled', etc., even by women who could be considered feminist because they support women's equality with men] (10, n. 5 [italics in original]).[29] It is clear, then, that across Spain the utility, validity, and relevance of feminism to women's reality are subject to an intense questioning that has ultimately apparently led to wholesale rejection. In her ironic explanation of this situation, Lidia Falcón observes that former Spanish feminists now assert that 'Ya hemos concluido con el feminismo' [We're done with feminism] (2000: 137) – ironic because, as the nation's foremost commentator on the situation of women, she is more aware than most of the continued need for a coherent feminist stand against the ongoing assaults of patriarchy. Nevertheless, the feminist philosopher Victoria Camps, and Justa Montero, a women's leader from Madrid, have both expressed profound reservations about the relevance of feminist activity and activism as they have traditionally been constituted in their country (see Andrews and Brooksbank Jones 233; Brooksbank Jones 28).

At this very elemental level, then, Petra Delicado subscribes wholeheartedly to this essential tenet underpinning post-feminism as well as Spanish difference 'feminism', for she repeatedly asserts that she is quite definitely not a feminist and she heaps scorn on many fundamental beliefs of feminist philosophy. Indeed, she appears unperturbed by her fellow male officers' allegations that debate aimed at securing gendered equality is little more than 'filípica feminista' [feminist tirades] (*Día de perros* 142), or 'reivindicaciones feministas' [feminist demands] (*Mensajeros de la oscuridad* 60, 163). In *Mensajeros de la oscuridad*, she herself mentions the 'pendencias feministas a las que había renunciado tiempo atrás' [the feminist squabbling that I'd given up on ages ago] (98), the very term 'pendencias' revealing her negative perception of feminist discourse, a stance confirmed in *Muertos de papel* with her reiteration of 'no soy feminista' [I am not a feminist] (123, 126). Within this novel she expounds on her line of thought, telling Garzón: 'tenga una cosa clara: no soy feminista. Si lo fuera no trabajaría como policía, ni viviría en este país, ni me hubiera casado dos veces, ni siquiera saldría a la calle, fíjese lo que le digo' [let's get one thing straight: I'm not a feminist. If I were I wouldn't be a police officer, I wouldn't live in this country, I wouldn't have married twice, I wouldn't even go out on the street, you mark my words] (123). That a feminist might avoid working within the conservative, traditional, patriarchal, and misogynist National Police perhaps goes without saying. Quite why Petra feels that a feminist could not live in Spain, nor marry, nor even step out into the street, is not entirely clear, but her reader can only surmise that she feels that contemporary Spain, with its continued gender inequalities, would not be a happy place for a feminist. Her words may also serve to ironically and pointedly highlight the widely held popular vision of the feminist as a rabid man-hater who refuses to work towards the perpetuation of the kind of patriarchal mores that are inherent to the police force.

The reasons for the rejection of feminism and its ideals in Spain seem multi-fold. Anny Brooksbank Jones ponders the issue at length, remarking, like those scholars cited earlier, that 'very few women today would describe themselves as feminists, and a significant number actively reject this term' (29). She then goes on to explain:

This is partly due to its [i.e. feminism's] demonisation, particularly in right-leaning media. But it also reflects a resentment among some older women of what they see as feminists' blanket condemnation of women who do not conform to their models [. . .] At the same time, however [. . .], there are many young women who now take key politico-juridical gains for granted [. . . and] others see feminism as a kind of reverse machismo, grounded in discredited stereotypes linked to battles which arose in very different social, political and economic circumstances and retain little or no contemporary relevance. (ibid.)

Josep Maria Riera and Elena Valenciano articulate a similar explication of the phenomenon, albeit with some minor variations on the theme. In their study of young women's attitudes in contemporary Spain they conclude that

el término 'feminismo' se plantea con cierta ambigüedad entre las jóvenes. No son antifeministas en el sentido clásico de rechazo desde una perspectiva 'feminista'; al contrario, en general se identifican con el feminismo como un movimiento social y pocas lo tildan de 'machismo pero al revés'. Pero tampoco lo ven como una necesidad, al menos en la imagen que tienen hoy del movimiento feminista. Piensan que es 'demasiado agresivo', que no 'deberían enfrentarse a los hombres', que las soluciones son más individuales que colectivas . . . (224–5; [ellipsis in original])

[young girls think about 'feminism' with a certain ambiguity. They are not anti-feminist in the classic sense of rejecting it from a 'feminist' perspective; quite the opposite: in general they identify with feminism as a social movement, and few of them brand it as 'reverse *machismo*'. But neither do they see it as a necessity, at least with regards to the view they hold nowadays of the feminist movement. They think it is 'too aggressive', that they 'should not confront men', that solutions can be sought individually rather than collectively . . .]

Interestingly, these views replicate almost verbatim the response of many Spanish difference 'feminists' to the feminist project both inside their country and beyond its borders. Pre-eminent among these figures are Milagros Rivera and Victoria Sendón de León,[30] both of whom have published substantially original philosophical contributions to the promotion of 'feminist' thought alternative to the kind of mainstream bourgeois, liberal feminism espoused by Oliver's Lònia Guiu, for example. Both Rivera and Sendón de León formulate an ideology founded firmly in the work of the Italian difference 'feminists', Sendón de León proposing a radical new 'feminism' originating in what she calls 'ginandria como significante de una visión mítico-simbólica de lo femenino o de la Mujer con mayúscula' [gynandry as signifying a mythic-symbolic vision of the feminine or of Womanhood with a capital 'W'] (1981: 234).[31] The text from which this citation is taken is her oft-quoted and influential *Sobre diosas, amazonas y vestales. Utopías para un feminismo radical* [Goddesses, Amazons, and Vestal Virgins. Utopias for a Radical Feminism] (1981),[32] the very title of which reveals the rather esoteric nature of her thought, founded in the female body and the significance of various goddesses and figures culled from world mythology.

Sendón de León claims that, despite her work suggesting a reading to the contrary, her 'feminism' 'no es – como se ha interpretado en muchos casos – una tendencia meliflua del feminismo que mira al ombligo y exalta infantilmente las cualidades femeninas de ternura, intuición y cosas por el estilo' [is not – as it has often been construed – a mellifluous tendency within feminism to contemplate its own navel and exalt in an infantile way the feminine qualities of tenderness, intuition, and that sort of thing] (1988: 141). What Sendón de León's brand of 'feminist' thought does do, however, is contest the validity of earlier forms of equality feminism, labelling it as a 'débil correctivo del machismo' [a weak counter-*machismo*] (1981: 223). Indeed, this particular thinker is vitriolic in her condemnation of it, claiming that the search for gender parity has led to –

la conciliación más simplista de la mujer con su 'partenaire' que ya le lava los platos o baña a los niños y hasta le deja trabajar fuera de casa. Toda la fuerza feminista se centra muchas veces en organizar viajes baratos a Londres para abortar o centros de información para atiborrar de píldoras diversas a las mujeres y enriquecer a los *trusts* farmacológicos. Para las más 'liberadas' su feminismo pasa por facilitar a los hombres prostíbulos gratuitos con toda una gama de sofisticaciones y numeritos. Las más 'responsables' toman su ferviente 'profesionalidad' como el precio que deben pagar para demostrar que valen, que pueden ser todo un 'hombrecito'. (1981: 223–4 [italics in original])[33]

[reconciling a woman in the most simplistic manner with her 'partner' who now does the washing up for her or bathes the children and even lets her have a job outside the home. Very often all the feminist energy is concentrated on organising cheap trips to

London to have an abortion or on information centres aimed at stuffing women full of assorted pills while making a fortune for drugs companies. For the most 'liberated' women feminism allows them to make free brothels available to men, offering all manner of sophisticated sexual shenanigans. Those in the most 'responsible' positions accept their fervent 'professionalism' as the price they have to pay to prove their worth, that they can be a 'real man'.]

This particular quote appears to show that one of Spain's principal contributors to a national corpus of difference 'feminist' thought and discussion works from a position which suggests that women will remain in the home and occupy their time with domestic chores – an issue to which I want to return a little later in this chapter. Sendón de León also seems to imply that in her opinion women do not necessarily have the right of autonomy over their own bodies, and intimates that those who enter the professional world become honorary men by dint of their very participation in the paid labour force.

This latter point is also explored by Milagros Rivera, Spain's other eminent difference 'feminist', in her key text entitled *El fraude de la igualdad. Los grandes desafíos del feminismo hoy* [The Equality Con. Feminism's Biggest Challenges Today] (1997). The '*fraude*', or 'con' to which she alludes is the way in which women were sold the belief that they could achieve parity with men by entering the workplace – but on the proviso that they give up all contact with their female body:

No es que las feministas de entonces quisiéramos ser como los hombres ni vivir como ellos; lo que queríamos era distinguirnos mucho de nuestras madres y poder hacer en la sociedad, si así lo deseábamos, todo lo que los hombres adultos, blancos y cultos podían hacer. El precio que se pagó por este intenso amor a la libertad fue, sin embargo, más alto que lo que valían los derechos que pedíamos. A cambio de ellos, a cambio de derechos iguales, se exigió a las mujeres emancipadas o emancipables que fingieran que no tenían cuerpo femenino: éste es el fraude de la igualdad. (1997: 9)

[It's not as if we feminists of those days wanted to be like men nor live like them; what we wanted was to be very different from our mothers and be able to do everything that adult, white, educated men could do – if we so wanted. The price that was paid for this fervent love of freedom, however, was much higher than the value of the rights we were asking for. In exchange for them, in exchange for equal rights, it was demanded that emancipated women (or those who could be emancipated) pretend that they did not have a feminine body. That is the great con of equality.]

Rivera's contribution to the debate – apparently somewhat more considered and measured than Sendón de León's impassioned diatribe – has been echoed far more recently by Carmen Alborch, Spanish Minister of Culture between 1993 and 1996 and a highly visible figure on Spain's contemporary cultural and political scenes. In 2002, she published *Malas. Rivalidad y complicidad entre mujeres* [Wicked Women. Rivalry and Complicity among Women], a weighty tome that achieved excellent sales and was later made available in cheap paperback editions. The book meanders through history, mythology, and a great deal of Spanish and Italian difference 'feminism' theory and posits a largely post-feminist vision of the situation of women in contemporary Spain, concluding that female solidarity is largely unattainable under the premises of equality feminism. Like Sendón de León and Rivera, Alborch also takes issue with the 'masculinization' of women as a result of the demands of the feminist movement of the 1960s, 1970s and 1980s, and talks about

mujeres en las que la lucha por el éxito y el triunfo han *masculinizado* – en el peor sentido de la expresión – algunos de sus hábitos, formas de comportamiento y recursos, forzándolas a adoptar los mismos lenguajes y ademanes bélicos de los hombres frente a sus congéneres, las demás mujeres, con las que se ven forzadas a competir desde la pueril concepción masculina del éxito y el triunfo. (18 [italics in original])

[women whose behaviours, lifestyle strategies, and some of their habits have been *masculinized* – in the worst sense of the word – by the struggle to succeed and triumph, forcing them to adopt the same bellicose language and gestures as men when dealing with their fellow women, with whom they have been forced to compete under the terms of the puerile masculine perception of success and triumph.]

Alborch's assumption that 'success' and 'triumph' are male categories forged in the patriarchy suggests that women's 'natural' way of behaving precludes subscription to such notions. Her view echoes that of difference 'feminists' such as Sendón de León or Rivera in Spain who, like the Italian theorists whose work they develop, posit the prevailing political *modus operandi* as a patriarchal one with which women should not and cannot legitimately engage, nor in which they should participate. Alborch's comments are all the more surprising because, as a female politician of some very considerable visibility, her reader might assume that in order to secure her position she had to engage in at least some of those very strategies she professes to abhor.

Through the medium of her detective, Petra Delicado, Giménez-Bartlett ponders and responds to many aspects of this difference 'feminist' vision of the demands and expectations of the Spanish woman who has, apparently, been led down the garden path of a utopian but unattainable equality by means of professional participation. It is in *Un barco cargado de arroz*, an outstanding work of fiction and easily Giménez-Bartlett's finest novel to date, that Petra enters into a detailed consideration of the effects that her job has had on her personality and on her private life. She realizes that her work for the force has affected her very significantly, and observes: 'Había llegado a pensar que la influencia del trabajo era mínima en mi estado interior, pero aquel caso estaba revelando la falsedad de esa idea' [I'd got to the point where I thought my work had only a minimal effect on my inner self, but the case was showing me how false this idea was] (66). Perhaps more importantly, she also begins to see that she is giving up her social life in order to fulfil the demands of her post:

> Estaba acostumbrándome a trabajar todo el tiempo, respetando cada vez menos los horarios de una persona civilizada. Si seguía de aquél modo, acabaría como uno de esos polizontes que carece por completo de vida privada y que sólo disfruta cuando está metiendo las narices en algún caso. Había conocido unos cuantos así [. . .] estaba actuando con negligencia en lo que atañía a mi vida personal, y eso no podía permitírmelo. (68–9)

> [I was getting used to working all the time, increasingly failing to observe a civilized routine. If I carried on like that I'd end up like one of those cops who have no private life whatsoever, and only enjoy themselves when they're sticking their noses into some case or other. I'd known a few like that [. . .] I was becoming negligent with regard to my personal life, and I couldn't allow that.]

In many ways, then, Giménez-Bartlett is reminding her reader of one of the key issues reiterated by Spanish difference 'feminists': that by working outside the home in a paid professional post women 'endanger' other aspects of their existence and identity. Nor is it any coincidence that she likens herself to 'cops' she has known – all of whom, we may infer, were male. By immersing herself in her career, by participating in every case on an equal footing – or with even more fervour – than her male colleagues, she has effectively become 'one of the lads', an honorary 'bloke', a 'male' workaholic – apparently with the unhappy consequences highlighted by Alborch, Rivera, and Sendón de León.

Within the same novel Giménez-Bartlett drives home the point that women really cannot have their cake and eat it, so to speak. Petra has not had a relationship with a man for a long time, despite her manifest enjoyment of sexual activity, and realizes that she does not even know any more what sort of male might attract her: '¿Cómo me gustaban ahora [los hombres]? ¡Ni siquiera podía contestarme a eso! Hacía tanto tiempo que no salía con nadie ni pensaba en ligar. Me encontraba demasiado absorbida por mi rutina y las responsabilidades del cargo' [What sort [of men] did I like these days? I couldn't even answer my own question! It was such a long time since I'd been out with anybody or even thought of picking up a man. I was far too absorbed in the routine and responsibilities of my job] (70).

Petra is not the only female character in *Un barco cargado de arroz* to articulate the belief, dear to the hearts of difference 'feminists', that women cannot expect to have it all. Silvia Caminal, the young female medical doctor who performs post mortems for the police, is also aware that her profession and a private life are not compatible:

> Soy buena en lo que hago, ¿sabes? Y creo que algún día seré la mejor. Saqué sobresaliente en todas las asignaturas de la especialidad. Tengo planes. Algún día estaré en la cúspide profesional [. . .] También sé que no tendré hijos y no me casaré si se trata de un matrimonio que pueda peligrar mi carrera. Ahora hay muchas mujeres que pensamos así, lo que pasa es que no suele decirse, queda mal. (42)

> [I'm really good at what I do, you know. And I think that one day I'll be the very best. I got top marks for all my specialist subjects. I have plans. One day I'll be at the very top of my profession [. . .] I also know that I won't have children and I won't get married if it's the kind of marriage that will get in the way of my career. There are

lots of women who think like that nowadays, but they don't usually talk about it because it doesn't look good.]

The reason it doesn't look good to talk about not wanting children in preference to a career is because in Spain – as in many other national arenas – the belief that women should prioritize communion with their bodies, their biology, their 'essence' is widespread. This 'return to the body', so to speak, would entail prioritizing motherhood over career development. And this assumption is held not only by men, but also by women, as the works of Sendón de León, Rivera, and Alborch seem to suggest.

But while Giménez-Bartlett flags up the issue of the incompatibility of professional development and motherhood or marriage for women, and provides the younger woman with space to voice her unequivocal rejection of the traditional female role, the views on the topic evinced by the childless, twice-divorced Petra are – in keeping with all aspects of her personality – rather contradictory, and she concedes to Silvia that she is still not sure if the decisions she has taken in her life have been the right ones (*Un barco cargado de arroz* 42–3). Indeed, in her study of the Delicado novels Kathleen Thompson-Casado repeatedly highlights the detective's very contradictory and ambiguous personality traits in an attempt to discern whether the character can be read as a feminist figure or not (2002: 74–5, 78, 79). Thompson-Casado observes that '[a]mbiguity [. . .] appears to be a purposely chosen central concept of these novels' (74), and Giménez-Bartlett of course calls readerly attention to this ambiguity in her very naming of her character as Petra (rock) and Delicado (delicate, or soft). The Inspector's stance illustrates well the paradoxes of female existence in the contemporary Spain she inhabits, a national context in which contradictory discourses regarding expectations of women's roles compete to be heard. Her ambivalence is apparent in her often very ambiguous responses to her professional standing and the philosophy of law enforcement, to the extent that I would suggest that she seems to shift between demonstrating anti-feminist attitudes that could be read as post-feminist or even unfriendly to other women, and a considerable diffidence towards the 'achievements' supposedly enjoyed by women like her in the professional and personal realms.[34]

Within the Petra Delicado texts there exist three primary areas of professional behaviour in which our protagonist's ambiguous structuring is made particularly apparent. I want to consider each of these in turn in order to show how Petra shifts between stances that on first reading seem symptomatic of her ambivalence but actually function to uncover how Giménez-Bartlett is working through the prevailing and often contradictory gendered ideologies which her character must negotiate. Petra demonstrates what Alborch and others deem to be 'masculinization' in the realms of language, her relationship to her gun – and thus, the use of violence –, and observance of the rigidity of the 'law' and its dictates. As I noted earlier in this section, vast swathes of Barcelona society – and specifically its less than salubrious underbelly – are uncovered as Petra peels back the veneer of gentility that covers the unpleasant side of the Catalan capital. In all of the novels to date any number of social groups and classes are shown to be implicated in the crime investigated within the text but, ultimately, the guilty party is always revealed to be an individual whose actions were motivated by greed or a desire for revenge or power. This pattern radically revises the norm established in Spain's earlier post-dictatorship *novela negra* to implicate the nation's governmental, financial, and other institutions in crime and corruption, and also stands in opposition to Oliver's ethos, made clear in the Lònia Guiu mysteries, which reproduces the belief in the culpability of the political and economic establishment and patriarchally determined power groups. Nor is Giménez-Bartlett particularly interested to focus on crimes perpetrated by men against women victims,[35] a key element of Oliver's detective novels.

One area in which Petra and Lònia Guiu might initially appear similar is in their use of strong language. Both women swear profusely – Lònia in Catalan and Petra in Castilian, and Giménez-Bartlett's character in particular deploys all the terms to describe both male and female genitalia that are now intrinsic to peninsular Spanish.[36] As Walton and Jones note, the hard-boiled novel was conceived as a form of writing nuanced *against* the elitist and the feminine (121). The language employed by its smart-talking hero was quite clearly constructed as masculine in this respect, and indeed, there still persist in many cultural environments powerful constraints on women's use of expletives. In the texts analysed here Lònia and Petra both use strong language when surprised or angry, to underscore humour, and in an attempt to appear tough when dealing with colleagues or suspects. It would seem that both Oliver and Giménez-Bartlett emphasize how their protagonists utilize expressive modes of this type to show that both detectives are equipped to usurp 'the masculine' in this, and other areas when necessary.[37] It must be remembered, however, that assimilating male behaviour in this regard is a formulaic and tokenistic route to 'equality' and does not in any way really signify professional parity with those men with whom Inspector Delicado shares the workplace or with whom Lònia has dealings. Language, then, and specifically *bad* language, is one of the sites at which the detective's ambivalent employment and personal situation as a woman who has allegedly achieved emancipation comes to the fore.

Petra's straight talking is initially a source of great disquiet for the old-fashioned Garzón, and during their first case he informs her that he would prefer to work with a male partner, apropos of her use of bad language (*Ritos de muerte* 37). While delivering a report to her he tells her that during the questioning of the first rape victim the girl had indicated that her attacker had grabbed her breasts while assaulting her. His vocabulary is so politically correct and formulaic that Petra has to ask him for clarification of his meaning, to which he responds that the victim had been subjected to 'succiones mamarias y cosas por el estilo' [oral contact with her breasts, that sort of thing] (37). Our candidly spoken policewoman takes exception to her partner's timid use of vocabulary, and discourses at length on the absurdity of his attempts to appear politically correct and his use of inflexible police style, much to Garzón's chagrin:

—¿Quiere decir que estuvo magreándole las tetas? ¿Eso quiere decir?

Me miró con antipatía.

—Sí, eso quiero decir.

¿De dónde había salido aquel polizonte, Dios, de algún seminario? ¿Por qué me cayó en suerte justamente a él? Ya había muchas mujeres trabajando en la policía, y más de una vez debía haberse cruzado con alguna, hablado con ella. ¿Por qué coño decía succiones mamarias? ¿Nunca soltaba un taco ante una mujer? ¿Exclamaba ¡testículos! en lugar de ¡cojones! en los momentos de tensión? (37)

['Do you mean he was groping her tits, is that what you mean?' He shot me a look of dislike. 'Yes, that's what I mean'. Good God, where on earth had this cop come from? A seminary? And why was it my bad luck to have ended up with him? There were lots of women working in the police force, and he must surely have come across some of them at some point and spoken to them. Why the fuck did he say 'oral contact with the breasts'? Didn't he ever swear in front of women? Did he exclaim 'testicles!' instead of 'bollocks!' when he was het up?]

By the sixth novel in the series, *Un barco cargado de arroz*, Garzón has become more than accustomed to Petra's use of colourful language, but other male colleagues, while deploying expletives within earshot of their female counterpart, are offended by her use of similar terms. Inspector Sangüesa, head of the financial investigations unit, upbraids Petra for continually harassing him for information, to which she responds: '—Sangüesa, no seas cabrón' ['Sangüesa, don't be a bastard' ('cabrón' translates literally as 'male goat')]. Her workmate's sense of gendered propriety prompts him to point out: '—Tampoco "cabrón" es el vocablo ideal para una abogada y una dama' ['"Bastard" is hardly a word that a lawyer and a lady should be using'] (272). Although the conversation ends good humouredly, Sangüesa's response serves to remind the reader that even within the police force, known for its tough talking and uninhibited vocabulary, gendered linguistic conventions are still observed by Petra's male colleagues and her directness can shock them. Her 'equality' with them, then (in this case specifically her assumption that she, too, can use the strong vocabulary in which they habitually indulge), is thus brought into doubt, and is an issue that again underpins Giménez-Bartlett's interrogation of the real gains of Spanish women at the end of the twentieth century and into the twenty-first.

Petra also uses linguistic violence to reinforce actual or threatened physical violence, a tactic that causes raised eyebrows in some of the social circles she frequents. During a genteel breakfast with the equally genteel Concepción Enárquez – the sister of Garzón's holiday romance 'conquest' – Petra threatens to beat up her partner if he fails to behave, much to Concepción's consternation: '—[. . .] si persiste en hacer el gilipollas lo que haré será romperle la cara de un puñetazo. —¡Caramba, inspectora!' ['[. . .] if he carries on behaving like a dickhead I'll smash his face in'. 'Goodness, Inspector!'] (*Serpientes en el paraíso* 171). In the same novel Petra also exteriorizes her aggression during a bar fight. She confesses to Fermín that she has always wanted to get involved in a brawl, but that she has never dared to because she is a woman (124). She and her colleague then proceed to beat up a group of young men without the slightest provocation, much to her enjoyment: 'Sentí que la sangre me burbujeaba, que un ramalazo máximo de excitación hacía presa en mí. Me acerqué, cogí a uno de aquellos chicos vociferantes por la solapa de su cazadora de piel y lo golpeé en la cara con toda la fuerza de que fui capaz. ¡Ah, qué sensación maravillosa!' [I could feel my blood effervescing, that a tremendous wave of excitement was taking me over. I approached the yelling lads, grabbed one of them by the lapel of his leather jacket, and smashed him in the face with all my might. Ah, what a marvellous feeling!] (125).

Petra and Fermín are fortunately saved by their friend, the judge García Mouriños, who drags them off to his apartment before the police can arrive and discover that two of their number initiated the fight. Once at the judge's home Petra proceeds to explain exactly why she wanted to participate in the punch-up:

—No era un capricho, señores. Me sentía mal y decidí reaccionar de forma masculina. Los hombres beben, luchan, lo sacan todo al exterior sin miedo. ¿Y saben qué hacemos las mujeres cuando hay algo que nos corroe, lo saben? [. . .] ¡Pues a callar y aguantar, eso es lo que hacemos, interiorizar! (127)

['It wasn't a whim, gentlemen. I wasn't feeling good and decided to react in the way a man would. Men drink, they fight, they just get it all off their chest without any fear at all. And do you know what we women do when something's eating us up inside? Do you know? [. . .] Well, we keep quiet and put up with it, that's what we do. We bottle it all up inside.']

Despite her own actions on this occasion – and in other scenarios as I shall detail later – Petra thus seems to conceive of violence as a male preserve but also seems to believe that aggression has some value and significance as a means of expression. I would posit, however, that her stance is disquieting for the female, particularly the feminist, reader of Giménez-Bartlett's novels. Vanacker has pointed out with reference to Anglophone woman-centred, female-authored detective fiction that excessive violence perpetrated by the investigator may leave a feminist reader 'off-balance and uneasy about identification with the protagonist'

(67–8). Such a reader may also be concerned that, rather than Petra's use of violence being directed towards the protection of other women, much as Shuker-Haines and Umphrey conclude to be the case in many women's genre fictions in English (77), or even in pursuit of her duty as a policewoman, she displays aggressive behaviours for the hell of it – a siting that places her in direct opposition to Lònia Guiu who tries to avoid violent encounters if at all possible. It is perhaps in this realm, then, that what commentators such as Milagros Rivera or Carmen Alborch see as the dangerous 'masculinization' of the working female comes to the fore most clearly within the series. And once again, as in the case of the detective's use of expletives, we must read Giménez-Bartlett's extensive exposition and analysis of this particular theme as a device constructed to lay bare the considerable anomalies of the professional woman's situation in contemporary Spain.

The other area of working activity in which Petra may be deemed to have 'usurped' certain 'male' behaviours or attitudes is in her relationship to her gun – a weapon with which she is of course equipped as a member of the nation's official police force – and its link to, and encouragement of, violent behaviours by our policewoman protagonist. In the context of Anglophone crime fiction (and specifically US texts as Great Britain exercises extremely strict control on gun ownership and the police are not usually armed) critics have observed that the female investigator who wields a weapon is invested with new, 'phallic' – and thus 'masculine' – powers. In their paper on woman-authored detective novels in English, Shuker-Haines and Umphrey analyse the relationship of Sue Grafton's Kinsey Millhone character to her gun, pointing out how it becomes 'a fetishized "old friend" with clear phallic overtones' (73). Similarly, Dilley discusses how Sandra Scoppettone's protagonist, Lauren Laurano, 'has comparatively little power or authority' because she is a woman, but that 'with the gun, she regains control over the situation' (45). These issues of power and control are neatly summarized by Linda Mizejewski who points out that in Hollywood movies 'the professional woman investigator [is] not just a dame with a gun, but a licensed woman in a hardboiled tradition: in short, the female dick' (13). Mizejewski goes on to discuss the many meanings of the word 'dick', but primary among them, of course, are 'detective' and 'penis', the one traditionally masculine, the other inherently so.

In Petra's case her relationship to her little Glock revolver – fairly lightweight and handy for carrying around in her handbag – changes as the series progresses, but ultimately comes to symbolize many of the attitudes and assumptions pondered by those Anglophone critics cited above. In *Día de perros*, for example, she and Garzón come face to face with a fighting dog that is about to jump and rip out their throats. Petra is unable to use her gun to shoot the animal because she has left the weapon in her bag in their police car. By the most recent novel, however, she has become used to carrying her firearm with her at all times, and it makes many – and brutal – appearances within *Un barco cargado de arroz*. For example, when threatening a small-time crook, Matías Sanpedro, Petra pulls out her revolver in order to gain the upper hand:

> Rebusqué en el bolso deprisa, saqué la pistola. Le atenacé la nuca con una mano y le metí el cañón en la boca, chocando abruptamente con sus dientes. Ahí los ojos le cambiaron de expresión, tenía pánico. Empezó a lloriquear. (54)

> [I scrabbled around in my handbag and took out my pistol. I gripped the back of his neck with one hand and shoved the barrel of the gun into his mouth, smashing it against his teeth. That's when the expression in his eyes changed, he was in a panic. He began to snivel.]

What we see here is what I will call Petra's 'phallusization'. In part this is her wholesale subscription to the strongly 'masculine' values of the police force, founded in brutality and violence (not all of which is gendered or directed solely against women), but it is also symbolic of her gaining an actual phallic substitute. For what does the above citation replicate if not a staple of literary, filmic, and media products – and, most likely, of pornography, too? In a plethora of cultural outputs the male rams his erect penis into a woman's mouth as he drags on her hair to violently wrench back her head to facilitate his enforced oral entry of her. Her widened eyes register her panic and fear as they roll in their sockets. Petra's gun, then, is her 'penis'; she has become a dick with a dick. Her status in this regard thus stands in direct opposition to that of Lònia Guiu, the PI without a gun whose vulnerability because she does *not* carry a weapon is repeatedly made clear by Maria-Antònia Oliver.

Petra's love affair with her revolver-phallus reaches its crescendo in *Un barco cargado de arroz* after an interesting relationship to penises develops throughout the earlier books in the series. In *Ritos de muerte*, the very first Petra Delicado novel, our protagonist forces a young man who falsely claims to be the rapist to undress in an interrogation room, and sits for some considerable time staring at his genitals in a successful attempt to make him confess that he was not involved in the case she is investigating (63–5).[38] By visually 'appropriating' the suspect's penis – on the beauty of which she also comments – Petra thus initiates the route to her own 'phallusization' which, from a reading of this incident at least, might appear to be prompted by penis envy.[39] In the third Petra novel, *Mensajeros de la oscuridad*, Inspector Delicado is sent postal packets containing amputated penises. This further development in her link to the penis indicates a sort of middle ground: she no longer simply observes male genitalia, she now has some of her own. However, these have been sent to her without her consent, thus placing her in an ambiguous relation to them. It is in the latest novel to date, then, *Un barco cargado de arroz*, that her bond with the phallus is resolved with her full appropriation and use of her service revolver, her very own little penis. Because she now has a dick all her own, Petra has become 'empowered' in a traditionally masculine way, just as, in the quotes cited earlier, Dilley, Mizejewski, and Shuker-Haines and Umphrey concluded occurs in Anglophone detective fictions that protagonize a female who wields a firearm.

In another telling scene, Petra fantasizes about showing her gun to Ricard Crespo, a 'mad' psychiatrist whom she meets while investigating the murder with which *Un barco cargado de arroz* opens, and with whom she will have a passionate affair (which, nevertheless, ends with the closure of the novel). She has invited her beau for dinner at her home, and as she cooks the meal considers how the evening might develop:

> En caso de que el encartado se pusiera pesado, no tenía más que largarlo y en paz. Además, en un momento de emergencia, siempre podía usar mi pistola reglamentaria. Una sonrisa inconsciente me vino a los labios. Imaginé la cara del psiquiatra loco viéndose encañonado por mi Glock. Casi deseé que se produjera algo parecido. (69)

[In the event that the accused got to be a nuisance I only had to
kick him out, end of story. Anyway, if an emergency situation arose
I could always use my regulation issue pistol. A subconscious smile
came to my lips. I imagined the mad psychiatrist's face when he saw
my Glock pointed at him. I almost hoped that something like that
would happen.]

The sex/power parallel made apparent from the earlier quote
is again clear in this citation. Petra is sexually excited at the
thought of Crespo's visit, and she imagines pointing her revolver
at him, showing him her phallus – again analogous with a sort of
primaeval male behaviour of exhibiting the penis to the female.
Equally, however, she is energized by the feeling of power that
aiming her gun at her guest will induce – both because she is
a police officer and because she can invert the more usual
gendered sex roles.

Interestingly, however, when Petra first meets Crespo and he
asks her to show him her revolver, the interplay of power between
them is far more ambiguous:

—[. . .] ¿Puede enseñarme su pistola?

Me quedé estupefacta. ¿A quién me enfrentaba, a un psiquiatra
loco, o a un espíritu burlón. Titubeé.

[. . .]

No llevaba ningún guión preparado para aquella situación, me
cogió desprevenida, y como una imbécil hice lo que me pedía,
saqué la Glock del bolso y se la mostré en la palma de la mano.
(27)

['[. . .] Can you show me your gun?' I was stupefied. Who was I
dealing with? A mad psychiatrist, or a joker? I hesitated [. . .] I
didn't have a script prepared for that sort of situation and I was
caught off guard. Like an idiot I did what he asked. I took the
Glock out of my handbag and showed it to him in the palm of my
hand.]

On the one hand, then, Petra gets out her phallus and shows it
to Ricard – a man who is apparently more than willing for a
woman to take the lead in matters sexual and otherwise. On the
other, however (and this is where the intense ambiguity of the
character's personality comes to the fore), she does what the
medic tells her to do – she complies with his request *because* he is
a man. Thus, although Giménez-Bartlett's protagonist is a feisty,

outspoken, independent woman with a gun all of her own, she is often seen within the novels that make up the series obeying orders given to her by men, a point to which I shall return later in this section.

One area in which Petra's ambiguous stance towards the gendered nuances of her professional endeavour come to the fore is when ensuring she receives just praise and reward for successfully bringing investigations to a close, for on several occasions she allows male colleagues to garner the congratulations for solving cases which she and Garzón had painstakingly unscrambled. Her modesty in this regard is initially made manifest in *Ritos de muerte* when, at the end of the narrative she asserts: 'no quiero que nadie piense que busco el aplauso' [I don't want anybody to think that I'm seeking the limelight] (254). Her refusal to participate in a press conference to discuss her work on the case she has solved means that the public is informed that García del Mazo, the 'boy wonder' of the Gerona police who was called in to try to get to the bottom of the multiple rapes, resolved the puzzling crime, and he is awarded the attendant merits. The closure of *Muertos de papel* is similar, as Petra is entirely unperturbed that Moliner, a male inspector, may take all the credit for having solved a case in which she and Garzón had invested a vast amount of time and energy, and claims: 'Seguir batallando por los laureles de un caso después de haber trabajado denodadamente en él, siempre me ha parecido un exceso' [To carry on fighting for the laurels in a case after you've tirelessly worked on it has always seemed over the top to me] (280). She then heads off to the beauty salon and to engage in a shopping spree.

Her attitude on both occasions seems to reveal that she understands that however much she might work towards the successful resolution of a case, it is more than likely that a male colleague will manage to manoeuvre himself into the limelight. Her comments might also be read as symptomatic of the profound sense of irony that characterizes Giménez-Bartlett's 'lady inspector'. Furthermore, the alacrity with which in the second example cited above Petra dashes off to avail herself of a 'pamper session' also suggests that in these earlier novels, at least, she still finds some time outside her professional schedule to devote to herself, that she is not just a cop obsessed with her job.

Significantly, though, given her apparent willingness to leave male workmates to collect the rewards for a job that she and

Fermín have done, we might read her stance as suggesting that for a woman a decent hair-do and the purchase of a pair of high heels and black stockings is perhaps of greater importance than protecting one's professional interests. Although her attitude appears to run counter to the image painted by Sendón de León or Alborch of the fiercely competitive cat-fighting career woman, it is highly evocative of Susan Faludi's and Germaine Greer's perception of the woman who inhabits the post-feminist space and functions within the post-feminist economy as a consumer-motivated and consumer-constructed individual. Greer sees post-feminism as a phenomenon of the marketplace controlled by multinationals, and says it has brought women little but the business suit, carefully coiffed hair, and excessive make-up (glossed in Falcón 2000: 135–6; Gamble 51).[40] Faludi claims that as a '*commercial* response to the women's movement, post-feminism offers women an adman's Faustian pact: the promise of 'powerful' sex appeal and 'choices' you buy with your very own credit card, in exchange for genuine power and self-determined choices for all women' (2000: 1647 [italics in original]) – a lens through which we might read some of Inspector Delicado's behaviours and attitudes.

Indeed, Petra often appears not to exercise the authority the reader might expect of a senior police officer. On the one hand her *notional* authority as an inspector is often undermined by her male colleagues, but she may also refuse to wield the power that her post affords her (just as the aforementioned difference 'feminists' suggest, women avoid exercising authority in their professional environment. In the third novel of the series Petra wryly observes, 'A ese estado habíamos llegado, a la total desmiti-ficación de mi autoridad' [We'd reached the point at which any authority I had no longer held any mystique whatsoever] (*Mensajeros de la oscuridad* 15). While it is indeed the case that Petra and Fermín enjoy a solid friendship based on mutual understanding and humour as well as a strong working relationship, her role as Garzón's superior is rarely, if ever, made clear. In fact, Kathleen Thompson-Casado quite correctly observes that 'it is Petra who initially desires to establish a collaborative investigative style' (2004: 146), and although the critic points out that Garzón at first rejects such an arrangement, in later novels in the series he has subscribed fully to the notion of his equal standing with his 'boss'. Indeed, in *Un barco cargado de arroz* the Deputy Inspector reminds her that 'cualquier cosa que tenga importancia profesional no la concibe usted sin mí' [you don't take any professional decisions without me] (311), thus confirming that his supposed position as her subordinate is questionable. What seems to be the case here, then, is that Petra and her sidekick evince very different attitudes towards the implementation of authority in their professional environment, for while the Inspector seeks a more collaborative, collegial working *modus operandi*, the Deputy Inspector is initially keen to preserve the hierarchy inherent in the police. While Petra's stance might be a result of her position as a newcomer to the job (i.e. she is unaware of the importance of the rigid pecking order within the force), and her youth relative to Garzón, the gendering of the dynamics of the pair's occupational relationship should not be overlooked, for her willing abrogation of power suggests that it is perhaps as a woman, specifically, that she does not wish to – or feels she cannot – exploit her authority, a pattern very much in keeping with observations by the Spanish difference 'feminists' cited earlier as well as the Anglophone post-feminist scholars also just quoted.

Petra does not relinquish her say-so only within her workplace, however. Within the novels she protagonizes there is strong indication that she acquiesces to some men in her private life, too. In *Ritos de muerte* Petra's first husband, Hugo, makes a number of appearances. He initially telephones the detective at home to ask if they can meet as he needs her to sign some documents pertaining to the sale of the final property they jointly own. Petra immediately slips back into the role of timorous, subservient wife, and agrees to his request: 'Asentí como si fuera imbécil y nos dimos una cita. Había vuelto a hacerlo de nuevo: temer su opinión, demostrarle sin ninguna necesidad que era respetable, cuidadosa, razonable, convencional. No lograría nunca sacudirme el encogimiento que me atenazaba frente a él' [I said yes like a moron and we set up a time to meet. I'd done it again: fear his opinion, show him, entirely unnecessarily, that I was respectable, careful, reasonable, and conventional. I'd never shake off the shrinking feeling that gripped me whenever he was around] (78). Her depressing submission increases as their conversation develops. Hugo insults her professionally, criticizes her for having become a policewoman, derides Garzón and his dress sense, and tells her she will never solve the case of the multiple rapist (78–80). Throughout this tirade Petra either remains silent or makes weak attempts to interject and pacify her former spouse – to no avail. Hugo's offensive slurs reach a crescendo when they do finally meet for lunch – in the company of Fermín and Hugo's impeccable second wife, and again Petra says nothing: 'Yo estaba allí, con una sonrisa mecánica clavada en la boca, preguntándome de qué manera saldría de aquello sin humillarme' [There I was, with a forced smile on my lips, asking myself how on earth I was going to get out of the situation without making a fool of myself] (153). Petra does seem aware of the debasement and manipulation to which she is subjected by her ex-husband but does not seem equipped to deal with them in order to extricate herself from her unpleasant predicament. Perhaps her socialization as a female has retarded her ability in this regard, for Petra has possibly internalized the notion – espoused and promoted by the difference 'feminists' too – that women should refrain from taking command and defer to the authority of a husband.

Despite the negative portrayal of Hugo, however, a noticeable characteristic of Petra's response to men is often a gentle grumbling that seems to suggest that she sees many of them as rather adorable, if childish, individuals who are often devoid of aggressive tendencies – a view that seems to replicate that expressed by the author herself.[41] In *Un barco cargado de arroz*, our heroine is initially very much attracted to Ricard Crespo because of his rather unkempt, unworldly appearance. Following a telephone conversation with him Petra muses on men:

> Los hombres son extraños —pensé—, territoriales y olfativos como las alimañas, pero capaces de una gran ternura y afectividad. A veces se comportan como cachorros de cocker y otras como lobos enfurecidos. Pero era inútil sacar sobre ellos un balance negativo, porque la verdad era que me resultaban más fascinantes que cualquier otro ser vivo, excepción hecha del colibrí. (198)

> [Men are strange, I thought to myself, territorial and olfactory like animals, but capable of great tenderness and affection. At times they behave like spaniel puppies, and at others like rabid wolves. But it was no good coming down on the negative side about them because they fascinated me more than any other living being – except for the humming bird.]

While Petra's observations – like many of her interventions within the novels she protagonizes – are laden with irony, her view would appear to be a fair measure of a more widespread attitude towards the opposite sex apparent from a reading of the Delicado series. Within these fictions women do complain about men, but mostly in a good-natured way and with a fair deal of acceptance of the manner in which they are treated by them. Earlier in *Un barco cargado de arroz* Petra had observed that 'ya lo decían todas mis amigas, era un clamor general: los hombres son un desastre en los últimos tiempos' [all my girlfriends said the same thing: men are a disaster these days] (81–2). The point had also been made in *Muertos de papel* and, in keeping with Giménez-Bartlett's position, the moans about men voiced by the women with whom Petra shares an afternoon at the sauna eventually turn into a generalized discourse of an understanding of the quirks and idiosyncrasies of the male:

> se enzarzaron en un rosario de comentarios sin desperdicio sobre los hombres, su manera desconsiderada de portarse, su debilidad interior, su incapacidad para afrontar los cambios de la edad . . . [. . .] Hubo acuerdo por unanimidad, y lo que habían sido denuestos se convirtieron como por magia en frases de aceptación e inexorabilidad para acabar siendo bromas, cada vez más subidas de tono. (79 [first ellipsis in original])

> [they got caught up in a string of stinging comments about men: their lack of consideration for others, their weak character, their inability to face up to getting older . . . [. . .] They all agreed, and what had been insults magically turned into words of acceptance and inevitability, finally ending up as jokes that became more and more risqué.]

Although in this sequence Petra is in a sauna with a group of women, this is an unusual scenario within the novels she protagonizes as she does not habitually form part of a female – or even mixed-sex – social group, except sporadically in *Día de perros* in which she socializes with Garzón and his two female lovers, and in *Serpientes en el paraíso* where we see her in the company of her colleague, his (new) lover, her sister, and the judge, García Mouriños. In the sauna incident, rather than evoking the sort of 'sisterhood' promulgated in Maria-Antònia Oliver's detective texts, however, Giménez-Bartlett's depiction of the scene – naked bourgeois women lolling in the comfort of an expensive spa while moaning about their husbands – is very similar to Faludi's description of the protagonists of a number of Anglophone post-feminist products, of whom she notes: 'women who are shown with "careers" and economic power [. . .] use these gains primarily to shop, obsess about their weight, and whine about loser guys' (2000: 1647–8). What Giménez-Bartlett is indicating here, it seems, is that Petra – and other Spanish women – have moved on and away from the notions of female solidarity and sisterhood illustrated in Oliver's overtly feminist fictions. Although the very concept of 'sisterhood' was in any case a problematic one for many schools of feminist thought, through the figure of Petra Delicado her author reminds the reader that within the post-feminist climate inhabited by her detective ideas such as this one are no longer considered particularly relevant.

At the most essential level of 'sisterhood', Petra fails to understand her biological sister, Amanda, who appears for the first – and only – time in *Muertos de papel*, a narrative characterized by the frequent bitter words and recriminations that pass between the siblings. Her empathy with women often appears somewhat limited, a situation made particularly apparent in the latest novel in the series. In *Un barco cargado de arroz*, Petra has to seek the assistance of Yolanda, a very young female member of the municipal police who is very much in awe of her older colleague, not least because of the stories she has heard about her (17). Yolanda invites Petra to call her by her first name and asks her many questions about her personal life (18) – possibly in the belief that because they are both women Petra will take her into her confidence. However, Inspector Delicado responds brusquely and extremely rudely and insists on using the formal 'usted' mode of address with the young officer (18–19). Although she later ruminates on her 'bad' behaviour (21, 31) she often feels unable to respond to friendly overtures from other women,[42] possibly because the moral of at least two of the novels seems to be that trusting other women can be dangerous and that it is thus best to simply avoid getting close to them. In *Mensajeros de la oscuridad*, Petra initially places a great deal of faith in her domestic assistant, only to later learn that the girl was in cahoots with the leader of the bizarre sect that sent her amputated penises, and that the younger woman had been placed in her home to spy on the progress of the investigation. A similar pattern is apparent in *Serpientes en el paraíso*. Throughout the narrative Petra responds in a friendly manner to Malena Puig, a resident of the elite housing scheme on which a corpse had appeared, only to realize at the end of the text that she had been consorting with the killer herself. The closure of these particular novels in the Delicado series echoes that of Oliver's *Antípodes*, referred to earlier in this chapter. But where Lònia Guiu's personal and professional beliefs do not preclude her from assisting women or from forming part of female gatherings and networks, Petra – perhaps also because she is a member of the police force – is shown to be increasingly more chary of doing so; perhaps having once been bitten she is now twice shy. We might also read Petra's stance as growing evidence that she is perhaps progressively subscribing to the force's patriarchal philosophy, and that, on the other hand, she evinces behaviours with regard to any possible female solidarity that clearly indicate that she inhabits the post-feminist realm. Similarly, Petra seems to experience little sympathy for the female victims of the crimes she investigates, an attitude made very apparent in *Ritos de muerte*, a response that again places her in counterpoint to Lònia Guiu.

Early on in her investigation of the rapes Petra takes an aerobics class, and suddenly realizes that of the young women also attending the session 'Cualquiera de ellas podía ser violada a la salida de clase, marcada con una flor. Todas me parecían susceptibles de ser empujadas a una pesadilla que destrozaría sus mentes y quizá también sus vidas. En cualquier momento, sin una auténtica razón' [Any one of them could be raped as she left the class, marked with a flower-shaped wound. They all seemed vulnerable to being pushed into a nightmare that would destroy their minds and also maybe their lives. At any moment, and with no real reason] (42). Significantly, though, her perceptiveness does not motivate an empathetic or sympathetic stance towards the girls attacked by the rapist, who evoke for Petra 'esos ratones que hemos cazado en una trampa [. . .] el pelaje suave, los ojos como dos minúsculos botones' [like little mice caught in a trap [. . .] with soft fur and eyes like two tiny buttons] (41). Despite their very obvious fragility, the very considerable social marginalization of all but one of them, and their position as victims of a vicious assault, Petra treats them in a brusque and unfriendly manner devoid of any of the subtleties or comprehension (15–18) a reader might expect from a policewoman – indeed, any police officer – interviewing a girl who has been assaulted.

Furthermore, although she constructs them as victims, she does not characterize them in specifically gendered terms the way that Oliver's Lònia Guiu genders women casualties of male aggression. Rather, Petra sees the girls primarily as members of 'la gran cohorte de jóvenes desheredados que andaba deambulando por la ciudad' [the great mass of disenfranchized youths who wandered around the city] (42). In this way she diminishes the gendered nature of their victimization, although she does flag up issues of social exclusion, a frequent preoccupation throughout the series. Petra's stance can thus be read as indicating a shift towards a more broad-based awareness of the dynamics of victimology, but is also indicative of the author's awareness of post-feminist discourses which construct as a fallacy the universal victim status of the female.[43] As Ann Brooks observes, post-feminism 'challenges hegemonic assumptions held by second wave feminist epistemologies that patriarchal and imperialist oppression was a universally experienced oppression' (2), a stance typified by Camille Paglia (1993) who – among others – criticizes second wave feminism as 'victim feminism'. Equally importantly, *Ritos de muerte* appears to be underpinned to some degree at least by an authorial understanding of the rhetoric of rape formulated by such writers as Roiphe (1994), Paglia (1993), and Sommers (1995 [1994]), which claims that many victims of rape are not 'really' such, and that responsibility for sex crimes should in some cases be assumed by women either individually or as a collective – a stance energetically rejected in the genre fiction of Maria-Antònia Oliver, as was noted in the second section of this chapter.

Key post-feminist scholars such as Katie Roiphe (1994), Rene Denfeld (1995), and Naomi Wolf (1994 [1993]) condemn what they perceive as the feminist construction of the female as victim within patriarchy of male physical aggression and of patriarchally-engineered socio-political inequalities based on gender, while also noting that women are as capable of violence as men. According to the Spanish feminist Lidia Falcón, however, the consequences of such a vision are multifold. They include the vilification of the maternal because, within the economy identified by Roiphe et al., the mother is capable of violence and 'emotional manipulation' (2000: 119–20); the construction in fiction and film of legions of wicked women who give free reign to their violent desires (2000: 126); and the denial of the existence of widespread physical violence against women by men (2000: 129) which had become a veritable tidal wave of killings, rapes, and batterings by the end of the twentieth century (2000: 131), an issue I shall discuss in detail in the next chapter.

In keeping with the post-feminist construction of the maternal signalled by Falcón, in the Petra Delicado series the mother is often portrayed as uncaring or irresponsible, or as a sinister character who merits the hatred and rejection of her offspring for whose delinquent behaviour she is also held responsible.[44] Petra's view also seems to replicate that identified by Naomi King who uses Julia Kristeva's theories to posit that crime fiction is full of devouring mothers (glossed in Cole 155). In Giménez-Bartlett's *Ritos de muerte* and the short story 'Muerte en el gimnasio' the mother features as a castrator and inhibitor. In the short story a man is murdered by the woman he spurned, and an overpowering mother and a stifling domestic environment are suggested as causal factors: if the victim's mother had not encouraged her son to leave his lover she, in turn, would not have killed him in a quest for revenge. In a more recent short story, 'La voz de la sangre' one of the protagonists – a sleazily theatrical, money-grabbing prostitute – is portrayed as the archetypal 'bad mother', one who abandons both of her children to the social services and continues her occupation as a sex worker.

In *Ritos de muerte*, the serial rapist is identified as 'Juan, un tipo apocado y sin carácter, castrado por su madre' [Juan, a spineless type of guy, with no personality, castrated by his mother] (181), a young man who, according to Petra's analysis, suffered from '[d]emasiada presión femenina, demasiados deberes' [too much pressure from women, too many obligations] (140), and whose symbolic emasculation by his mother is posited as the cause of his actions:

> Un joven sometido a una férrea disciplina despersonalizadora podía llegar a estallar, dedicarse a ser diferente y aun opuesto en otra parte, incluso vengarse de un elemento femenino tan totalizador. Y escoger chicas débiles para hacerlo, demasiado temeroso de la ciclópea figura materna. (149)

> [A young man subjected to a rigid, depersonalising discipline could end up exploding, devoting himself to being different and even contrary in another environment, even seeking revenge against such an overpowering female presence. And choosing weak girls for the purpose, because he was so afraid of the Cyclopean maternal figure.]

In this first novel in the series Petra also describes in great detail the joyless, sanitized interior of the home the murderer shares with his mother and cousin, an apartment in which no personal objects are visible. This depiction of the cheerless rooms is evocative of that of the home of the murdered bodybuilder in 'Muerte en el gimnasio', 'un piso cutre cargado de flores secas y tapetes de ganchillo' [a tacky flat stuffed with dried flowers and crocheted doilies] (202). Not only are these 'bad' mothers castrators and inhibitors of their sons' personalities, then, they are also incapable of fulfilling their 'motherly' role to create a warm, welcoming home environment in which their offspring can flourish, providing instead a sterile, impersonal lodging devoid of a space which the young men can call their own or in which they can express their personalities.

Petra's awareness of the deficiencies of interior design apparent in the homes that some male criminals share with their mothers is part of a much wider interest she evinces in homemaking. Her eye for detail could of course be born of the police officer's imperative to observe and take mental note of what is seen, but seems to be linked to the personal importance for her of attractive interiors. This facet of her personality is apparent in many novels as she describes with minute precision the living rooms of friends, colleagues, or suspects, and reaches its apogee in *Serpientes en el paraíso* in which she spends a great deal of time in the beautiful houses in El Paradís, the luxury housing estate on which she must investigate a murder. Within this text her concern about the appearance of her own home is articulated, and as she awaits a visit from Malena Puig she runs her eye over her furniture and decoration in the hope that it will meet the other woman's exacting criteria (235–7).

Inspector Delicado's interest in decoration and furniture certainly suggests a new ('feminine'?) approach to sleuthing.[45] However, this element of the series can also be read as a further indication of Petra's siting within a post-feminist economy informed by difference 'feminist' thought, a central tenet of which is the notion of woman's return and removal to a welltended domestic space. Lidia Falcón has noted that among former fellow activists, youthful participation in the Spanish feminist movement has given way to a denigration and rejection of the value of their early political involvement, and that this goes hand in hand with a move back into the domestic environment they had hardly occupied as young women (2000: 249). In a hugely emotive chapter of *Los nuevos mitos del feminismo* [Feminism's New Myths], Falcón describes in detail, and from a very personal standpoint, how many of her middle-aged female friends have protagonized the shift she identifies, and notes that they have exchanged 'la excitación de la lucha' [the excitement of the battle] and 'la alegría de las victorias obtenidas' [the pleasure of the victories that were won] of their feminist commitment (249) for mortgages, hours and hours spent choosing furniture and accessories for their new homes and, most significantly, 'privacidad' [privacy] in their own domestic 'nest' (245) – a 'room of their own' that is apparently not a space in which to engage in any intellectual or culturally creative activities.

Cruz and Zecchi replicate many of Falcón's observations, although they say that women in Spain are expected to be domestic goddesses as well as public and professional figures: 'se multiplican los discursos políticos y culturales, tanto masculinos como femeninos, que proponen un modelo de mujer que, aun inserta en la esfera pública (profesional), añora la privada, mientras redescubre "valores" tradicionales como el matrimonio, la domesticidad y, sobre todo, la maternidad' [we are seeing an increase in both male- and female-generated political and cultural discourses that propound the notion of a woman who, while still participating in the public (professional) realm, pines for the domestic space as she rediscovers traditional 'values' such as marriage, domesticity and, above all, motherhood] (11). They also conclude that the praise of the home and attendant female subservience within it enjoy more currency now than they did during the Franco regime (11).

In Petra's case, after '[d]emasiados años de apartamentos con muebles funcionales y gran congelador' [too many years of apartments with functional furniture and a huge freezer], she purchased 'una casita con jardín en la ciudad' [a little house with a garden in the city centre] (*Ritos de muerte* 7) which she lavishly refurbishes and decorates, paying particular attention to install a fitted kitchen, in which she aims to prepare delicious dishes following complicated recipes. The lengthy description of the process of creating a little 'nest', and of the time and money invested in the task, is uncannily similar to Lidia Falcón's portrait of the effort expended by her former feminist friends, whom she calls 'las feministas de la privacidad' [privacy feminists] (2000: 245), to create a beautiful home in middle age, revealing a significant shift in their interests and priorities. However, Petra does not have a spouse or children to care for – indeed, she seems quite content having sent two former husbands on their merry way – and in this respect falls somewhat short of post-feminist familial expectations, and nor does she clean her own house – for that arduous chore she employs a daily help. Despite Petra's intentions to become a 'domestic goddess', then, she performs relatively little housework. Her aim to become a gourmet chef within her own kitchen comes to fruition rather infrequently – a situation, I would suggest, that again highlights the detective's ambiguous siting within the gendered economy and underscores the heavy sense of wit and irony that pervade the series: an irony that often functions to call attention to the paradoxes of life as a professional woman in a post-feminist reality.

Another way I think Petra is 'returned' – or returns herself –, so to speak, to the realm of what has traditionally been the 'feminine' (in *opposition* to the kind of feminism espoused by Lònia Guiu, for example) is through her relationship to the media which facilitates her 'objectification', another key issue of concern for some post-feminist scholars. Despite proving herself as a detective by solving a number of particularly difficult cases, when the force is invited to send a representative to participate in a television chat show, she is chosen, not for her sleuthing skills – which by the third novel in the series have become formidable – but because, as her boss explains, 'Siempre queda mejor una mujer' [a woman always goes down better] (*Mensajeros de la oscuridad* 8). He elaborates his point, telling her: 'todo el mundo piensa que una mujer policía es ideal para las tareas humanas y diplomáticas' [everybody thinks a female officer is best for tasks needing the human touch or involving a PR role] (223). Petra is aware that his stance is offensive and highly unoriginal, but decides to participate in the television programme in an attempt to please and 'quedar bien' [look good] (7). Faludi has signalled that women living within the post-feminist economy, which she says is largely generated by the media and advertising, view the media as the only possible means of confirmation of their status as females (2000: 1647–8), a rhetoric which might help to understand Petra Delicado's response to the opportunities for media exposure in the opening pages of *Mensajeros de la oscuridad*. The detective's attitude might also be read as echoing the current scramble to appear on 'reality television', and it is therefore perhaps unsurprising, given the penchant for humiliation of participants that underlies this type of product, that within *Ritos de muerte* Petra should be publicly embarrassed and professionally ridiculed on a television programme. During an interview with a female journalist, the three economically disadvantaged victims of the series of rapes investigated by Petra accuse the detective of harsh treatment and lack of empathy, declarations which fuel a press outcry aimed at removing Petra from the case. What Inspector Delicado's media forays also ultimately reveal, once again, is the ambiguous siting of the professional female in contemporary Spain (as elsewhere): despite her willingness to appear on the television Petra's endeavours in this regard function to highlight her superior's sexist assumption that a woman officer is better suited to such tasks, and this particular medium is the device that launches attacks from all sides on her professional endeavour.

Ultimately, what many of the attitudes and ideas explored in the Petra Delicado series possibly combine to reveal is the disbelief in the likelihood of a gendered equality of the type implicit in the words and deeds of a character such as Oliver's Lònia Guiu.[46] Petra's doubt about the imminent prospect of equal opportunities – despite her education as a lawyer and her present senior post within the police force – is apparent in her stance with regard to accepting recognition for a job well done, to the exercising of authority by women, to the return of the female to the domestic space, and towards the relationship between women and the media, among other notions. Inspector Delicado's view on the unlikelihood of the rapid achievement and implementation of real equal rights (rather than the 'legal' equality of the type I discuss later) is undoubtedly based on her own experiences as a woman and as a police officer, but it should be noted that her opinion also echoes ideas that are central to a great deal of Spanish feminist thought and writing.

The alleged invalidity of equality feminism and the rejection of gender parity as an opportunity or aspiration for women is a cornerstone of Spanish difference 'feminism' which has developed this perspective from Italian difference 'feminism' (see de Grado 40). The two principal Spanish exponents of this particular body of thought, Sendón de León and Rivera, have both written extensively about the concept of equality. I want to cite Rivera at some length on this particular topic, as her words serve to bring together her take on equality and the 'masculinization' of the female noted earlier in this section, and to reveal the roots of her particular line of thought:

> el propio triunfo del principio de igualdad de los sexos sembró la alarma entre sus defensoras y protagonistas, las mujeres emancipadas [. . .] Sembró la alarma ante el peligro real de que lo de la igualdad fuera de verdad en serio y se rompiera el ya delgado hilo de oro que nos enlazaba con el orden simbólico femenino y materno. Convirtiéndonos así, si el hilo se rompía del todo, en mujeres con las raíces al aire, sin memoria de una genealogía propia, simulacros de hombres, ya que hombres, en realidad, no queríamos llegar a ser ni en pintura, ni queríamos tampoco vivir como ellos. (1997: 62–3)

> [the very success of the principle of equality of the sexes caused alarm among the liberated women who were its champions and leaders [. . .] What caused this alarm was the real danger that the equality might indeed be true and that the fine golden thread that joined us to the female and maternal symbolic order might break. If the thread broke completely we would become rootless, with no memory of our own genealogy, simulacra of men, because in reality the last thing we wanted was to become men or to live like them.]

Sendón de León also replicates the assertion that women do not want equality with men: 'Nos ronda el fantasma de un mito o el mito de un fantasma: la igualdad [. . .] ¿Iguales en qué? [. . .] Quiero la diferencia. Me repugna profundamente la igualdad' [We are stalked by the ghost of a myth, or the myth of a ghost: equality [. . .] Equal in what way? [. . .] I want difference. I find equality deeply repugnant] (1981: 112–13).[47] More recently Alborch has claimed that 'la ideología igualitarista del feminismo puede enrarecer y enturbiar las relaciones [entre mujeres]' [feminist egalitarian ideology can rarefy and cloud relations [between women]] (35). Ana Rubio Castro, in her measured, scholarly overview of difference 'feminism', observes that fighting for equality can endanger the feminists' corner, but she qualifies her assertion by pointing out that demanding *only* equality with men leads to a situation in which *only* legal reparation is offered as a means of addressing gender disparity, and that legislation often simply confirms and perpetuates the marginalization of and discrimination against women (185–7). In a similar vein, Cristina Piris has opined that 'L'alliberament sembla tenir un preu massa car, si paral·lelament no s'introdueixen canvis substancials en la vida dels homes i en l'organització de la vida pública' [liberation would seem to have too high a price if in tandem substantial changes in men's lives and the organisation of public life are not introduced] (76).

Within the volume that contains Piris' paper, Charo Altable Vicario also discusses the concept of equality, stating, like Rubio Castro, that legal parity has largely been achieved, but she goes on to ask: '¿dentro de qué modelo se pedía esa igualdad e igualdad de quién con quién? [. . .] ¿Y por qué esa igualdad era de las mujeres con los varones y no de los varones con las mujeres en los valores y las habilidades que hemos desarrollado? [within what model was this equality sought, and equality of who with whom? [. . .] And why was this equality that of women with men and not men with women when it came to the values and abilities we have developed?] (31–2). Neus Campillo – among many other female Spanish commentators on the situation of women in Spain – reminds us that it is dangerous to even believe that sexual equality has been achieved (54). The bottom line in this debate, according to Lucía Etxebarria, novelist, writer, and analyst of women's affairs, is that hers is a nation 'que ya asume, teóricamente *pero no en la práctica*, la igualdad de derechos y deberes de hombres y mujeres' [which has accepted in theory – *but not in practice* – the equality of the rights and responsibilities of men and women] (2000: 8–9 [my italics]).

It is perhaps this reality, and an acknowledgement of the perceived dangers of a simple sex 'equality', that underpin many of Petra's responses to, and stances on, gender parity. On the one hand our detective strives for, and achieves, an equality of sorts in becoming 'one of the lads' within the police force. How real or valid or valuable this type of 'equality' might be, however, is questionable. On the other hand, however, it may indeed be the case that Giménez-Bartlett's character perceives that for some women, at least, equality has been achieved in some areas. Her comment at the end of *Muertos de papel* – 'actualmente se vive como juego aquello por lo que nosotras habíamos organizado una revolución' [women nowadays think of what we fought a revolution for as a game] (37) – reveals to the reader that Petra not only perceives herself as belonging to a generation that fought for women's liberation, but that younger women of today do not believe equality is worth chasing because they think they have achieved it. It is this latter view that in my opinion perhaps echoes Giménez-Bartlett's stance – in the face of assertions such as those articulated by Etxebarria, or Lidia Falcón's devastating conclusion in her latest work, *Las nuevas españolas* (2004), that young Spanish women are marginalized from equal employment opportunities, that they continue to be the victims of acute gendered violence, and that they are sceptical about any hope for their futures.

In conclusion to this discussion of Petra's siting in a post-feminist environment informed by Spanish difference 'feminism' (as well as by other lines of thought or schools of thinking) that is apparent from a reading of Giménez-Bartlett's detective fiction, I want to analyse the notion of individualism as expounded within the novels and assess how it underpins not only post-feminism but also difference 'feminism', and how such a concept is articulated in the context of the genre. In the Anglophone world, where post-feminism was first theorized, younger scholars such as Denfeld, Roiphe, and Wolf propounded a generally 'individualistic, liberal agenda rather than a collective and political one' (Gamble 298). Similarly, the Spanish difference 'feminist' Milagros Rivera explains the fundamental significance of the personal, the individual to her school of thought and she classifies it as 'la política en primera persona' after the Italian difference 'feminists' (1994*a*: 181 *et seq.*; 1994*b*: see especially 31, 33). For the Italians the concepts of *différence* and difference, as theorized particularly by the 'French feminists' – principally Luce Irigaray (see, e.g. Edgar and Sedgwick 115–16; Gamble 216–17) – tie in with the individuality and individualism highlighted in Spain by thinkers such as Rivera. I would stress that while notions of the individual and the personal inform both post-feminism and difference 'feminism', they signify something rather different for each line of thought and, as I noted earlier in this section, I do not want to suggest that post-feminism and difference 'feminism' are one and the same either in Spain or elsewhere – rather that they appear to share many fundamental tenets and points of view. What I see as an important similarity is the way in which both philosophies have apparently informed perceptual and discursive responses to female experience in contemporary Spain. For example, in *Malas*, Carmen Alborch, as a pre-eminent commentator on, and advocate of, difference 'feminism', proposes that 'Cada mujer debe singularizarse. La batalla por la *unicidad*, por ser única e irrepetible, ser una y no la otra, es uno de los temas más profundos a los que nos enfrentamos las mujeres' [every woman should be an individual. The battle for *uniqueness*, to be unique and irreproducible, to be oneself and not somebody else, is one of the most important issues that we women have to face] (33 [italics in original]).

With reference to television cop shows, Lorraine Gamman has pointed out that even when an independent, tough female police officer is featured, it is her isolation and also her uniqueness that prevail, rather than her positioning to propound themes of sexual discrimination (11). Although her comments refer to the televisual medium, they serve, I think, to highlight a key aspect of the Giménez-Bartlett's Inspector Delicado series. And with particular reference to Spanish women's narrative of the 1990s, the US-based critic Carmen de Urioste, also notes that while the autonomous, individualist female is often found at the centre of such texts, this character is usually unique, a 'one-off', rather than part of a wider feminist movement, philosophy or awareness. Although Urioste does not mention Giménez-Bartlett among the list of authors she analyses, her comments are a fair reflection on the Petra Delicado novels:

> Las escritoras de los noventa están elaborando modelos femeninos – mujeres con autonomía propia, con comportamientos independientes, con una sexualidad y un deseo hasta hace poco no reconocidos – divergentes de los patrones hegemónicos [. . .] Sin embargo, es necesario apuntar que uno de los problemas de esta narrativa se encuentra en que muchas de las novelas [. . .] presentan la crisis de una mujer burguesa con alguna independencia que ha llegado a la edad adulta con un cierto grado de inconformidad que verbaliza a lo largo de la narración [. . .] dejando en el anonimato a otras clases sociales u otros modelos de mujer con menor grado de educación. (207)

> [Women writers of the nineties are creating female role models – who are autonomous, independent, who experience sexuality and desire that hitherto went unrecognized – who are different from the hegemonic type [. . .] It must be noted, however, that one of the problems with this type of narrative is that many novels [. . .] portray the crisis of a bourgeois woman with a certain independence who has reached adulthood feeling a certain degree of inconformity with her lot which is articulated throughout the

narrative [. . .] but which does nothing to reveal the plight of the members of other social classes or other types of women who are less educated.]

While it is the case that the novels and short stories in the series do focus largely on the activities and thoughts of the middle class, Petra and her bourgeois acquaintances, because the police officer has perforce to move among all sectors of society, the lives and penuries of those living on the socio-economic margins of Barcelona are also uncovered and commented on. Although, as I noted earlier in this section, Giménez-Bartlett's protagonist does not specifically gender the victims of crime, within the texts the existence and experiences of the poor, the homeless, the victim-ized, and the marginalized are portrayed in sufficient detail for the Inspector Delicado series to be at least partly removed from the tendency identified by Urioste in this regard.

Alicia Giménez-Bartlett has, in keeping with many of her contemporaries, written thoughtful, reflexive, woman-centred fic-tion of outstanding literary quality, which has also performed extremely well in the national and international markets. Rather than her texts articulating the kind of audible feminist demands immediately apparent from a reading of much Spanish women's writing of the 1980s, however, her series is part of a more contemporary phenomenon identified by Ana Maria Spitzmesser. In a recent study, the critic says that 'the novel written by women in Spain today evolves exclusively around the female private self. The larger social significants like religion, conscience, capital, labor, justice or even power are alien to these texts' (82). While it is undoubtedly the case that Petra *must* seek 'justice' for the victims of the crimes she investigates because she is a police officer, the exposition within the fictions she protagonizes of an ideological corpus entrenched in notions of post-feminism and difference 'feminism' does lead to the kind of 'interiorist' text identified by Spitzmesser. And privileging Petra's voice, point of view, and personal musings within the Inspector Delicado series can be read as Giménez-Bartlett's primary device for brilliantly and humorously analysing the paradoxes, ambiguities, and diffi-culties with which women who inhabit a post-feminist economy often informed and underpinned by difference 'feminist' ideas must contend.

NOTES

1   This is not to suggest that such series abound. Indeed, the female-authored woman sleuth as protagonist of a series of texts is something of a rarity in Spain. Margarida Aritzeta – whose fiction is analysed in both chs 2 and 3 of this study – has published a number of detective novels featuring the police investigator Coia Moreno, while Blanca Álvarez (whose *Las niñas no hacen ruido cuando mueren* [Girls Don't Make a Noise When They Die] is discussed in the next chapter) has written several texts centring on the figure of Baby Villalta who is at once a criminal and an amateur investigator of a very unusual kind.

2   Catherine Davies reminds her reader that first wave feminism was absent from Spain, mainly as a result of the strength among the oligarchy of Catholic ideology (14). She goes on to point out that during the decades of second wave feminist activism in many other parts of the world, Spanish women were often reluctant to become involved in the movement because they felt a profound aversion to all-female organizations reminiscent of Fascist groups that were imposed on the nation's women during the dictatorship. Additional impediments to feminist activity were the continued influence of the Catholic Church in all spheres of life, and the relative absence of women in the workforce (16).

3   Primary among those who formalized this discourse was Lidia Falcón, whose works such as *Mujer y sociedad. Análisis de un fenómeno reaccionario* [Women and Society. An Analysis of a Reactionary Phenomenon] (1969) served as consciousness-raising texts towards the end of the dictatorship within a country that had experienced very limited feminist activity since the demise of the Second Republic.

4   For an overview of the multiplicity of women's groups that existed in Spain during the 1970s and into the 1980s see SESM's article, 'El movimiento feminista en España. De 1960 a 1980' [The Feminist Movement in Spain. From 1960 to 1980], and the article by Montserrat Cervera et al.

5   Throughout this study I will adopt my own convention of referring to this particular line of thought as difference 'feminism', enclosing the second part of the term in inverted commas in order to signal my profound disagreement with the idea that a philosophy that promotes an exclusively female genealogy, that focuses on the primacy of the female body, that exhorts women to refuse to participate in the wider political apparatus, and that promulgates such notions as the female return to the domestic space – among other retrograde and reactionary notions – can ever possibly be considered a truly feminist one. My view is echoed by feminist thinkers, scholars, and philosophers inside Spain who condemn difference 'feminism' as inherently dangerous to the project of female emancipation within a nation that suffered from the imposition by a right-wing dictatorship of very 'traditional' norms for female behaviour long after such models were

obsolete in the rest of Europe. For criticism of Spanish difference 'feminism' see Amorós 1986: 52–4; Amorós 1997: 415 *et seq.*; Gil Ruiz 161 *et seq.*; de Grado 43 *et seq.*; Larumbe 2004: 268 *et seq.*).

6   For an excellent overview of the origins of Spanish difference 'feminism' see Amorós 1997: 417 *et seq.* For a thorough summary in English of the debates and issues at the centre of this school of thought in Spain see Vanessa Knights' review article.

7   Oliver's first detective narrative was a short story entitled 'On ets, Mònica?' (1983) ['Where Are You, Monica?' (1991)]. It featured the sleuth who would appear in all of her subsequent genre fiction.

8   The original Catalan title refers to an old rhyme sung in Majorcan Catalan and is untranslatable into English. Patricia Hart explains the origin of McNerney's title for the English translation in her introduction to *Blue Roses for a Dead . . . Lady?* (vii).

9   Oliver's crime fiction has also been translated into a considerable number of other European languages (see Broch 1995).

10   Alicia Giménez-Bartlett also uses a first-person female narrator, but her detective character, Petra Delicado, engages in far more 'interiorist' musings than does Lònia whom Oliver deploys specifically as a mouthpiece for an ideology founded in female solidarity. Just as the two authors articulate very different approaches to feminism and the function and position of women in Spain, however, so they use their protagonists to put forward divergent stances on the functions of the female first-person narrative voice. It is possible that Oliver insists on the *ex*teriorisation of her protagonist's thoughts and views and their deployment as a vehicle for articulating the concerns of a global society of women (rather than her own personal angst) as a concerted means of rejecting the interiorist narrative point of view which Geraldine Cleary Nichols sees as so dangerous to the female literary project in Spain (1989: 9–11). In another study Nichols has commented on the assertions of the eminent Spanish literary critic José Carlos Mainer to the effect that *male* literature in Spain adopted the interiorist stance during the 1980s (Nichols 1995: 201–2). Again, we may read Oliver's textual strategy as a rejection of what – according to Mainer – appears to have been a defining feature of (male) Spanish letters at the time Oliver wrote her first two Lònia Guiu novels.

11   Writing in 1995, Àlex Broch noted of Maria-Antònia Oliver that she is 'An active feminist' (1995: 56), while more recently the author herself has affirmed her feminist credentials (these comments were made on 6 July 2004 during Oliver's discussion of her detective fiction at the conference called *Murder and Mayhem in the Mare Nostrum* which I organized with colleagues from Manchester Metropolitan University and Monash University at Monash's Prato Centre near Florence).

12   Melissa A. Stewart has also signalled the evolution of Lònia's character throughout the texts she protagonizes, observing: 'In the three novels [. . .] the author has crafted an increasingly complex Lònia

while continuing to confront serious issues and, at times, experiment with certain self-reflexive techniques' (186).

[13]   The oppressive and restrictive nature of the family for women during the Franco period is a concern of many female Spanish writers. Montserrat Roig has claimed that 'feminists question the family [. . .] because it is at the core of their annulment as social beings' (cited in Davies 17), while the critic Francisca López notes that numerous contemporary female authors in Spain condemn marriage as an 'abomination' (182 *et seq.*). In her book-length study of post-Civil War female narrative from Spain, María Jesús Mayans Natal identifies five key types of familial organization that prevail in the literature of the period. Although some of them may appear to afford women a limited function as the 'matriarch' of the group, in the final analysis they are all profoundly and dangerously detrimental to the female (see Mayans, ch. 1).

[14]   The politicization of women's work in the domestic sphere was of course also central to the Anglophone feminist movement (see Oakley 1974, 1985). Interestingly, Larumbe claims that in the case of Spain 'women's work' (i.e. running the home and household chores) had been highly valued in rural areas, but that once the exodus to the cities began in the 1960s and greater value was attached to employment that generated income, then the traditional significance of domestic labour was seriously eroded (2004: 27–8).

[15]   Although McNerney translates 'odi' as 'deep grudge', the original Catalan is better translated as 'hatred', thus indicating the depth of antipathy that Lònia feels towards her mother.

[16]   The title of *Estudi en lila* can also be read as a possible reference to Conan Doyle's *A Study in Scarlet* (1887). Purple is also the colour that has long been associated with the Suffragette movement, and the title of Oliver's novel could thus also be understood as a nod to early feminist activities.

[17]   Molinaro observes that neither author clarifies what constitutes rape nor questions the detectives' assumption that the victim is telling the truth. Nor are the victims able to express themselves nor consider the crime that has been perpetrated against them (109). She also points out that the novels featuring rape – *Estudi en lila* and Giménez-Bartlett's *Ritos de muerte* – focus only on the effects of rape, not on the event itself, and that only one type of rape is considered (110). Furthermore, in the context of Oliver's novels the ethnicity of victims other than Sebastiana and Elena Gaudí is 'virtually erased' (ibid.).

[18]   This ruthless removal of any woman who endangers the successful outcome of a crime or the continued prosperity of an ongoing illegal business run by men has been called 'the disposable female syndrome' by Linda Barnes, a textual strategy to which I shall return in ch. 2. In this particular case the two murder victims – an office cleaner and an old, drunken woman – are particularly 'disposable' because they are from socially and economically marginalized groups of Melburnian society.

[19]   As I discuss in the next section of this chapter, Giménez-Bartlett's

Petra Delicado starts a brawl in a bar for the fun of it and physically intimidates suspects – for no apparent reason. It is this type of violence, then, that the reader may consider to be gratuitous. On the other hand, however, as I note in this section of the study, Lònia Guiu is shown to use violence as a tool for protecting either herself or other women. The only textual exception to this norm occurs at the end of *Antípodes*. In this scene Lònia slugs Cristina, the wealthy heiress whom she had at one time attempted to save, as a response to the other woman's duplicity – although the detective claims that the slaps she gives the other are a form of 'payment' for the deaths of the 'granny' and the cleaning woman in Melbourne. Significantly, although Henry, her former lover, is revealed to be equally scheming, Lònia does not engage with him physically, citing his lack of character as a reason.

20 The fictional detective Lluís Arquer (named for Lew Archer) was the brainchild of Jaume Fuster, Oliver's husband.

21 The significance attached to 'justice' and 'the Law', specifically with reference to their gendering, is assessed further in *Estudi en lila*. Lònia recalls that when she first arrived in Barcelona she worked as an assistant store detective in a large department store. She initially believed that her employment was morally legitimate and appropriate to a 'good citizen'. Her radical, politically savvy flatmates, however, took great pains to explain to her that shops that sell essential goods at hugely inflated prices are the thieves, robbing the working class who should have access to such items, and that in collaborating with the off-duty policemen who worked as store detectives she was colluding with the regime. Once Lònia had been informed of her housemates' point of view, she became increasingly aware of the fact that most female shoplifters were subjected to humiliating victimization by the male security staff working in the shop – including suggestions of sexual harassment and 'shaming' the thieves by telling their families and neighbours (*Estudi en lila* 115–17; *Study in Lilac* 95–6).

22 It is also my premise that I am operating as a feminist *critic* on Oliver's – and other writers' – fictions. Geraldine Cleary Nichols, a leading scholar in the field of Spanish women's writing, describes the feminist critic's function thus:

> para ser una crítica literaria feminista hace falta orientar las estrategias de interpretación a fines políticos, reconocer y amplificar las voces sumergidas [. . .], respetar otro (des)orden de significado, privilegiar el detalle juzgado insignificante. Es enseñar a leer lo anómalo, los súbitos silencios en el discurso, los pequeños rotos o descosidos en el tejido; a entender cómo el ser 'pasivo' (mujer u otro marginado) disfraza – literalmente – su grito. (1992: 26)

> [in order to be a feminist literary critic it is necessary to direct analytical strategies towards political ends; to recognize and

make heard hidden voices [. . .]; to respect another sort of (dis)order; to emphasize those details deemed insignificant. It is about showing how to read the anomalous, the sudden silences in discourse, the little holes or flaws in the fabric; it is about understanding how the 'passive' subject (a woman or other marginalized individual) quite literally disguises her cry.]

23 One possible exception to this norm are Francisco García Pavón's full-length novels featuring 'Plinio', a Civil Guard from La Mancha, which appeared from 1968 onwards, proving immensely popular among a Spanish and international readership.

24 Dove characterizes the police procedural as a genre that 'must be built around a mystery', focuses on 'the procedures followed by policemen in real life', and within which 'the detective [. . .] does those things ordinarily expected of policemen, like using informants, tailing suspects, and availing himself of the resources of the police laboratory'. Furthermore, 'policemen in the procedurals almost always work in teams, sharing the responsibilities and the dangers, and also the credit, of the investigation, with the result that the resolution of the mystery is usually the product of the work of a number of people' (2).

25 Although I am not a member of that particular school of Hispanism that insists on citing the birth dates of authors under analysis I do so here to highlight the fact that both women came to maturity during the dictatorship and would have been exposed to similar political and feminist rhetoric during that period and the 'Transition' to democracy.

26 The writer made this point on 29 June 2003 during a talk on the construction of her Petra Delicado character at *The Hispanic Detective* conference I organized at Royal Holloway, University of London. In an interview with Óscar Palmer, Giménez-Bartlett also observed that she was drawn to the detective genre because 'te permite la posibilidad de que en broma se puedan decir cosas muy serias' [it allows you to make some very serious points in a light-hearted manner] (Palmer 1999: np).

27 Spain is policed by a number of forces. The oldest of these – founded in 1844 – is the Civil Guard, or Guardia Civil. This highly militarized force works across the country and performs a wide range of functions: police patrols of (particularly rural) areas by car; anti-terrorist activities (especially in the Basque Country); mountain patrols in the Pyrenees to control smuggling and movement of terrorists; motorway patrols to assist drivers in cases of accident and breakdown; nation-wide control of firearms and explosives, as well as implementation of hunting laws; immigration controls at Spain's international borders. The other major force in Spain, the Cuerpo Nacional de Policía [Spanish National Police Force] – which until 1978 was called the Policía Armada [The Armed Police] – was once the most feared of Franco's police, but did away with all of its

military-style ranks and organizational structures in the years following the demise of the dictatorship, and has worked hard to overcome
corruption and uphold a truly democratic ethos. This force is the
closest to the county or city constabularies of the UK, and officers
(uniformed in the lower ranks, plainclothes in the higher ones) work
from police stations – usually in larger towns and cities. Petra
Delicado works in the National Police Force, women having been
first admitted to its ranks in 1984. In addition to investigating the
kind of crimes that Petra protagonizes, the National Police are also
responsible for issuing identity cards to Spaniards, guarding some
public buildings, overseeing and controlling private security firms, as
well as functions relating to immigration, deportation, extradition,
and refugees. Many towns and cities also have a Policía Municipal
[Municipal Police], a local police force with limited powers, that
imposes local laws, oversees traffic and parking, and assists the
National Police with crowd control. Under the 1979 legislation
granting regional autonomy, the regions were also permitted to
establish their own police force. In Catalonia this is the Mossos
d'Esquadra (founded 1989), also mentioned in the Delicado series.

28 'Modelados en barro' appeared in a slim volume entitled *Damas del
crimen* [Ladies of Crime] that was given free with *Qué Leer*, a popular
book magazine that has enjoyed very considerable success in Spain.
'La voz de la sangre' was published as part of a collection called *12
cuentos cruentos* [Twelve Cruel Tales] that was also offered free by the
FNAC bookshop chain with the purchase of two other titles in the
Punto de Lectura paperback collection. As a consequence, both of
these stories are very difficult – if not impossible – to obtain
commercially.

29 Kathleen Thompson-Casado also alludes to the way in which the
term 'feminism' (what she calls 'the "f" word') likewise becomes
almost an expletive in the Petra Delicado novels (2002: 77).

30 Milagros Rivera's full name is María-Milagros Rivera Garretas. She
has published influential – if controversial – texts under both her full
and abbreviated names. The bulk of her work dates largely from the
1990s, and thus appeared over a decade later than Sendón de León's
most significant works.

31 Sendón de León offers the following clarification of 'ginandria'
[gynandry]:

> La posición ginandra es un intento por recomenzar tomando
> un camino más rupturista pero más creativo, más profundo,
> ambiguo y peligroso, sacrificando la divulgación masiva por
> una opción más personal, más radical, más solidaria.

> La ginandria no es un sueño trasnochado de matriarcalismo.
> Nace de la conciencia de una posición privilegiada, biológica-
> sentimental-lúdica, de la mujer sobre el varón. Conciencia de

superioridad y de fundamentación. La mujer es clave privile-
giada del cambio en los códigos eróticos, sociales, intelectu-
ales, preceptuales y políticos.

La ginandria es el rechazo a la integración que se pretende; es
la búsqueda de un proyecto propiamente femenino desde la
instauración del sujeto-mujer. (1981: 224–5)

[The gynandric stance is an attempt to start afresh, taking a
disruptive but more creative route, one that is more profound,
more ambiguous, more dangerous, sacrificing widespread dissemination for options that are more personal, more radical,
and more supportive.

Gynandry is not an outdated dream of matriarchalism. It is
born of the awareness of woman's biologically, emotionally,
and ludically privileged position over men. An awareness of
superiority and biological essentialism. Woman is the privileged key player in the codes governing erotic, social, intellectual, perceptual, and political exchange.

Gynandry is the rejection of the integration that was aimed for;
it is the search for a truly feminine project founded in the
confirmation of woman as subject.]

[32]   'Radical feminism' in the Spanish context is not to be confused with
Anglophone radical feminism (see Brooksbank Jones 8).

[33]   This is a reference to the fact that, prior to the passing of Spain's
abortion law in 1984 by the Socialist government, Spanish women
who wanted to abort usually had to travel to London to terminate
unwanted pregnancies. Airlines such as the now defunct Spantax
offered cheap flights from Spain to the British capital which, it was
very widely rumoured, would on Fridays be full of 'weekend abort-
ers'.

[34]   It is this ambivalence, together with Petra's aforementioned rejection
of many of the values of feminism, that combine to underscore her
awareness of the post-feminist environment she inhabits and which
impinges so significantly on her choices as a woman. In the conclusion to their text on feminist literature Sara Mills et al. note that in
the popular contemporary perception it is posited that 'women in
the 1980s do not really need feminism at all; they have become
so-called *post-feminists*: women who are the competent, independent
equals of men and who therefore no longer need to 'compromise'
their femininity or their equally important roles as wives and
mothers. The fact that such women are actually a very small middle-
class minority within society as a whole is, of course, never said' (227
[italics in original]). Although Mills et al. were writing in the late
1980s, the Anglophone situation they highlight translates very clearly
into the Spain of the 1990s and beyond which is the backdrop to the
Petra Delicado series.

[35]   Giménez-Bartlett's first book in the Petra series does of course deal

with the case of a serial rapist. As I discuss elsewhere in this chapter, however, it is my contention that it is not the novelist's primary aim to specifically gender the victims of the crime.

36   In her gloss of Calero Fernández, Miranda Stewart notes that 'in Spain [. . .] many more swearwords relate to the male genitals than to the female [. . .] Those relating to female genitalia are more likely to be offensive [. . .] However, the majority of those relating to male genitalia have highly positive connotations [. . .] Hence, it could be argued that society's views of men and women are encoded in this ambivalence' (156). The fact that Petra in particular uses swearwords related to the female genitals can thus perhaps be read as further evidence of her ambivalence towards the role and position of women in contemporary Spain.

37   Miranda Stewart says that in Spain 'men use swearwords, and in particular the more powerful ones, more than women, [and] working-class men and women swear more than university students' (157–8). Using bad language thus has not only gendered but also class connotations in Spain.

38   This kind of action of course constitutes 'breaking the law'. However, later on in the novel Petra points out to Fermín that demanding the male suspect strip was no worse than the indignities to which male members of the force subject women they are interrogating. Her action also has the desired effect of ensuring that the 'suspect' confesses that he is not related to the case. Thus, despite the 'illegal' nature of Petra's actions in this regard, I would assert that because the technique she uses is seen as a fairly routine police procedure and achieves the desired results it stands in direct opposition to the stance adopted by Lònia Guiu in *Estudi en lila*, for example, in which the PI colludes with Elena Gaudí in the (very definitely illegal) castration of her attackers.

39   By this I do not mean a strictly Freudian envy for the fleshly penis, but a desire for the empowerment that owning a 'phallus' supposes.

40   I would note here that Petra is rarely textualized as being obsessively preoccupied with her appearance. Interestingly, it is Oliver's Lònia Guiu – who expresses no concern at all with what she might look like – who is particularly interested in make-up, specifically her vast collection of lipsticks. The 'feminizing' function of these is subverted and negated, however, because the PI never uses them – she simply places them in a locked display case.

41   In her non-fiction work entitled *El misterio de los sexos* [The Mystery of the Sexes] (2000*a*), Giménez-Bartlett asserts that: 'Me gustan los hombres. Los encuentro en su mayoría encantadores, y me parece tendencioso pensar en varones haciendo especial hincapié en su propensión al uso de la fuerza' [I like men. I find the majority of them delightful, and I think it's tendentious when thinking about them to place particular emphasis on their propensity for the use of force] (17–18).

42   An exception to this rule of thumb does, however, occur in *Un barco cargado de arroz* when Petra agrees to have a beer with the young

forensic medic Silvia Caminal. During their brief conversation they exchange the kind of opinions and confidences that would usually form part of any standard conversation between friends (42–3).

[43] Interestingly, many of the victims on which the novels in the Petra Delicado series are predicated are men. Whether this is an indication of the pre-eminence of the male within the texts and the ideology that underpins them, however, is unclear. Petra's social conscience, and her understanding of the devastation that crime and social marginalization can cause, develop markedly to reach a high point in *Un barco cargado de arroz*. In this novel all murder victims are male. What is key within Giménez-Bartlett's texts, however, is the clear indication that, unlike Oliver's Lònia Guiu, Petra does not evince any awareness of a specifically gendered victim status.

[44] What Falcón perceives of as the post-feminist (or possibly 'backlash') portrayal of the bad mother seems to contradict the celebration of the maternal by such difference 'feminists' as Sendón de León whose work, as noted earlier, is founded on the significance of the female (specifically the female body), and the pre-eminence within the female economy of figures such as 'la Gran Diosa, la Diosa madre' [the Great Goddess, the Mother Goddess] (1981: 228) – an ideological contradiction that appears irreconcilable. Given the cultural prevalence of the violent and manipulative mother figures that Falcón identifies, however, it would seem that Petra's stance can indeed be read in conjunction with the trend towards a vilification of the maternal. Significantly, Michèle Ramond points out that in much Hispanic women's writing the 'Diosa Madre esplendorosa' [the splendorous Mother Goddess] has become a terrible, overpowering figure with whom all links must be severed (51), an assertion that suggests that Giménez-Bartlett is one of many authors to question the validity of the positive maternal archetype.

[45] Her eye for interior detail is commented on humorously and ironically in *Muertos de papel* in which the principal clue to solving the crime is what Fermín calls 'la teoría del borlón' [the theory of the tassel] (70), as Petra resolves the case to hand when she notices that a victim's decoration is an exact replica of that featured in a women's magazine she reads at her hairdressing salon.

[46] Lònia knows that such a parity is not a reality, but she articulates a fervent belief that it may one day exist and in her words, actions, and attitudes she works towards achieving it.

[47] Although much of Sendón de León's work dates from the 1980s, I would assert that her ideas have had a particular resonance among later difference 'feminist' thinkers in Spain, and that they contributed to the perpetuation of notions such as those explored in the Petra Delicado novels and stories.

Chapter 2

Mujeres que Mueren, Mujeres que Matan: Female Victims and Women Criminals

The Female Victim

Crime narratives are predicated on the supposition that a criminal action usually implies the presence of a victim.[1] In the classic text, this role is most often occupied by the ubiquitous 'body in the library' or, in tales which are altogether bloodier, messier, and nastier, by the chaotic cadaver, dismembered and disembowelled. Bodies of both types appear in crime novels by women authors from Spain and they are almost always female. In this chapter, then, I want to examine the multiple textual significances of these corpses, as well as briefly considering victims of other types of crimes – some of which were mentioned in Chapter 1. I shall also analyse the textual functions of the female offender: an individual who may also have suffered criminal victimization because of her sex. In this section of the chapter, I shall read the figure of the female victim within a range of novels and short stories in conjunction with a selection of theoretical material pertaining to gendered violence. I want to show how the chosen authors use their fictions to foreground their contemporary reality – one characterized by apparently unremitting violence against women in today's Spain;[2] while at the same time they revise some essential tenets of the sub-genres in which they write. In the second section of this chapter, I focus on the female criminal. I again read the chosen texts through aspects of Spanish and international gendered criminology, and suggest that the very considerable number of women wrongdoers that appear in female-authored fictions function as a mechanism for addressing and attempting to overcome the criminal victimization to which many women are subjected.

The human victim is often considered essential to the crime and detective genre. He – or she – is the object or presence that kick-starts the narrative, and is considered by Slavoj Žižek to be 'crucial' to the human dynamics on which the text is predicated:

> The corpse as object works to bind a group of individuals together: the corpse constitutes them as a group (a group of suspects), it brings and keeps them together through their shared feeling of guilt – any one of them *could have been* the murderer, each had a motive and opportunity. The role of the detective is [. . .] precisely to dissolve the impasse of this universalized, free-floating guilt by localizing it in a single subject and thus exculpating all others. (59 [italics in original])

Gill Plain has said that in detective fictions bodies 'appear at the beginning of the novel as a "tabula rasa" upon which the script of detection will be written' (31), and although her comment in this case refers specifically to Agatha Christie's books, other critics who write about other authors concur with her assertion. As Sarah Dunant summarizes: 'Without the body, without the murder, there would be no fiction' (12). Similarly, David Lehman has pointed out the importance of a body to the construction of many types of detective text, and comments on 'the backward structure of detective novels: It begins with a corpse and works its way backward [sic]' (193). Although Lehman, along with Plain and Dunant, clearly positions the victim as the foundation stone of the investigation reconstructed in the detective tale, he also proposes that the victim is not as significant as other individuals in the text:

> The eternal triangle in the detective novel consists of the culprit, the sleuth, and the victim. Of the three, the victim is the least important. The victim exists for one purpose: to get killed, and quickly [. . .] We customarily meet the victim just long enough to realize that he or she is a thoroughly expendable character. (6–7)

Anne Cranny-Francis also makes this point, and claims: 'The victim of the crime is conventionally characterized minimally so that reader attention is focused on the detective' (1988: 70). This view is replicated in the Spanish context by Joan Ramon Resina in *El cadáver en la cocina*, his study of post-dictatorship crime fiction. Resina agrees with Plain's belief that, despite their function as the motor for detective texts, victims' bodies are 'empty signifiers' (Plain 31), and observes: 'En el panorama de la literatura policíaca las víctimas constituyen un repertorio de personajes no realizados, de tramas encapsuladas en la tarea de ser pretexto y punto de partida para la detección' [In detective literature, victims constitute a range of undeveloped characters, of plots that are a pretext and starting point for the investigation] (66). He thus sees the victim as a mere ploy, a textual device contrived, in most cases, to legitimize the existence of a detective story.[3] His stance is echoed by another Spanish critic, Román Gubern, who maintains that in those novels which adhere to generic norms the victim's death is 'completamente despersonalizada, instrumentalizada y despojada de todo sentido trágico' [completely depersonalized, instrumentalized, and devoid of all sense of tragedy] (14).

The body, in its function simply as narrative keystone, does indeed often conform to the pattern identified by Gubern and elicits little – if any – horror or compassion from either the detective or the reader of the text, inured and anaesthetised as the latter has become to the textualization of the corpse, and aware as he or she is of its alleged role as a purely literary device.[4] But this writing-off of the victim on page 1 is contested by the crime novelist, Sarah Dunant, in an essay on her craft in which she claims that 'In the hands of a good crime fiction writer [. . .] the body has a life after death [. . .] Far from being forgotten, the dead person stays around on the slab as a main character, albeit without words' (13). She goes on to point out that the victim occupies a central space both in the text and in the reader's imagination because the detective must bring the dead body figuratively back to life again by reconstructing its existence, personality, and relationships (ibid.). The victim is therefore resurrected and is not forgotten.[5]

Dunant's essay deals specifically with women writers and female corpses. Of the latter she notes that when they appear in male-authored tales they are usually faceless. Their features are either

mashed or mutilated or simply do not merit mention.[6] Sometimes, the only part of their bodies that is textualized is the vagina,
the site of the crime and of man-made violence (17). Oddly,
Dunant does not make the link between the facelessness and lack
of any personal identity of these victims and the ability of the
detective novel to 'bring the dead back to life' by means of
the investigator's digging around in their past. This very reconstruction of the corpse's former incarnation as a person is a
powerful means of redeeming and resurrecting female victims
who are textualized not as individuals but as mere symbols and
symptoms of the gendered aggression directed against them.

Dunant's extensive analysis of the role and significance of the
dead female in crime fictions might thus seem to invalidate
Lehman's careful gender neutralization – as 'he or she' – of 'the
body in the library'. In a similar vein, in one of the earlier studies
of feminism and crime narratives Maureen Reddy observed that
within the genre women are far more likely to be victims than
murderers (35), and Linda Barnes has identified what she calls
the 'disposable female syndrome' to be a constant feature of
crime narratives (cited in Walton and Jones 95).[7] In her work on
film, Carol Clover coincides with Lehman's tripartite vision of
characterization in the detective novel, but where Lehman avoids
gendering the victim, Clover takes care to point out that the role
is sexually determined: 'There is something about the victim
function that wants manifestation in a female, and something
about the monster and hero function that wants expression in the
male' (13). And although Clover works with a different medium, I
would suggest that her comments signal an underlying trend in a
number of cultural products that also includes the crime text,
within which, Paulina Palmer notes: 'the investigator and the
perpetrator of the crime are generally portrayed as male, with the
third term in the triangle represented by a woman – more often
than not in the ultra-passive role of corpse!' (94).[8] It is this
passivity, usually associated with the feminine, that prompted
Kathleen Gregory Klein to go so far as to venture that 'the victim
[. . .] is, despite biology, always female' (1995*a*: 173). She bases
her argument on her theory that in the criminal/victim
dichotomy that underpins detective fiction, the genre reproduces
the Cartesian binaries of the mind/body and male/female.
Because 'the victim is always controlled, subordinated [and]
gradually becomes less visible, fading almost into irrelevance'

(ibid.), so the victim is always gendered as female. If we recall that Lehman declared the victim to be the least important element of a crime text, we might conclude that it is no coincidence that this lack of importance stems from the gendering as female of this particular character.

The pages of many male-authored detective fictions are littered with women's lifeless bodies that have been sexually misused by male protagonists. This imperative to kill and then leave the prey to be seen by others might perhaps respond to male voyeuristic desires, as Dunant suggests (17), and in this regard the disfigured female victim, denuded of clothing and any last vestige of dignity or personal identity, evokes the shaved, splayed, penetrated female of the pages of photographic or filmic pornography. It could be argued that woman's status as victim in some male crime fiction, then, is possibly an expression of a wish for control of the feminine, as is heterosexual pornography, which is of itself a violence visited on the female body.[9]

Many male writers of crime fiction across the globe allegedly formulate these textual fantasies of control as a response to women's move into the public arena. With specific reference to what she sees as 'an explosion in images of sexual violence towards women' (17) in recent decades Sarah Dunant states: 'The more visible and noisy women have become [. . .], the more they have become the target of fictional violence and sadism' (18). In an earlier work that perhaps sets the tone for Dunant's more recent commentary, Delys Bird and Brenda Walker observe in their study of Australian crime narratives that out there in the 'real' world 'women's public role seems often to have been to provide a legitimized outlet for male aggression' (15). The fêted US writer of feminist PI novels, Sara Paretsky, also ponders the issue of the rise in gendered victimization in her country, both in society and in fiction. In an interview, she discusses evidence of the trend apparent in North American cultural products:

> Since the passage of the initial Civil Rights Act, the emergence of women in significant numbers into the professions that had previously been mostly closed to them is resolved and OK for some men, but for others, it's a terrifying, emasculating experience. And when you feel terrified and helpless, your response is great anger toward the people you perceive as causing it. And this is being played out in what has become increasingly more graphic and

furious material about the destruction of women – through rape, dismemberment, snuff films, etc. (13)

If women read books or see films that tell them they are likely to become a victim the minute they step over the threshold of the domestic domain, they will probably prefer to remain inside and forgo the benefits of occupation of the public space. As Sarah Dunant notes, the message of some contemporary crime fictions embellished with a dead female is this: 'put another set of locks on the doors, girls, because however strong you are, the bad men are worse than you think' (20).

If some male crime authors write women victims to vicariously fulfil and perpetuate patriarchal control fantasies, why would female novelists consider portraying other women as victims of crime? Priscilla Walton and Manina Jones suggest that by writing a different sort of female victim women authors can assert female agency (95–6), while in her gloss of Terry Castle, Paulina Palmer contends that a female sleuth, a female perpetrator, and a female victim serve to centre a text on the female, thus keeping things 'between women' (93). Dunant claims that she and some other female writers of crime stories revised the norms of man-made aggression because in their texts they 'didn't revel in it [i.e. violence]' (18). She also acknowledges that women writers who replicate male-authored patterns of gendered violence are on shaky ideological ground (19), a point I have discussed within the Spanish context with reference to Maria-Antònia Oliver's fiction (Godsland 2002*a*: 354–7).

Like Dunant and her fellow female Anglophone detective authors, many Spanish women writers of crime fictions also portray female victims in their texts and consider the implications of gendered violence.[10] In line with Walton and Jones's thesis that when penned by a woman the crime story can sometimes function as a site of female agency, many women novelists from Spain explore this possibility not only through the figure of the detective, as discussed in Chapter 1, but also by means of the articulation of woman-authored violence as a response to victimization by patriarchy, a point to which I shall return below. Spanish women who write female victims are also voicing their own concerns and those of their countrywomen about the extent of male violence against women in contemporary Spain.[11] Although they pen fiction, their stories and novels also serve to reverse what appears to have been a long-standing collusion – until very recently – to downplay the extent of the problem in the media and official discourses.

Writing in 2002, Lidia Falcón claimed that after the death of Franco –

> Twenty-five years had to go by before the media would begin to reflect on the massacre of women in our country. This being, of course, a much lesser preoccupation demanding much less coverage than that of terrorism. While terrorism occupies the front pages, editorials and covers of all newspapers and news magazines, and provides the lead story in television news programmes, the murder of women remains relegated to the local press and crime pages. (2002: 20)[12]

Maite Súñer makes a similar point in her book-length collection of interviews with, and writings by, Spanish women who have been victims of many types of violence, including murder attempts, at the hands of the men in their lives. She is a little more positive than Falcón, however, in her view of how the media is finally managing to overcome its reluctance and reticence to report on the problem:

> Desde que, en diciembre de 1997, la granadina Ana Orantes fue quemada viva por su ex marido tras haber denunciado en un programa de televisión días antes cuarenta años de palizas a manos de este, las noticias de los malos tratos están en las primeras páginas de nuestro país. Hasta este momento, unas cuantas líneas en la sección de sucesos era la máxima relevancia que podía esperar cualquier información sobre mujeres maltratadas. (19)

> [Since December 1997 when Ana Orantes from Granada was burnt alive by her ex-husband for having denounced him a few days earlier on television for forty years of beatings at his hands, stories about violence against women are front page news in our country. Until then, a few lines in the news section of the papers was the most coverage of abused women that you could hope for.][13]

The increased media attention given to crimes committed by men and directed against women during the late 1990s and the early years of the twenty-first century was perhaps a result of activity by women's groups to expose the widespread nature of the problem. However, it may possibly – in part at least – have been a response to the Spaniards' traditional penchant for bloodthirsty

crime news and contemporary thirst for 'reality show' style programmes and information,[14] rather than to a real concern about
the underlying issues.[15] Reports of this sort of crime are also often
dramatized and exaggerated, and in the press, at least, merit
particularly lurid headlines which counteract and negate the
outrage at the nature of the violence and the supposed pity for
the victims that journalists would have their readers infer from a
reading of their articles (see Fernández Díaz 2003). Even during
2004, the year that witnessed an unprecedented increase in media
coverage as a result of impending changes in legislation introduced by the new Socialist government (a point to which I shall
return at the end of this section), the tone of articles in the
quality press reporting violence against women still tended to be
overly dramatic, but underscored by an insincere pathos that
functioned to invalidate any possible concern evinced for the
victims of such crimes.

Perhaps as a mechanism to overcome this long-standing sensa-
tionalism and that inherent to many male-authored crime fictions, crime stories and novels by the Spanish women analysed in
this study tend to be far less vividly detailed in their portrayal of
aggression against women than are many texts published by
Spanish men during the past three decades or so, much as
Dunant suggested to be the case with her own books in the quote
included earlier. As in the English-speaking world, crime tales in
Spain written by men abound with female bodies found floating
in the sea, hanging from rafters, lying on beaches or mean streets
or plush sofas, among other scenarios. With rare exceptions,
however – and Olga Schiller Bulowa in Vázquez Montalbán's *Los
pájaros de Bangkok* is one of the few examples to come to mind[16] –
Spanish male writers' female corpses perform the function of
symbolic dead woman noted by Dunant. On the other hand,
when the women authors studied here narrativize victims of their
own sex, they often delve into the bleak realities of victimization;
for these writers, the casualties of gendered murder (and other
sorts of violence) are not just textual symbols of a patriarchal
obsession with bashing and butchering women, but individuals
whose lives and bodies (and also minds if the woman is not killed)
have been rent asunder by their victim status.

Importantly, because their female victims are portrayed with
reference to the human effects on them of crime and violence,
many women writers thus revise and rewrite the generic norm

identified by Lehman, Resina, and Gubern of the insignificance of the victim (other than simply as an initial motivator of a fiction). For the Spanish female authors whose fictions I will analyse here, the victim should be important because she is – or was – an individual with a life, a family, dislikes, preferences, and opinions; she is not the 'thoroughly expendable character' identified by Lehman (7). Rather, much as Dunant has suggested, by writing the victim an author can 'keep her alive', even after death – although it should not be forgotten that many dreadful crimes perpetrated against women leave them alive to relive the horrors of their assault. (I shall return to victims of this sort after my consideration of those who are killed in the fictions analysed.) In the texts selected for study, the faceless female corpses of many male crime fictions become women who, after meeting a violent death, are 'resurrected' through the telling of their stories. Even though her demise renders her silent, some other woman – be it a professional or amateur investigator, or a friend or relative – speaks for her and makes known the victim's tale.

The texts analysed in this chapter also revise and rewrite the assumption that victims are somehow to blame for their victimization. Echoing a widely held point of view, Resina claims that within crime fictions 'La víctima siempre es responsable de su propia muerte. Él o ella se lo han buscado' [the victim is always responsible for their own death. He or she was asking for it], and he goes on to note that in many Spanish post-dictatorship detective fictions penned by men, fault is shown to lie in the victim's rejection of prevailing social mores (1997: 68). Lehman is less subtle, and affirms that victims are done away with 'For as a rule these are nasty people and leave no one heartbroken when they exit the scene; guilt is one thing, remorse quite another' (8).

When blame of this sort is gendered, however, it acquires a rather different hue. In many male-authored crime fictions and other cultural products such as film, women are not butchered or raped or mutilated because they are social misfits or because they are 'nasty people'. Rather, they are victimized 'just' because they are women, as Greg Forter makes quite clear in his study of masculinity and the crime novel.[17] If we recall the observations made by Bird and Walker, Dunant, and Paretsky, women are made into victims by male novelists and by men in general because they dare to step out into the public arena and occupy a space hitherto deemed to be a male preserve. The Spanish women writers

examined here question in detail the possible reasons for victimization of the female, and they take particular issue with the
notion of victim complicity, as I shall discuss below.

Numerous female crime authors from Spain contest the gendered voyeurism that appears to be inherent to the genre as
established by male writers, and their tactic often functions to
de-sexualize the female victim and helps to personalize her in
ways discussed earlier. In texts featuring the murder of a woman,
one way in which the female novelist might overcome the overtly
sexualized voyeurism of some male texts is to devote relatively
little narrative attention to the dead female, as Isabel-Clara Simó
does with her protagonist, Sara, in *Una ombra fosca, com un núvol de
tempesta* (1991) [literally, A Dark Shadow, Like a Storm Cloud,
translated by Patricia Hart as *A Corpse of One's Own* (1993)].[18]
Simó's description of her protagonist's body is brief, and she
rejects the more usual sexualized symbolic value of the dead
female, and instead attributes to Sara's corpse a religious significance. The novelist suggests a symmetry with a Christ figure: the
white, shroud-like blanket that is used to cover her body, the arms
spread out like a cross, and the death in a public place surrounded by onlookers. Sara's body thus assumes new significances: her killing is an 'example' to other women who may attempt
to function outside the limits of the role society affords them and
she thus 'pays' for perceived female 'sins'. I would suggest that
her corpse can also be read as emblematic of all of those women
who are victims of male violence:

> els homes de blanc de l'ambulància tiraren una manta a sobre el
> cos, les cames doblegades, el braç estirat, els ulls tancats, de la Sara,
> que jeia morta [. . .] Semblava una altra Sara, amb el front
> enfosquit pel regalim de sang. Un front amb una ombra fosca,
> fosca com un núvol de tempesta. (171–2)

> [the men in white from the ambulance threw a blanket over the
> body, the legs bent, the arm stretched out, the eyes closed, of Sara,
> who lay there dead [. . .] She looked like a different Sara, with her
> forehead darkened by the trickle of blood. It was a forehead with a
> black shadow on it, black like a storm cloud. (*A Corpse of One's Own*
> 166–7)]

While some male-authored voyeuristic presentations of dead,
or otherwise, victimized women are fuelled and sustained by
textual undercurrents that are clearly very highly eroticized,

others, according to Dunant, are hidden behind pseudo-legal or pseudo-medical discourses. In this regard she identifies the 'voyeuristic image of a female corpse sexually mutilated, and served up with a helping of spurious police/forensic jargon to make us feel a tad less guilty about reading it' (16).[19] The Spanish texts which best exemplify the revision of this 'male' writing strategy are Blanca Álvarez's *Las niñas no hacen ruido cuando mueren* [Girls Don't Make a Noise When They Die] (1998), and Yolanda Soler Onís's *Malpaís* [Bad Country] (2003), to which I shall return later. Álvarez's second crime novel for adults, *Las niñas no hacen ruido cuando mueren* continues the story, begun in *La soledad del monstruo* [The Loneliness of the Monster] (1991), of Bárbara Villalta, 'Baby para los conocidos, Bab para las burlas, treinta y dos años, ciento doce kilos, ciento cincuenta y tres centímetros de altura, miope y asqueada, odiando a diestro y siniestro' [Baby to those who knew her, Bab to those who made fun of her, thirty-two years old, one hundred and twelve kilos, one metre fifty-three tall, short-sighted, totally pissed off with life, and hating people left, right, and centre] (13).

As the story opens Bárbara is in the police morgue to identify a young girl upon whose body no ID documents had been found. The first paragraph details the pathos of the corpse and the older woman's reaction to it:

Muerta parecía transparente. La piel era como un cristal mate que dejaba ver las venas azules y finas simulando dibujos de un mapa fijado en el instante anterior a su destrucción. Bárbara Villalta miraba el cuerpo tendido de aquella niña y no acababa de imaginarla quieta para siempre. Por un momento quiso creer que no era Rosa el cuerpo frío que identificaba: aquel no era su sitio, entre el olor a formol, desinfectantes y orines. Rosa no soportaría dormir con el gesto tranquilo entre azulejos desconchados y cajas metálicas que guardaban vagabundos sin identificar. (11)

[In death she seemed transparent. Her skin was like opaque glass that showed the fine blue veins that looked like the lines drawn on a map just before her death. Bárbara Villalta looked at the body of the girl lying there and couldn't imagine her being still for ever. For a moment she wanted to believe that the cold body she was identifying wasn't Rosa; she didn't belong in that place, among the smell of formaldehyde, disinfectant, and urine. Rosa would never put up with quietly sleeping among the chipped tiles and metal boxes where unidentified tramps were stored.]

Although the novel contains many more passages which describe Rosa's corpse, they cohere with Álvarez's textual ideology of the female victim as evinced in this opening paragraph. Rosa's seventeen-year-old body has not been sexually ravaged, nor is it arrayed in a manner that even insinuates any possible eroticization. Rather, its fragility, defencelessness, and silence are all highlighted – features that often do not merit a mention when the female victim is textualized by a male writer. What is more, Álvarez reformulates the practice identified by Dunant and mentioned above of imbuing 'official' responses to the female corpse with an underlying voyeuristic tendency. In siting Rosa's body in the municipal mortuary, surrounded by the smells and signs of medicine and officialdom, but focusing on the tragedy that such a death supposes, not only for the dead girl but also for Bárbara, Álvarez takes issue with the device noted by Dunant. Perhaps most importantly of all, and in spite of Rosa's situation as a runaway vagrant, her scant friends, and her lack of family ties, Álvarez's victim is redeemed from her apparent position as a nonentity, as the 'unimportant' victim in crime fiction, or as the dead female of the detective text, or of contemporary reality. The novelist achieves this 'personalization' through the minute and careful reconstruction of the girl's existence in Bárbara's memory, a narrative that makes up much of *Las niñas no hacen ruido cuando mueren.*

Rosa's corpse on page 1 is the device on which the rest of the text is constructed, in much the same way as critics have indicated is usual in crime fiction. Álvarez's tale is not a traditional detective story, however, for although it opens with the pathetic result of a crime, it is far less concerned with identifying whodunit – although it eventually does so – than with reconstructing and saving from oblivion the memory of its young victim while also enquiring into society's incessant victimization of the female. Using Rosa's lifeless body as its starting point, *Las niñas no hacen ruido cuando mueren* details how Bárbara had met the girl and her friend, Chelines, a young, aristocratic drug addict from Seville, when they were living on the streets and squatting in abandoned buildings. The girls had moved to Bárbara's apartment, inherited from her murdered partner, and a relationship based on trust and mutual understanding had developed, during which the older woman had learned of Rosa's unhappy life in the north of Spain, her reason for deciding to leave home. However, Chelines' husband, to whom she had been given in an arranged marriage, her mother, and their hired henchmen were searching for her to oblige her to sign over her ownership of the empty building in which she and Rosa were hiding as its market value was considerable. When Chelines refused to conform to their wishes they set fire to the property in order to murder her and thus claim her inheritance, but Rosa, who was inside the building at the time of the arson attack, was killed 'by mistake'.

As is common in the Spanish *novela negra*, in this novel it is the collusion of patriarchy and big business that prompts criminal activity. And while Rosa is the victim of this dangerous duo, she is also the victim of a society that cares little for runaway girls, even dead ones. As Bárbara is told by the policeman in charge of the mortuary where Rosa's pathetic remains are stored: 'Y ya van cuatro en este jodío mes. Sin familia, sin nadie que los reclame . . . ¡Malditas mocosas! Un par de hostias bien atinadas y se les iban las ganas de ir jodiendo al personal' [That's four dead girls already this fucking month. No family, nobody to claim them . . . Bloody little brats! A couple of good slaps and they'd soon stop fucking us around] (13 [ellipsis in original]). But Rosa is not the only victim in Álvarez's unwaveringly brutal text. Chelines is a drug addict whose habit is fuelled and encouraged by a mother keen to gain control of her daughter's money and property, an inheritance from her grandmother. She is habitually raped by a brutal husband to whom she was 'sold' to preserve her family's financial interests. Bárbara herself is an emotional cripple detested by her own mother and derided and verbally assaulted by all and sundry, while Rosa's father rapes his wife and obliges her to drink in order to control her, forcing her to keep him company while he watches violently pornographic videos.

In contrast to Álvarez's portrayal of unrelenting and unremitting physical violence against women of all ages, of all social groups, and from all parts of Spain, the Catalan Margarida Aritzeta's *El verí* [The Poison] (2002) is in many ways a much gentler text, although many of its central premises parallel the concepts foregrounded in *Las niñas no hacen ruido cuando mueren*. In Aritzeta's novel, Martina and her brother Tomàs find their aunt dead in the attic room in which she has been kept a virtual prisoner for decades. The description of the corpse is reminiscent of Christie's tidy, bloodless, neatly arranged bodies that are discovered in well-appointed rooms in *haute-bourgeois* homes: 'el llum va projectar tota la duresa del seu esclat sobre el rostre esblanqueït de la dona, recalcada a la butaca d'orelles, al costat del balcó aparedat' [the harsh light shone on the pale face of the woman resting in the winged armchair near the walled-up balcony] (13).

In some ways this orderly corpse that opens the novel is the 'unimportant' body that merely functions as a pretext for the narrative of detection: an enquiry into the life, family, and circumstances of the dead aunt all inevitably follow on from the discovery of her remains and the realization that she had been poisoned. On the other hand, however, it is this very investigation into her life that serves to overcome the more usual unimportance of the victim as a character rather than simply a literary device. Just as Rosa is rescued from oblivion in Álvarez's tale, because Bárbara recuperates and retells the young girl's story, so in *El verí* Caterina Maduell, alias 'la boja' [the madwoman] (5) who has spent most of her adult life sequestered in the loft of her sister's farm house, is resurrected from her marginalized position in family myth and imagination and comes to occupy her rightful place as an individual. The telling of Caterina's story as a result of her mysterious death by strychnine also symbolically releases her from the locked rooms she had inhabited. The novel is therefore not only a vindication of the female victim but also furnishes a commentary on the 'imprisonment' of women in rigid and unfulfilling social roles during the Franco dictatorship, a point developed in Chapter 3 with particular reference to the parallels between gendered and regional subjugations.

The studious de-sexualization of aunty's corpse in Aritzeta's text is replicated in Yolanda Soler Onís's *Malpaís*. Winner of the 2003 Premio Tristana de Novela [Tristana Prize for the Novel], *Malpaís* is something of a hybrid text that draws generically on both the hard-boiled *novela negra* and the police procedural for its structure, themes, and laconic style. Protagonized by Gumersindo ('Sindo') Roca, an overweight, socially awkward, loner police officer whose personality and attitude to women are akin to those manifested by male hard-boiled private eyes, the novel recounts the minutiae of the investigation into the apparent murder and subsequent burning of Elda Meyers, a French sculptress and long-time resident of the Canary Islands. Soler Onís dispenses with a comprehensive narrative description of the charred remains of the victim and instead offers her reader only the lengthy report on the case prepared by the forensic medic (48: 168–71). This particular textual strategy, combined with Sindo Roca's failure to view the body because he arrives late on the scene, ensure that the reader is not presented with a detailed image either of the corpse in the burned-out building in which it was found, nor on the mortuary slab. The writer thus evades the kind of voyeurism inherent to so many crime fictions in the presentation of the cadaver, and any sexualization or fetishization of the dead woman is thus precluded – an authorial ploy that is confirmed in the revelation that the forensic medic is a hetero-sexual woman (whose gaze upon the body would thus have been a purely scientific one, and not that of a possibly voyeuristic male). What is also important here is that this de-eroticization of Elda in death in some way negates or erases her extreme sexualization while alive, for she had enjoyed intimate relationships with a large number of men, including Sindo Roca.[20] Soler Onís, like the women authors of several other crime fictions analysed later in this section, thus uses the de-eroticization of the female body in death as a distinctive narrative strategy to contest the validity of patriarchal socio-sexual mores which position the female as 'pro-miscuous' and as a sexual object if she engages in sexual activity with numerous partners.

This particular textual technique also underpins Isabel Olesti's 1999 novel *El marit invisible* [The Invisible Husband], although here 'Christie-esque' or scientific conventions for describing the mortal remains of the deceased are dispensed with and unpleas-ant details abound. The body belongs – or belonged – to the narrator's mother, and is found by her son lying in the shower of the family's squalid Barcelona apartment. Despite the fact that during her life the mother had been used and abused as a sexual object by her multitudinous lovers, she was never an eroticized figure. Rather, her sexuality is textualized as tawdry and pathetic, a view confirmed in the depiction of her dead body:

> La meva mare estava arraulida damunt el plat de la dutxa; l'aigua li petava al cap i li marcava una ratlla torta als cabells. Les mans – tacades de sang – premien amb força el baix ventre. On els esquitxos no arribaven hi havia llapissades vermelles, com si hagués volgut aferrar-se a les rajoles. Tenia unes quantes regateres seques a les cuixes, la resta era un líquid rosat que el desguàs de l'aigüera no podia engolir perquè el seu cos l'obstruïa. (38–9)

[My mother was huddled on the shower tray, the water coursing down on her head and etching a crooked line through her hair. Her bloodstained hands tightly clasped her lower abdomen. There were red streaks where the spray from the shower hadn't reached, as if she'd wanted to grasp hold of the tiles. There were a few dried runnels of blood on her thighs. The rest was a pinkish liquid that couldn't go down the plug-hole because her body was blocking it.]

The body that had been the site of innumerable sexual incursions is now reduced to a soggy mass blocking the drain in the shower, so in spite of this woman's (often enforced) sexualization by Spanish men during the Franco regime – an issue developed in the next chapter – her posture in death is the very antithesis of any eroticization. In fact, the revulsion and horror that the image of her corpse evokes in the reader serve to summarize *El marit invisible*'s constant textual allusions to the mother's status as a victim. She is not only the victim of a murder, but also of a political system that persistently crushed and controlled the members of a number of marginalized groups – economic, political, gendered, religious, or linguistic. As a poor Catalan woman whose promiscuity veered far from the norm of sexual propriety imposed on women in Francoist Spain, whose political sympathies lay with left-wing separatists at the other end of the political spectrum to the official dictatorship line, and whose religious beliefs led to her affiliation with the Pentecostal movement rather than the government-backed Catholic church, the mother was multiply marginalized and as a consequence was multiply victimized by the state apparatus and its official and unofficial representatives, an issue analysed in greater detail in the final chapter of this study.

Olesti positions the mother's corpse and her sexualized body while still alive as the slate on which are inscribed the multiple political and gendered discourses of the Franco regime. Similarly, in Ángela Vallvey's *La ciudad del diablo* [The Devil's City] (2005) the cadaver of a young woman who has been stabbed to death is the narrative keystone around which the novel's dissection of the socio-political events surrounding the dictator's death is built. Clara, the victim, is found naked and bloody outside the doors of a chapel in her home village of San Esteban, near Toledo, in early November 1975 as Franco lies dying in Madrid. The fictional death is investigated by don Alberto, the young priest unfortunate enough to have discovered the grisly remains, and Ricardo, an eleven-year-old pupil at the local primary school, a Spanish version of 'Sherlock Holmes y [. . .] un pequeño doctor Watson' [Sherlock Holmes and [. . .] a little Dr Watson] (160), as the priest puts it. The narrative reflects both of their points of view, swinging between ponderous considerations of religious and litur-gical matters and the prevailing political situation, and segments of text that purport to convey the impressions of a young boy and his incomprehension of the events that are taking place around him. As such, then, it replicates many of the elements not only of the classic ratiocinative tale but also of the police procedural, both genres which, although nuanced ideologically in different ways, expound in detail the mechanics of an investigation and can offer asides on the lives and thoughts of the sleuth. Within *La ciudad del diablo* the enquiry into Clara's murder by the Civil Guard is also alluded to, but it is never narrated in the detail the author devotes to Alberto and Ricardo's investigation. This writ-erly device can be read as part of a wider strategy to negate textual space to the formal, official concerns of state, thus privileging the point of view of Spain's citizens, rather than its leaders, a stance that is also apparent in the very different narrative treatment afforded the two deaths that occur in the novel – as I detail below.

From the very beginning of her work, Vallvey establishes a number of contrastive features between the deaths of Clara and the dictator, intended, it seems, to focus readerly attention on the girl's demise in the face of the overwhelming media coverage and national interest in the imminent end of the country's head of state. Thus, while the death of the female is unexpected and private and occurs in, and has repercussions on, a tiny microcosm of Spanish society, the impending end to the life of the male political leader is a very public affair, is expected by the populace, and will affect the future of Spain and its international standing. However, because Clara's passing away is afforded more textual attention and has a greater impact on life in the village portrayed in the novel, Vallvey conveys to her reader her perception of the considerable significance of the violent end of this woman. Fur-thermore, it is this death, rather than the dictator's, which prompts extensive narrative analysis of the relevance of conserva-tive Catholicism to the Spain of the time, of the dynamics of inter-personal relationships in San Esteban, of the pace of social, political, and religious change within the country, of the nation's bloody past, and of contemporary sexual standards and the role and position of women. These latter themes are explored through the figures of Ricardo's mother and aunt, but particularly in the character of the deceased herself who was an unmarried mother known to initiate and enjoy affairs with a number of men, all of whom were married. Once again then, and in keeping with a tendency observed in other crime texts by Spanish women novelists, the female victim's corpse is carefully de-sexualized in *La ciudad del Diablo* – because, despite being found naked it is discovered by a priest, a man who expresses no sexual interest in women (similarly to Olesti's novel in which the dead woman is found by her son). The victim is thus 'redeemed' of any sexual 'sins' she may have been perceived to have committed in life.

A similar dynamic underpins Teresa Barbero's 1998 novel *Planta baja* [Ground Floor]. The narrative opens with the bald statement, 'La encontraron al anochecer cerca del acantilado' [They found her at dusk near the cliffs] (13), and throughout the first chapter of the work the narrative returns frequently and almost obsessively to the body found on the beach, each reference serving to furnish more detail about the corpse – the open eyes, the long hair, the polka-dot blue dress, and the dribble of blood emanating from a gunshot wound. *Planta baja* does not recount the investigation into the young woman's murder; an extensive police enquiry proves unnecessary because her husband confesses to the crime. Ágata, the victim, had maintained many affairs, and as a result of her latest extra-marital relationship had decided to abandon her spouse who, in a fit of jealousy, shot her.

Barbero's project within the novel, however, is two-fold: to analyse the processes that led to Ágata's murder, and to document the chain of events set off by the young woman's death among a group of comfortably off inhabitants of Spain's capital. Thus, where Clara's killing in *La ciudad del diablo* sets in train textual disquisitions on religion, politics, gender issues, and so on, so in *Planta baja* the murder with which the tale opens is the starting point for an analysis of the lives and human relationships of a number of characters. The reader learns that one of Ágata's lovers was Raúl, a teacher from Madrid who was holidaying with his wife, Nadia, at the beach resort where the woman's cadaver was found. The murder causes Raúl profound worries and his marriage to Nadia founders. So, too, does the couple's friendship with Marta and Aurelio, not least because Marta is the lawyer appointed to defend Ágata's husband. All of these characters, as

well as Nadia's parents, visit Julia, the first-person narrator of the
novel who is a writer, in the ground-floor sitting room of her
home in Spain's capital to confess their links to the dead woman,
and seek her advice on how to extricate themselves from an ever
stickier situation.[21] Their self-absorbed discourse on their own
failings and weaknesses also prompt the middle-aged Julia to
reassess her own life and agonisingly mull over the sterile little
world she inhabits and the opportunities she has lost over the
years. Barbero makes clear that, had the murder not occurred,
then her characters would simply have continued with their
bourgeois existence, and the aggression, hatred, jealousy, fear,
and ultimately death that ensued from the finding of Ágata's body
would not have floated to the surface. In this regard, then,
Barbero proposes an interesting revision to woman-authored
crime writing in Spain, because rather than the demise of a
female murder victim setting in motion a police (or amateur)
enquiry or leading to a reconstruction of her life, in *Planta baja*
the female body is the foundation-stone for an analysis of other
people's lives and the ways in which they are affected by the
death.

Barbero also makes clear that despite Ágata's frequent infidel-
ities she could in no way be blamed for her death. Indeed, the
author evinces evidence of her sympathetic stance towards her
victim, noting that she did not deserve to be 'asesinada por celos,
abandonada por su amante, corriendo a buscarle desesperada-
mente y encontrándose, no con el hombre amado, sino con la
muerte en una playa desierta' [murdered because of jealousy,
abandoned by her lover, desperately rushing to look for him and
finding death on a deserted beach rather than with the man she
loved] (85), and that Raúl had tossed her over 'como una colilla'
[like a cigarette end] (83). As in numerous other texts analysed in
this section, Barbero steadfastly avoids eroticizing Ágata's corpse,
even though in life the young woman had engaged in a great deal
of sexual activity with many men. Authorial support for the victim
and the writerly refusal to present her cadaver for voyeuristic
consumption thus combine to remind the reader that Ágata's life
should not have been ended because the men she knew perceived
that she had transgressed moral and sexual codes. The notion of
victim complicity in a crime such as this is also negated by this
means. Similarly to many other writers, Barbero textually
'redeems' her victim, and reformulates a strategy found in many

male-authored crime fictions that proposes that the transgressive female deserves to die or be otherwise punished.[22]

The de-eroticization of a woman's body, which in life had been the site of a great deal of heterosexual sexual activity, is repeated in another of Margarita Aritzeta's crime novels, *El cau del llop* [The Wolf's Lair] (1992). Set in Tarragona, it tells of the discovery of two female skeletons in the basement of a building that once housed a notorious bar – The Wolf's Lair of the title. Police sergeant Parra and the female detective Coia Moreno are assigned to the case, and after a lengthy investigation involving a corrupt police commissioner, a bishop and a set of compromising photographs, and the prerequisite fights, car-chases, double-crossing, and false clues essential to the hard-boiled detective text, the pair of intrepid investigators identify the bodies as belonging to two prostitutes who used to frequent the bar and who had disappeared some years earlier.

Their corpses merit barely a mention. The tale opens with a description of two workmen clearing out the cellar of the building, moving boxes, cleaning away dust and dead rats, until one of them comes upon something altogether more sinister:

> Sota les caixes d'ampolles hi havia un bon tou de calç. L'home va clavar la pala i va tirar una paletada de calç al cabàs. La va tornar a clavar i va arrencar una calavera. Se li va glaçar la sang. Aviat es va adonar que entre la calç hi havia les restes del que havia estat un cos humà. (7)

> [Under the boxes of bottles there was a big pile of quicklime. The man dug deep with his spade and threw a shovel of quicklime into the basket. He stuck his spade in again and pulled out a skull. He froze. It soon dawned on him that the remains of what had once been a human body lay among the quicklime.]

These briefly textualized corpses are undoubtedly the starting point for a police murder investigation, the principal narrative concern of Aritzeta's tale. On the other hand, however, the novelist is keen to assure her reader throughout the text that the victims' lives as prostitutes do not warrant their description after death as the object of male voyeuristic desire. Instead, she takes the de-eroticization of the female body to the extreme by skeletonizing it, and highlights the pathos of the pile of bones that had once been women. She is also quick to point out that although the prostitute is by virtue of her profession the woman who most blatantly occupies the public space, her presence in streets and bars does not in any way justify her murder; in other words, her victims did not deserve to die. *El cau del llop*, like many other women's crime fictions from Spain, also details other sorts of victimization of women. The prostitutes are killed and covered with quicklime, but gendered violence and discrimination assume many other forms. Sergeant Parra verbally abuses both Coia Moreno, his fellow detective, and his wife who must run their home as well as working full-time as a nurse. A female suspect is attacked in her home, Coia's apartment is broken into – thus violating the space in which she most needs to feel safe, and the mother of the murderer was obliged to give up her illegitimate child due to social pressure.

Aritzeta's portrayal of the murderer is also of concern in *El cau del llop*, however, as it seems to offer a rationale for his penchant for murdering innocent women. Following an exhaustive and exhausting enquiry Moreno and Parra identify the killer as Jeroni Carrera, the son of Puri, a former co-owner of The Wolf's Lair. They decide that Moreno will disguise herself as a prostitute in order to lure the suspect into revealing his true colours or to extract from him a confession and, sure enough, Jeroni is goaded into action with a handy kitchen knife. Unable to save herself, Moreno screams blue murder and is rescued by her bigoted *machista* sidekick, a timely reminder, as in Maria-Antònia Oliver's novels analysed in Chapter 1, that while female intellect and investigative skills may solve the crime, male physical strength is often needed to defuse a dangerous situation. Together Moreno and Parra compel Carrera to confess to his nefarious past deeds.

During the scene featuring detective Moreno and the sharp knife, Jeroni Carrera seems to be absent; he is initially motionless, shakes and trembles, and is deathly pale, later screaming insults in a hysterical manner. His 'abnormality' is compounded over subsequent pages, for during the interrogation 'Va tornar a la timidesa, es va retreure més encara [. . .] fins que es va tornar insociable del tot' [He became timid again, and retreated into himself even more [. . .] until he became completely withdrawn] (141). Later on he turns mad and violent once again: 'Tenia els ulls brillants, els punys estrets. Quan va tornar a parlar semblava que havia concentrat tota la violència en la seva veu, una veu monòtona però esmolada i tallant com una destral. Parlava per a ell mateix, en veu alta' [His eyes were bright, his fists clenched.

When he started talking again it sounded as if he'd concentrated all his violence in his voice, a voice that was monotonous but as sharp and cutting as an axe. He was talking out loud, but to himself] (142).

The pathologization of this killer of prostitutes, his status as supposedly a social aberration or abnormality, is compounded in his apportioning the blame for his homicidal tendencies to his over-indulgence in alcohol and to his mother who was forced to abandon him as a child and who could not care for him even when he was older because, as a prostitute herself, she was always controlled by a male pimp. Mother blame and its link to mother murder are explored later in this chapter, and perceived maternal responsibility for an offspring's deviance was discussed in Chapter 1, but what merits attention and comment here is Aritzeta's suggestion, implicit in the characterization of Jeroni Carrera, that he kills women because he is not 'normal', because he is somehow inherently mad, bad, and dangerous to know. While it may be the novelist's intention to suggest that Carrera was brutalized by his military service (he killed the prostitutes during periods of leave from the army), the pathologization of the man serves an exculpatory function that is very much at odds with the constant victimization experienced by other female characters in *El cau del llop* and very many other Spanish women's crime fictions (as well as in Spanish society).[23] In fact, Jeroni Carrera probably is not unusual in any way. He is just one more man for whom the female is a disposable commodity and whose very existence as a woman merits her victimization at his hands.

It is unclear how far Aritzeta's excusatory characterization of the male murderer as a homicidal maniac is simply a ploy to draw attention to societal discourses that attempt to explain away violence directed against women. Her description of Carrera is indeed very similar to that of the unbalanced criminal male portrayed in the media and constructed in popular perception. A worrying example of the ideology that underpins such depictions is developed in Pérez Abellán's volume dedicated to the real-life stories of men who have killed their wives and partners. He offers male jealousy of various female bodily functions as one of the primary motivators of murderous behaviour:

Los asesinos de mujeres las matan porque envidian su sexo, su cualidad reproductora, la posibilidad casi infinita de gozar con el amor, y su fortaleza moral. A veces, la causa de esta celotipia abarca todo lo exclusivo del universo propio de la mujer, su aparato reproductor, las partes del mismo, vagina y clítoris, y la carga mensual por ser hembra, la menstruación. Por increíble que parezca, a algunos de estos terribles asesinos les gustaría suplantar el papel de su víctima y tener la regla [. . .] y hay quien mata a la pareja porque no puede convencerla de que tenga el hijo que él desea, desesperado por no poder parir en su lugar. (2002*b*: 11)

[Men who kill women do so because they envy their sex, their reproductive capabilities, their almost endless capacity for deriving pleasure from love, and their moral fortitude. Sometimes the cause of this jealousy is everything that is unique to the female: her reproductive organs, and their constituent parts: the vagina and clitoris, and the monthly burden that women must bear – menstruation. However incredible it may seem, some of these terrible murderers would like to take their victim's place and menstruate [. . .] and there are those who kill their partner because they cannot convince her to have the baby they so desire, and become desperate because they are unable to bear a child in her place.]

However preposterous and nonsensical such assertions may seem to the feminist reader, Pérez Abellán's works sell well and are widely available in Spain. And his professional success does not appear to preclude him from making ludicrous claims that do nothing to vindicate the female victims portrayed in his *Mi marido, mi asesino* [My Husband, My Killer] (2002). Indeed, his discourse implies, rather, the pathologization of the female body and the excusal of the male killer.

Conversely, however, female Spanish scholars and journalists are publishing a considerable number of texts for both a specialist, academic readership and the general public in which they ponder an array of other reasons for male violence and disabuse their readers of the notion of the pathological male killer.[24] In *Maltratadas* [Abused Women] (2002), for example, Maite Súñer asserts that the widespread perception of the aggressive male as lower-class, mentally ill, or alcoholic – or a combination of all three – is entirely erroneous:

Respecto a las características del agresor, atrás quedaron las teorías que intentaban asimilar su figura a la de un alcohólico o un enfermo de escaso nivel cultural. Los hechos han ido demostrando que, muy al contrario, la figura del hombre que maltrata se da en todos los niveles culturales y sociales, y que, salvo en casos aislados, su comportamiento no se debe a ningún trastorno mental. (21)

[With regard to the characteristics of the abuser, theories that tried to equate him with the alcoholic or the poorly educated mentally ill have been discarded. Facts have shown that, very much to the contrary, the male abuser is present at all socio-cultural levels, and that except in isolated cases his behaviour is not due to any mental illness.]

By 2004, a year of intense debate in Spain about gendered violence, the national media had taken up this message, and Súñer's words were repeated almost verbatim in an article by Jesús Rodríguez that appeared in the weekend supplement of *El País*, in which he reported that 'el único perfil del agresor es que no hay perfil. Son hombres normales [. . .] En un 80% no son enfermos mentales. En una cifra similar no son alcohólicos ni adictos a la droga' [the only thing that male abusers have in common is that they are all different. They are normal men [. . .] 80% of them are not mentally ill. A similar figure are not alcoholics or drug addicts] (40).

If the majority of men who murder, beat, and rape women are not the drunk illiterates of popular lore, why do they direct violence against the female in the many ways portrayed by Spanish women crime writers? In response to this question many scholars point not to male aggression – whether pathological, alcohol-induced, or otherwise – but to the victim herself, and particularly her changing socio-political role, as the source of the problem. The increased personal, political, and professional liberation of women has been considered a contributing factor to their victimization. Indeed, in the Spanish context, Inés Alberdi and Natalia Matas, authors of a recent report on violence against women in Spain, concluded:

La violencia masculina de mayor virulencia se acrecienta ante la libertad de las mujeres [. . .] La rebeldía de las mujeres ante un sometimiento que ya no están dispuestas a soportar refuerza el mecanismo de la violencia desatada. Es correcto entender el recrudecimiento actual de la violencia contra las mujeres como una reacción desesperada del machismo. (Cited in Nogueira 31)

[The worst male violence increases in the face of women's liberation [. . .] Female rebellion against a type of subjugation that they are no longer willing to put up with reinforces the mechanisms of the violence that has been unleashed against them. The current increased brutality of violence against women can be understood as a desperate reaction on the part of *machismo*.][25]

This view ties in with the assertions of literary critics and novelists cited in the introductory section of this chapter who posit increased violence against women in detective fiction (and in society) as a backlash against the female occupation of public spaces and places. Other observers and academics working in the field also generally concur that male desire for gendered supremacy lies at the root of the issue, thus echoing the reasons offered by feminist critics for violence against women in crime fiction. Caputi and Russell say that 'the objective of violence against women is to preserve the social and domestic hierarchy in which the man is the master and the woman the servant' (cited in Falcón 2002: 25). In the Spanish context Marta Fernández Morales endorses their assertion, claiming that 'El hombre que ataca a la mujer sólo por el hecho de serlo lo hace para establecer su posición de poder sobre ella y reafirmar su papel privilegiado. La violencia se convierte así en un efectivo instrumento de control' [A man who attacks a woman just because she's a woman does so to establish his position of power over her and reaffirm his privileged role. Violence thus becomes an effective means of control] (48). These discourses combine to remind women that their sex alone renders them vulnerable to assault at any time, much as Anny Brooksbank Jones surmises in her exhaustive study of women's status in contemporary Spain (95), and Mercedes Carbayo-Abengózar observes in her overview of the history of feminism in the country (2000: 122).

The fictional men who direct violence towards women in the pages of Spanish female crime novels, and the real-life males who engage in gendered aggression and about whom sociologists, criminologists, and others have treatized at length do not, however, always kill their victims; very often they victimize women in multiple ways other than murder. At an international conference on the gendering of violence Ángela Sanroma Aldea, Director of Women's Affairs for the Castilla-La Mancha autonomous region, declared that women are habitually subjected to aggression because of their sex:

Es evidente que la mujer como individuo, como persona, puede sufrir cualquier tipo de acción, violenta o no, y ser víctima de un delito contra las personas igual que el hombre, pero, a diferencia de éste, es también víctima de una serie de delitos por su condición de mujer, como consecuencia de factores socioculturales, que permiten que se produzcan agresiones en los tres ámbitos en los que desarrolla su vida: en el ámbito familiar, en el medio social y en el medio laboral. (13)

[It is clear that a woman as an individual, as a person, can be subject to all manner of actions, violent or not, and can become victim of a crime against her person, as can a man. But unlike the male, she is also victim of a series of crimes because she is a woman, as a consequence of socio-cultural factors that pave the way for aggression in the three arenas in which she lives her life: the family, the social environment, and at work.][26]

Indeed, writing in 1976, Lidia Falcón made a point about the constant aggression that women in Spain seemed forced to endure at the hands of men, an observation she repeated verbatim in a much more recent work, thus suggesting that her view – and the situation – perhaps remain unchanged:

todas somos víctimas diariamente de la agresión menor: el piropo obsceno, los comentarios insultantes o despreciativos, el roce furtivo en el metro y en la calle, el enfrentamiento verbal y la humillación constante a nuestra dignidad de personas. Antesala de mayores agresiones, de brutalidades infames, a que nos condena el sexo. (Cited in Falcón 2002: 19–20)

[as women we are all victims of minor forms of aggression on a daily basis: the obscene 'compliment', the insulting or deprecating comments, the furtive grope on the Underground or in the street, the verbal confrontations, and the constant putting down of our human dignity. These are the precursor of more serious aggression and of terrible brutality to which we are condemned because of our sex.]

The vast range of crimes and aggression to which women are subjected because of their sex is also identified by Nina Molinaro, who opines that the crime genre is the most suitable literary forum for articulation and analysis of female victimization: 'the kinds of transgression to which detective fiction attends could well benefit from a feminist intervention in order to investigate crimes usually visited upon women, such as rape, incest, domestic abuse, and sexual harassment and discrimination' (100). While some

Spanish women writers within the genre – such as Alicia Giménez-Bartlett – avoid the kind of 'feminist intervention' with regard to female victim status proposed by Molinaro, very many writers use the genre to explore the effects on the female victim of an array of different crimes.

As I have shown in this section, within many of the crime narratives analysed, Spanish women writers not only assess the multiple significances attached to the female corpse, but also catalogue the other forms of gendered violence, aggression, and harassment listed by Falcón and Molinaro and of which women appear to be victims on a daily basis. This is particularly the case in *Las niñas no hacen ruido cuando mueren, El marit invisible,* and *El cau del llop,* while in *El verí,* Aritzeta considers the subjugation to which women can be subjected because of their sex. Maria-Antònia Oliver and Alicia Giménez-Bartlett both portray female rape victims – albeit in rather different ways, as I concluded in Chapter 1 – and the Mallorcan author also examines the consequences for women of many other sorts of gendered sexual violence as well as the causes of the problem. Women are also shown in some crime fictions as victims of the domestic violence signalled above by Molinaro. This particular problem is seemingly extremely widespread in contemporary Spanish society and many women victims take the step of denouncing their abusive male partner. Indeed, in early September 2005 *El País* reported that in the past two years alone the names of 90,000 men had been added to the register of abusers (*El País* 03. 09. 05). The issue received extensive attention in Spain from women's groups, the media, and the national government, resulting in the passing of the 'Ley Orgánica 1/2004, de 28 de diciembre, de Medidas de Protección Integral contra la Violencia de Género' [Constitutional Law 1/2004 of 28 December, Measures for Full Protection against Gendered Violence] (*BOE* 29. 12. 04), at the end of 2004 aimed at meting out tough sentences to men who subjected their wives, partners, or ex's to violence. In the next section, then, I want to study the textual function of women who murder a male spouse in response to victimization of this sort at their hands, as well as analysing a number of other fictional female felons.

Women Criminals

If the female victim is a constant of women's crime fiction from Spain, so too is the woman criminal. The literary abundance of woman-authored female felons in Spain may appear to be a somewhat exaggerated reflection of reality, though, not least because, as the Spanish criminologist Miguel Clemente Díaz has remarked, 'No cabe duda [. . .] que la palabra delincuencia suscita una serie de características que la asocian al sexo masculino' [there is no doubt that the word delinquency suggests a set of characteristics that associate it with the male] (41). And despite the considerable number of female characters in Spanish women's crime fictions who turn their hand to illegal activities, Spain long had the lowest female crime rate in Europe (Clemente Díaz 28). However, public opinion in Spain apparently labours under the conviction that over the past few years Spanish society has witnessed an upsurge in the number of women breaking the law, a perception the Madrid-based lawyer Andrés Canteras Murillo (409) and the sociologist María del Mar Lorenzo Moledo (87) say is unfounded.

If female murderers and big-time thieves are something of a real-life rarity in Spain, why do women authors from across the country display such a penchant for textualizing them in the pages of their novels and stories? Some of the more humorous texts featuring female felons – a number of which are analysed both in this section and in the next chapter – might be read as a tongue-in-cheek literary response to the kind of public concern commented on by Canteras Murillo and Lorenzo Moledo, as just noted above. The use of humour, irony, and parody when narrating the exploits of colourful female criminals does much to question and contest any public perception that Spain is populated by increasing numbers of dangerous women who break the law. It is also my contention that within these texts the female crook can often function as an escapist role model for the female reader, not least because the authors studied here often characterize their women criminals as likeable individuals with whose wider life experiences, aims, and expectations the female reader can usually identify. And because the fictional female miscreants are often successful, authors not only humorously propose a criminal lifestyle as a possible female *modus vivendi*, but by this means also reinforce reader sympathy with their characters. What is more, most crime fiction by Spanish women re-writes the social and literary norm of often 'over'-penalizing the female criminal (i.e. handing out a punishment disproportionate to the significance or severity of her misdeeds), presenting instead women crooks who avoid legal sanctions. In this way, they question the validity of the portrayal in genre literature by many male crime writers of the unhappy ending meted out to the woman delinquent, as well as the judicial response to many real-life female criminals. Importantly, too, because many of their criminals' actions are motivated by prior victimization by the male (an individual or a group of representatives of the patriarchy), writers are furnishing their female readership with fantasies of contesting victimization, while also articulating the extent of violence against women in contemporary Spain. Their protagonists are victims of male physical, psychological or sexual terror, or of economic and social marginalization, prior to their incursion in illegal activities, and what such authors offer their reading public is perhaps a sort of symbolic generalized revenge, in the name of Everywoman, through the actions of their characters.[27]

In this part of the chapter, I want to analyse the portrayal of women criminals in a number of texts published both in Castilian and in Catalan. I will consider the gendered ideology inherent in the textualization of female murderers, and with reference to selected criminological and sociological studies consider the extent to which the authorial view of their characters' motives reflect those identified by scholars who work with 'real' women homicides in Spain. I then want to move on to assess how and why selected novelists characterize other female law-breakers, particularly thieves.

In his study of the detective genre, the Spanish critic Juan del Rosal identifies criminals' motives as the relatively few time-worn classics of '*codicia, venganza, la pasión y el miedo*' [greed, revenge, passion, and fear] (323 [italics in original]). Although his work was published several decades ago and his comments do not specify the sex of the fictional offender, his brief list serves to summarize very well the reasons why female criminals in woman-authored fictions in Spain are shown to resort to a life of illegal activity. Explanations of the causes of real crimes committed by women appear to coincide with those that del Rosal says prevail in fiction. The British feminist Barney Bardsley has claimed that women resort to breaking the law 'for money; from anger; for success; for kicks – and out of pure need' (14). While female offenders in Spanish women's crime novels and stories very rarely commit any offence – and much less murder – simply 'for kicks',[28] those characters who do kill seem sometimes to be prompted by anger and revenge – and more often by the fear signalled by del Rosal. Within a range of novels and stories, female protagonists end the lives of an array of victims, but bumping off a husband seems to numerically outnumber the murder of other individuals. This particular textual tendency not only reflects the fear that del Rosal says prompts some fictional criminals, but also remits to a reality identified in Spain by the journalist Francisco Pérez Abellán. Although the title of the work, *Ellas matan mejor. 50 crímenes cometidos por mujeres* [Women Make Better Murderers. 50 Crimes Committed by Women] (2000), reveals its rather sensationalist nature and draws attention to its author's penchant for exaggerated journalistic prose, Pérez Abellán does point out that among the cases he researched –

> La mayoría de los crímenes de las mujeres son para liberarse del acoso o del terror al que las someten los varones. Matan a sus maridos porque las maltratan, les dan mala vida o amenazan a los hijos. En general se defienden de agresiones continuas o de situaciones insoportables. (2000: 15)

> [The majority of crimes committed by women are to free themselves from assault or the terror to which men subject them. They murder their husbands because they mistreat them, because they make their life impossible, or because they threaten their children. They usually defend themselves from continual aggression or unbearable situations.]

Husband-killers of the sort characterized by Pérez Abellán in *Ellas matan mejor* are not in short supply in crime fiction written by women in Spain. Beatriz Pottecher's 1985 novel *Ciertos tonos del negro* [Certain Shades of Black] provides an excellent example. Protagonized by Elsa, an Argentinian, it recounts her disastrous marriage to a wife-beating social failure, Daniel, and her subsequent move to Barcelona from Buenos Aires where as a young girl she had enjoyed a comfortable lifestyle. Once in Spain she experiences a vertiginous descent into poverty and marginalization and her unhappy marital situation worsens, so when her husband suffers an asthma attack, Elsa effectively 'kills' him by refusing to call for medical help. She had been so browbeaten by the now deceased Daniel, however, that his demise does not necessarily signal her full reinsertion into society nor the resumption of the personal freedom lost upon her marriage, and it takes her some considerable time to take the action necessary to overcome her situation. This she does by entering into a drug-peddling deal with Laurio, a notorious character from the seamy Barcelona underworld. Having learnt that ridding herself of men is easy and supremely useful, however, Elsa kills him, too, and then returns to her native Argentina with the proceeds from the sale of the drugs.

Pottecher thus seems to suggest that in refusing to assist her ill husband and allowing him to die Elsa is motivated by the need or desire (both of which can be prompted by fear) to rid herself of a man who abused her and who was responsible for her socio-economic and personal ruination. The notions that this man deserved his end and that his wife's behaviour was justified are also textually implicit, and are reinforced by the observation that Daniel was an abuser and the fact that Elsa evades punishment for this murder and that of the drug dealer. Genaro J. Pérez takes his analysis of the novel even further, noting:

> Elsa se ha vengado del patriarcado, a través de su marido dejándolo morir, y de la sociedad machista mediante el asesinato de Laurio. Además, ha burlado las leyes de la sociedad al traficar con drogas. La novelista se burla de los valores patriarcales, puesto que Elsa no sufre punición alguna por haber matado sino que disfruta independencia económica al final de la novela. (2002: 41)

> [Elsa has her revenge on patriarchy by letting her husband die, and on *machista* society by assassinating Laurio. Furthermore, she cocks a snook at social rules by dealing in drugs. The novelist makes fun of patriarchal values because Elsa suffers no punishment at all for the killing; rather, at the end of the novel she enjoys economic independence.]

Barcelona is also the setting for Lidia Falcón's only crime novel to date. Elena, the protagonist of her *Asesinando el pasado* [Murdering the Past] (1997) appears to be a happily married member of the city's middle class and leads a tranquil life as a housewife. But bourgeois appearances veneer an altogether more sordid reality, for not only is her husband having an affair, but Elena has never confessed to him that she was formerly married to a minor criminal from the port area either. Her past, however, comes back to haunt her in the form of her first husband who reappears after many years and blackmails her with the threat of revealing to her present spouse that her first marriage was never annulled and that she is therefore a bigamist, and that the young girl Elena's friends and relatives believe to be her sister is in fact her daughter, offspring of the blackmailer. Motivated by fear of the damage that her first husband's revelations could cause to her child, Elena seeks him out one night among the mean streets of a poor part of town and kills him. She confesses to her crime but is not believed by the police who deem her admission of guilt to be the rantings of a middle-aged female attention-seeker. She thus avoids any punishment at all for her offence.

As in Pottecher's novel, in Falcón's text the woman who kills her husband escapes imprisonment, an important textual device for signalling to the reader that the author of the fiction believes her character's crime to be justifiable. And just as Pottecher's Elsa enjoys a 'happy ending' of sorts – making a large sum of money and returning to her native Buenos Aires – so in *Asesinando el pasado* Elena protagonizes the kind of closure perhaps more appropriate to a romantic novel: she and Félix, her true love, leave Spain to spend the rest of their days in a tropical paradise redolent with overtones of a redeeming primitive innocence. Falcón is also careful to construct the central figure within her tale as a loving and caring mother (under the guise of being her daughter's older sibling), as a loyal and patient wife, and as a responsible, trusted member of the city's bourgeoisie. Because Elena is the archetypal 'good' woman, and because both her husbands are portrayed as thoroughly unpleasant – one is a blackmailer, the other is unfaithful, and both are sleazy – the reader is skilfully induced to applaud the character's murder of spouse number one (as well as the abandonment of husband number two).

Women who rid themselves of their spouses – and other male members of their families – also feature in Julia Sáez-Angulo's fascinating, off-beat collection of short stories entitled *¡Es tan fácil matar!* [Murder is So Easy!] (1991). Women who kill husbands whose laziness and lack of consideration are a source of veritable torture for their wives are portrayed as being entirely justified in their actions. In 'Un luto deseado' [A Desired Mourning], Covadonga pushes her unfaithful, good-for-nothing partner from a sixth-floor window after many years of married life characterized by his unwillingness to perform any work at all and her exhaustion working the 'double shift' at home and in her profession. 'Mañana de domingo' [Sunday Morning] protagonizes Bibiana, an artist, whose creativity has been stifled by her marriage to a lazy fool who refuses to obtain paid employment or even to satisfy her sexually, a man described as 'aquel inútil y vago que la chuleaba de la forma más descarada y vil sin darle siquiera la satisfacción de la carne' [that useless, lazy specimen who sponged off her in the most shameful and despicable way without even fulfilling her sexually] (114). Sick of her situation, she stabs her mate in the back as he sits eating toast one fateful Sunday morning. Although the open ending of this story fails to furnish commentary on Bibiana's judicial fate following the homicide, she is certainly rewarded with personal freedom and a return of her artistic flair. Immediately after the stabbing she feels calmer – 'notó que los latidos de su corazón se habían aplacado' [she noticed that her rapid heartbeat had slowed down] (119) – and she calmly picks up her jacket and goes out for a walk. In 'Un luto deseado', Covadonga avoids any punishment because her husband's death is attributed to an unfortunate accident while fixing a window blind, and his demise brings a much desired respite from her life of virtual slavery in both the professional and domestic realms.

As in the novels by Pottecher and Falcón, then, Sáez-Angulo's murderous protagonists kill their husbands because the men made the women's existence a living hell, and their motivation thus reflects Pérez Abellán's comments recorded earlier. The stories contained in *¡Es tan fácil matar!* make extensive use of humour – usually to the detriment of the male. This textual strategy, combined with the kind of positive portrayal of the female and the very negative characterization of male figures that also underpin *Asesinando el pasado*, conveys an authorial stance which seems to condone husband murder when this is a consequence of abuse of the wife.

Yet another spouse murderer who gets off scot-free features in Álvarez's *Las niñas no hacen ruido cuando mueren* (1998). Within this novel, which documents the unremitting violence to which women are subjected by men in all walks of life, Álvarez presents an important exception to her rule of gendered aggression. Chelines' grandmother is the matriarch of an aristocratic Andalusian family and she murders her good-for-nothing husband after he has fulfilled his breeding function and provided her with two children. Her staff are all perfectly aware of her crime, but so great is their loyalty to their kind mistress and so strong their willingness to observe class hierarchies that they never denounce her. This particular facet of Álvarez's fiction is an unexpected one, not least given that all other victims within her novel are women, and explicit within her commentary on the homicide is the author's reflection on the legitimacy of getting rid of an unwanted husband:

> A todos les pareció justa la muerte [del esposo] si eso hacía feliz a la señora. Las mujeres veían en ella algo parecido al ángel vengador de sus maridos y convirtieron en chascarillo el asesinato como símbolo de revancha transmitido de madres a hijas en el lavadero mientras corrían ríos de envidia por tan gallardo carácter. (136)

> [The [husband's] death seemed fair to everybody if it made Madam happy. The women saw in her something like their husbands' avenging angel and turned the murder as a symbol of revenge into an amusing story passed from mothers to daughters in the laundry where rivers of envy flowed at such a daring personality.]

As in other texts analysed here, the female killer is portrayed in the rosiest terms: she is adored by her staff, is an excellent manager of her estates, is a generous, sensual lover, and defends cultural endeavour and liberal politics. I would suggest that once again, then, the woman author offers her reader a particularly positive representation of her homicidal protagonist as a primary means of justifying the murder she commits – even though in this case 'la señora' is not acting in response to any discernible victimization or abuse at the hands of her eventual victim, but seemingly because her partner was an unnecessary hindrance in her life.

These Spanish women writers thus craft their crime fictions to make clear that in the authorial view, at least, their characters are fully justified in indulging in a spot of spouse-murder, but in so doing the novelists ironically and playfully invert the more usual Spanish – and international – reality of murder of the wife or female partner by the male. Indeed, the *Guardian*'s Giles Tremlett has termed the killing by heterosexual Spanish men of their spouses, partners, and ex's 'the country's most lethal plague, wife-killing' (Tremlett 2002), and widely cited figures place the number of such murders in Spain in excess of sixty each year for the first few years of the new millennium. In the Spanish context, women crime writers' penchant for husband-murderers can perhaps also be read as an ironic revision of earlier national literary models, particularly seventeenth-century wife-murder theatre.[29] Writerly up-turning of real-life paradigms also means that novelists and short story writers remind their reader of the aggressions to which women can be subjected by a male companion within the domestic space, and at the same time they subvert and challenge this victimization by constructing the female as the aggressor, thus empowering not only their protagonists but offering fictions of agency and contestatory behaviours to their readers, too. Significantly, their stance reflects a swing in public and media opinion that suggests that in Spain, as elsewhere, husband-killing is sometimes deemed acceptable.

The fictions analysed above also subvert to some degree widely held perceptions of the woman who resorts to violence (specifically murder) to free herself from an intolerable marriage or partnership. Scholars have noted that real cases featuring women who kill their male partner as a reaction to their own victimization can generate negative perceptions and repercussions of these women by the media and in public opinion. In her study of media 'stories of fighting back', Marian Meyers observes that 'self defence appears justified only when the woman's actions occur within the framework of patriarchal notions of appropriate gender roles and behavior. Women who step outside that boundary may be represented as unjustified in fighting back' (80). In her paper that analyses real cases of violent women, Margaret Shaw says that the female who responds in kind to aggression is often portrayed as a 'helpless' victim, a stance that oversimplifies the situation (120). Similarly, Barney Bardsley has commented on press portrayal of women who murdered their spouse, noting that they were often constructed by the media as victims who, having borne a lifetime of abuse and brutality, finally fought back (130). These paradigms and perceptions are thus revised very significantly in woman-authored Spanish crime fiction of the type studied here. Although the murderous protagonists on whom I focus my analysis are victimized by their respective spouses, they are characterized as being far from the 'helpless victim' identified by scholars such as Shaw and Bardsley as existing in the real world. Furthermore, the fictional figures examined here also 'step outside the boundary' of what Meyers sees as 'appropriate gender roles and behavior' (among their number are a bigamist, an *outré* artist, and a woman with many lovers), but their authors opine that they are justified in fighting back, again in contrast with Meyers' assertions.

Perhaps significantly the kind of explanatory and exculpatory discourse for husband-killing devised within the selected narratives has also begun to pervade the media in Spain, and in this regard the authorial stance advanced in crime fictions by women can be read as part of a wider discursive tendency. A real case, which in Spain attracted extensive press attention and comment, was that of Teresa de Jesús Moreno Maya, known as 'Tani', a gypsy woman who in 1995 shot dead her husband after seventeen years of abuse at his hands. When, five years into her fourteen-year sentence 'Tani' was transferred to the Alcalá-Meco prison in Madrid, the daily *El Mundo* described how between 2,000 and 3,000 demonstrators had gathered at the gates of the jail to demand the assassin's immediate pardon and release, and the piece makes clear the (female) journalist's supportive stance of the prisoner (*El Mundo* 25. 10. 00). In a further piece, which appeared in the quality daily *El País*, Alicia Giménez-Bartlett, one of the crime writers whose fiction I analysed in Chapter 1, also underscores popular perception of 'Tani's' crime as a justified one to which the judicial system should have responded with sympathy. The novelist notes that the murderess had been the victim of 'golpes, humillaciones y terror' [beatings, humiliation, and terror] at the hands of a husband the writer classifies as a 'torturador' [torturer] (Giménez-Bartlett 2000*c*).[30]

Although in her 2000 article cited here Giménez-Bartlett expressed her understanding of 'Tani's' motives for murdering her spouse, husband-killers do not feature in any of her Petra Delicado fictions to date. A figure whom the writer does portray, however, is the 'woman spurned' who takes the life of the lover who rejects her. Thus, *Serpientes en el paraíso* concludes with the identification of Malena Puig as the murderer of Juan Luis Espinet who had been found dead in the swimming pool of the condominium where each lived with their respective spouse. Malena and the victim had been lovers, and Espinet was the father of her daughter. When he ended their affair and Malena discovered that he was the local Lothario who maintained casual relationships with any number of women, she killed him. Similarly, in the short story 'Muerte en el gimnasio', Charo, a cleaner in a gymnasium, 'cooks' her bodybuilder lover to death by locking him in the sauna and turning up the heat after he informs her of his decision to end their relationship. Giménez-Bartlett thus reproduces within her fictions an archetype that is not necessarily structured to elicit readerly sympathy in the way that the spouse murderers studied earlier in this section quite clearly were. And because both Malena and Charo are appre-hended by the forces of law and order – and will presumably be incarcerated for their crimes – the sort of justificatory discourse identified in other writers is absent here, textual strategies that again reflect the author's move away from the kind of rhetoric found in other writers who condone their characters' spouse-killing antics.

The model of the murderous 'woman scorned' also underpins María José Cavadas' short story, 'Día de caza' [The Shoot] (1996) – albeit with some important revisions. The tale is set among Spain's landed elite and centres on Mercedes, a member of the wealthy group who is engaged to be married to the son of a landowner. When she discovers that her intended has maintained a homosexual affair with a gamekeeper, she shoots the employee to exact revenge and in order to preserve her social position. She is never punished, however, because the others in her social circle close ranks to protect her. After all, it is reasoned, her victim was a barely human member of the lower classes and he had compro-mised the group's façade of respectability and morality by daring to speak out about his liaison with his rich lover. The point Cavadas makes here, then, is not that the victimized woman kills an abuser in a justified act of retribution, but rather that if a female member of Mercedes' class murders a rival to her part-ner's affections then the social group will work towards ensuring that she is not punished for her actions. 'Día de caza' is thus one of a very limited number of crime fictions by Spanish women to explore the nuances of the consequences for the female killer of belonging to a privileged social group.[31]

Group complicity in protecting a woman murderer from being apprehended and incarcerated is also key to ensuring that Álvar-ez's Baby Villalta escapes punishment. In *La soledad del monstruo*, Álvarez's character killed the woman she – erroneously – believed to be her lesbian partner's assassin in a frenzied knife attack. It is clear from a reading of *Las niñas no hacen ruido cuando mueren* that every member of the Huelva *demi-monde* and criminal fraternity within which Baby moves is fully aware of her crime, yet nobody is willing to report her to the police and thus bring about her almost certain incarceration. Because Baby is a lesbian and is also a physically repugnant misanthrope she can perhaps be read as the type of woman who moves beyond the boundaries of what Meyers – who was cited earlier – called 'appropriate gender roles and behavior'. Álvarez redeems her character, however, by refusing to submit to notions of legal justice and permitting Baby to escape punishment for her crime. In a way, then, this particular authorial stance reflects Álvarez's wider project of exposing the relentless and multitudinous violences to which women are subjected in all walks of life, but textualizing some forms of 'payback' or revenge. So while Chelines' grandmother kills off her husband and Chelines herself murders her mother, Baby stabs to death the woman she thinks killed her lover. But Baby gets 'the wrong man' – who is in fact an innocent woman – a timely reminder that despite Álvarez's rather celebratory portrayal of the killer grand-mother, the author also wants to alert her reader to the possible dangers inherent in the actions of women who respond in kind to violence.

The problematic ethical issues of murder by women, which are largely elided by writers such as Pottecher, Falcón or Sáez-Angulo, for example, in their justificatory textualizations of husband-killers, but which are unearthed by Álvarez, also underpin a number of other women's crime fictions from Spain. In both Álvarez's *Las niñas no hacen ruido cuando mueren* and Isabel Olesti's *El marit invisible* daughters kill their mothers for similar reasons: primarily because the older women thwarted their offspring's attempts to lead an independent existence, were the source of their children's profound frustration, or exerted other, more nefarious, pressures on their lives. Chelines, one of Baby's few friends in *Las niñas no hacen ruido cuando mueren*, kills her mother because she never helped her daughter to overcome her heroin addiction, sold her off into an arranged marriage that would further her own financial interests, colluded with Chelines' wife-raping spouse to make the younger woman's life a living hell, and finally murdered her friend Rosa. A similarly bleak tale emerges from Olesti's novel that is in essence an investigation into the

history of the homicide victim and her family in order to elucidate the reasons for her killing. Remei, her daughter and the
individual finally identified as her murderer, endured poverty and
marginalization and eventually reclusion in a psychiatric hospital
as a direct result of her unstable family environment, her
mother's sexual promiscuity, incarceration in the family's dank,
smelly apartment, removal from school by her mother at an early
age, and parental refusal to allow her to visit the man she loved.
When finally released from the mental institution in which she
had been interned, Remei meets up with her long-lost lover and
returns to her former family home where, in circumstances that
remain unknown to the reader, she kills her mother.

Just as Baby Villalta in Álvarez's novel avoids detection because
the citizens of Huelva appear to have entered into a pact of
silence to protect her, so in Olesti's story Remei will escape justice
because her brother, who solves the crime, will take no action to
report what he knows. Chelines' fate remains unclear, but the
repeated allusions throughout *Las niñas no hacen ruido cuando
mueren* to her imminent death as the result of many years of
heroin addiction suggest that her drug habit will perhaps kill her
before any 'formal' justice can be meted out.

The avoidance of legal retribution in this – albeit tragically
ironic – manner would certainly tie in with Álvarez's narrative
tendency to pardon her fictional murderesses and ensure that
they never fall into the hands of the Law. But I would suggest that
she is once again flagging up the profound ambiguities inherent
in textually condoning murder by women, just as she did in her
narrative treatment of Baby's assassination of an innocent woman.
Although Álvarez is clearly aware of the kind of humorous
characterization often inherent in the portrayal of women who
bump off their abusive husbands as her depiction of Chelines'
grandmother makes apparent, as a writer she evinces a concern
with violence exercised by women against women – indeed, just as
her fiction is shot through with a ceaseless concern for the
multiple forms of aggression to which her countrywomen seem to
be routinely subjected by men.

While Álvarez thus alerts her reader to these ideological and
ethical pitfalls, the victimization of the mother in *El marit invisible*
also sits very uneasily with allowing the perpetrator to quite
literally get away with murder and also merits comment. The
demonization of the maternal in female-authored crime fiction

from Spain (specifically, apportioning blame to the mother figure for unruly offspring) was analysed in Chapter 1, but in the cases investigated by Giménez-Bartlett's Petra Delicado, although blame for perverse and criminal offspring was laid at the door of the female parent, she was never the victim of an avenging child as is the case in Álvarez's and Olesti's stories. Attributing culpability to the mother, however difficult she may have made her daughter's life, would seem to set a dangerous precedent that lays the blame for female victimization (at least in some cases) at the woman victim's door and contradicts the tendency to counter and reject notions of victim complicity that are more usually expressed in women's crime fiction from Spain. What Olesti makes repeatedly evident in her novel, however (as I analyse in more detail in the next chapter), is the mother's status as a victim in all aspects of her existence. Because she is victimized sexually, socially, economically, politically, and also as a consequence of her Catalan identity, she is not equipped to protect or nurture her children, a situation which leads ultimately to disaster because her daughter, too, suffers multiple victimization as a result. Olesti thus skilfully re-writes the more usual paradigm of violence against women: the mother is not killed by an abusive male but by her own child. That Olesti allows Remei to avoid incarceration for her crime, then, is far from indicating the kind of tongue-in-cheek celebration of murder encountered in crime texts by Spanish women that feature a husband-killer. Rather, it is a nod to the acknowledgement that Remei's status as the latest in a very long line of women who have suffered extreme and prolonged victimization is motivation for her crime, and escaping imprisonment cannot be read in this text as an authorial pardon for murdering a woman.

Not all of the female criminals textualized by contemporary Spanish women writers are murderers, however, as the overview of Oliver's and Giménez-Bartlett's detective novels in Chapter 1 revealed. In addition, some authors portray thieves whose *modus operandi* seems alluringly flamboyant. The two novels that best exemplify this tendency are *Escapa't d'Andorra* (1989) [literally, Escape from Andorra, translated by Sheila McIntosh as *Wild Card* (1992)] by the Catalan writer Assumpta Margenat, and Matilde Asensi's *El salón de ámbar* [The Amber Room] (1999). Both protagonize successful female thieves whom their authors portray as young, daring, likeable, and intelligent, a textual ploy intended to create readerly empathy with the characters, a considerable degree of complicity in the robberies they carry out, and a certain vicarious pleasure in their exploits.

Rossi, the quirky, plucky character at the centre of Margenat's tale takes the decision to spend a winter season working as a supermarket checkout girl in Andorra, an important European ski resort and a tax-free haven for Spanish and French shoppers. Upon discovering that she is one of a very considerable number of women employed as wage-slaves and that some of her female colleagues and friends are also subject to sexual harassment by male employers and managers, the young heroine resolves to symbolically overcome collective gendered economic inequality and also boost her own flagging finances by stealing a considerable sum of money from the shop in which she works. She carries out the heist in collusion with her sister, and their careful preparations pay off, for the affable Rossi manages to divert her boss's attention wearing a low-cut blouse while her sister empties the company safe. Their crime is in many ways a playful revision of male-engineered robberies, for it requires no physical strength, no violence, no black masks or 'swag sacks' to carry out. In defiance of the norms of a genre that, as Maggie Humm has pointed out, tends to place very considerable emphasis on action protagonized by the male (238), Margenat's revision of the thriller is a study in non-action. Importance is given, rather, to patience, careful planning, and maintaining a low profile, and the text reveals that the non-active female, rather than the action heroine, can become empowered, thus offering an ironic alternative role model to readers.

Margenat furnishes further ironic commentary on the gendering of her characters' law-breaking. In order to take the stolen cash across the border into Catalonia, Rossi rolls up each of the banknotes bearing the venerable face of His Majesty King Juan Carlos I emitted by the Bank of Spain and hides them between the applicators of a box of tampons. In this way the patriarchal world of finance and big money is subjugated to female biology in a highly amusing manner, thus inverting the more usual relationship between the two whereby women must sell their labour or their bodies for a minimal slice of the world's economic pie. Importantly, too, Rossi's own 'escape from Andorra' will underline her rejection of some elements of globalized, corporate patriarchy – although in carrying out a robbery for personal enrichment she of course acknowledges that money is essential to function within that system. Rather than leaving the Principality by car or bus on the man-made motorways that snake into the tiny country, she opts to cross into Catalonia on horseback through wild mountains, thus avoiding detection but also reiterating her rejection of the exploitative capitalism that feeds on the day-trippers who arrive in motor vehicles. The 'escape' of the text's title thus has two connotations: one that is clearly a reference to Rossi's physical getaway from the Principality and is a nod to thriller titles, and a second, tongue-in-cheek one that alludes to her flight from the boredom and exploitation of the frenetic world of the duty-free supermarket.

In a further ironic negation of the virilist assumptions that underpin the thriller, Rossi and her sister use the code 'fer . . . "un jersei"' (17 [ellipsis in original]) ['knitting a sweater' (*Wild Card* 15)] to refer to their intended theft. Deploying this term also indicates a subversion of a domestic activity traditionally performed by women and which clearly has no criminal overtones whatsoever. In fact, our daring protagonist rejects any association with domesticity by living off instant soup and takeaway pizzas, behaviour that can be read as a parodic allusion by Margenat to the gastronomic excesses and fondness for cooking evinced by Spain's most famous male detective and *bon viveur*, Manuel Vázquez Montalbán's Pepe Carvalho.

A character as engaging as Margenat's Rossi is sited at the centre of Matilde Asensi's *El salón de ámbar*. The publisher, Barcelona-based Plaza y Janés, organized no advance publicity for the novel that was the civil servant-turned-writer's first book. It nonetheless sold over 12,000 copies shortly after its launch – a not inconsiderable number in a nation that has one of the lowest per capita levels of book buying in Europe – and has now run to several editions including economically priced small-format paperbacks that are sold at news-stands and in kiosks as well as in bookshops. Asensi has since gone on to write four more highly successful mystery novels, *Iacobus* [Iacobus] (2000), *El último catón* [The Last Manuscript] (2001), *El origen perdido* [The Lost Origin] (2003), and *Todo bajo el cielo* [Everything Beneath the Heavens] (2006), all of which are historical adventure mysteries, a feature which has led to her being likened to Arturo Pérez-Reverte, Spain's leading author of historical thrillers.

The best-seller status of her first book, however, is undoubtedly a consequence not only of its gripping construction as a taut thriller, but also of the characterization of its protagonist Ana, professional art thief and antiques dealer from Ávila, Spain's famous walled city. Ana is a successful businesswoman, owns a town apartment and a countryside retreat, never performs any domestic chores since these are taken care of by an old servant, and travels the world to steal valuable pieces of art. Although the reader learns little of her physical appearance, it is clear that she is very lithe and agile, a useful attribute when scaling walls or fences to purloin precious artworks for the international gang of art thieves of which she forms part.[32] And in addition to this list of fortunes she finds herself an equally wealthy, cultured lover – and fellow master criminal – whose code-name, *Cavalo* [horse], alludes not only to his function within a gang whose members identify themselves as pieces on a chess-board, but also to his sexual prowess.

The title of the novel is a reference to the amber room in the Catherine Palace, south of St Petersburg, that disappeared during the German invasion at the time of the Second World War and was never heard of again.[33] Asensi's tale proposes that the marvellous Russian amber carvings had been taken to Germany where they were hidden in a secret subterranean bunker in the shape of a swastika, and that details of their whereabouts were painted in code on the back of a portrait belonging to a wealthy German. *El salón de ámbar* relates how the crime ring to which Ana belongs is approached by an individual who wants them to steal a painting for him – the very canvas on the rear of which the secret instructions for finding the amber have been written, a fact of which Ana and her fellow criminals are at the time unaware. After careful planning by all members of the group, Ana is despatched to Germany to enter the castle where the picture is stored, steal it, and take it with her back to Spain. The description of the building's lavish architecture, Ana's approach to it in the dead of night, and the fact that it is inhabited by a dangerous man of questionable moral character serve to structure it as the house of terror of the gothic imaginary, and it is into this edifice that the young woman must go. Despite the gothic setting, however, Ana is far from being the gothic heroine who is imprisoned within the castle, and with the help of her high-tech surveillance equipment and her physical fitness she enters the building, removes the picture, and leaves as silently as she had come.

Once back in Ávila, however, she discovers the strange cipher on the rear of the canvas. She devotes some considerable time to decoding it, a feat she manages with the help of her phenomenal IT skills, and realizes that the secret message indicates the whereabouts of the amber stolen from Russia during the war. Once she understands that the fabulous treasures of the amber room lie within reach, she enlists her fellow criminal Cavalo and together they travel to Germany in search of a fortune that they will not have to share with the other members of their gang. Their odyssey through the underground labyrinth where the amber panels are hidden becomes increasingly dangerous as they realize that they are being followed by somebody whose desperation to own the carvings is so great they will stop at nothing – not even murder – and Ana and Cavalo are only saved by the intervention of the latter's twelve-year-old daughter and her computer know-how.

As in Margenat's *Escapa't d'Andorra, El salón de ámbar* revises many gendered assumptions underpinning the thriller. Primarily, of course, Ana adopts and revels in all of those behaviours generically posited as the realm of the male, and the (female) reader of the text may not only greatly enjoy the protagonist's exploits but may remain entirely unperturbed by them. As the action heroine, Ana is in many ways the antithesis of the dangerous, treacherous *femme fatale*. Indeed, the traitor in Asensi's novel proves to be Roi – code-name of Prince Philibert de Malgaigne-Denonvilliers – an urbane, charming, handsome Frenchman who is the mastermind of the gang with which Ana works, and whose textual position as the *homme fatal* within the narrative ironically undermines the validity of the more usual female construct.

Within *El salón de ámbar*, Asensi also uses her character to invert traditional gendered relationships to art. Historically, most of the great European painters, sculptors, and other producers of works of art have been male. Women's link to the world of artistic endeavour was long that of model and muse, as the object of the artist's gaze, as virgins or nudes on a canvas, for example. The male artist paints or sculpts her figure, and the male patron purchases and owns the work (and may also appear as the subject of a canvas, but rarely, if ever, constructed for sexualized, voyeuristic scopophilic consumption as are many female figures). Within Asensi's fiction, however, Ana of course steals art, and the painting she removes from the castle in Germany and which holds the ciphered clue to the secret whereabouts of the amber room is of a group of male figures, while another, far more rustic canvas, depicting '[u]n viejo de larga barba y rostro maligno' [an old man with a long beard and malignant features] (62) is roughly stuck to the back of it. Ana's breaking of multiple layers of taboo is thus compounded, for she not only becomes the (temporary) owner of pieces of art, she is a woman who possesses images of men, and she has of course come by them illegally. It should also be remembered that Ana is aided and abetted in her activities by her aunt Juana, although no love is lost between the two women. A nun in an Ávila convent, the older woman stores the gang's stolen goods in the cellars of the building until such a time as her niece can dispose of them quietly and safely, but in return she demands from Ana significant sums of cash to pay for her services and to buy her silence. Personified in this figure, then, is not only a reversal of the role afforded women within the Catholic church (that of silent and silenced virginal mother), but also an ironic inversion of the holy life and deeds of Ávila's greatest daughter, Saint Teresa.

The humorous, tongue-in-cheek portrayal of Rossi and Ana as likeable, daring young women who successfully pull off robberies that will enhance their economic position ensures that *Escapa't d'Andorra* and *El salón de ámbar* can be read as escapist fictions. However, a number of other features of these novels also suggest that their authors intend them to be read as enjoyable escapist literature. Like many of the writers studied earlier in this section who portray women who quite literally get away with murder, so Margenat and Asensi allow their protagonists to escape with their bounty and go unpunished for their crimes. Furthermore, and again in keeping with a number of the novelists studied above, the authors of *Escapa't d'Andorra* and *El salón de ámbar* ensure that the victims of their characters' misdeeds are never women, a strategy which goes some way to revising the victimization of the female that might seem to be a norm of much male-authored crime fiction and is a reflection of the Spanish social reality. In Spain – as elsewhere – women are also generally marginalized econom-ically in relation to the male as they tend to earn on average less than men and own fewer assets (see Falcón 2000: 9). Because Rossi and Ana enrich themselves, then, Margenat and Asensi perhaps intend to ironically draw reader attention to the more usual economic situation in which the female finds herself, and humorously propose a means of overcoming it. Similarly, I think both texts can be read as containing implicit commentary on the motives for theft committed by women. Spanish criminologists have noted that such factors as poverty, lack of education, and inadequate living conditions are common to the life experiences of female offenders (Canteras Murillo 209–17; Pollino Piedras y Vela Ferrero 13–14; Miura 9). These features do not in any way characterize either Margenat's Rossi nor Asensi's Ana who enjoy relatively happy personal circumstances. The characters' rather pleasant lives function to underscore the playful escapism of both novels, while at the same time establishing an implicit contrast with the unhappy existential factors and economic need that characterize the backgrounds of very many women who steal in real-life scenarios. Indeed, the contrast between the hardship that apparently prompts large numbers of female thieves and the motives evinced by Rossi and Ana is significant. The actions of these two fictional felons seem to be encouraged by the postmodern motivation to conspicuous consumption, a tendency that in Spain has combined with a traditional concern with image and 'keeping up appearances'. Ana and Rossi want to run a car, they want to enjoy a social life, they want to possess material goods, and so they steal, and in portraying them as likeable and daring, and in allowing them to get away with their crimes, Asensi and Margenat seem to suggest that their protagonists are entirely justified in resorting to robbery. Their rationalization of their characters' felonious exploits also rewrites a rule implicit in crime fiction – particularly woman-authored stories – that the economically poor individual (usually the detective) is an incorruptible moral stalwart because material inferiority means moral superiority (Young 105). In *Escapa't d'Andorra* and *El salón de ámbar*, then, as in many of the novels studied earlier in this section, being female and committing a crime do not equate with lack of moral probity. And because law-breaking women are portrayed in such a positive light within so many female crime texts from Spain, the reader understands that writers are offering up a literary revision of attitudes to women crooks that may be prevalent in wider society, and are suggesting crime as a response to gendered victimization.

NOTES

1   The postmodern revision of the crime genre, such as that essayed by
     Pynchon or Auster, for example, often fails to contain a victim.
     Indeed, it is often unclear if a crime has been committed at all.
     Despite the postmodern experimentation with the genre in Spain by
     writers such as Eduardo Mendoza or Antonio Muñoz Molina, Span-
     ish texts are generally more faithful to traditional models and usually
     contain either a crime that is investigated by a detective, or feature a
     crime and the individual who carries it out.

2   The status of the female as victim and male as aggressor is a constant
     feature of social perceptions and cultural productions in the West
     and elsewhere. Karen Lynch (2003) has proposed that within fem-
     inist detective fiction and woman-authored Gothic novels this pattern
     is replicated in a replay and revision of the gendering of sadism and
     masochism.

3   Despite his comment about the generalized nature of the victim as
     simply a textual building block, Resina goes on to say that Manuel
     Vázquez Montalbán's detective novels constitute something of an
     exception in this regard, because within them the victim performs an
     important ideological function. He claims that Vázquez Montalbán's
     theory of victimization reveals the chasm that exists between the
     beliefs of the victim and those of his or her fellow citizens. Because
     the victim is different, he or she endangers social cohesion and has
     to be sacrificed (1997: 66).

4   I use 'alleged' advisedly, for as numerous critics have pointed out,
     when the victim is gendered as female – and particularly when the
     criminal is male – texts are constructed on a set of political premises
     that permit and promote gendered victimization (see, for example,
     Forter's *Murdering Masculinities* and Dunant 17).

5   This is particularly the case, of course, in novels featuring forensic
     medics or other scientists, such as the popular series by Patricia
     Cornwell or Kathy Reichs, a sub-genre that is absent from Spanish
     literature as yet.

6   Significantly, the *femme fatale*'s face also lacks importance in *noir*
     narratives. Tom Reichart and Charlene Melcher note that in *noir*
     film:

> The camera, and the audience, would examine her [the *femme
> fatale*] slowly from spikey stiletto to coifed hairdo, concentrat-
> ing in particular on the long, elegant leg thrust resolutely
> forward from the fold of her too-tight skirt. When the camera,
> and the hero's eyes, finally rested on her face – dramatically
> concealed behind a swooping curl cascading over one eye – the
> audience knew exactly who she was. (287)

Clearly, then, the highly sexualized body is primary to the representation and perception of this female, as it often is to the portrayal
of the female victim's corpse. The relative unimportance of the face

is made clear not only by its revelation after every other physical feature has been minutely exposed, but also because when it finally comes into focus it is in any case half hidden behind a coil of hair which in turn functions to re-emphasize the primacy of the sexual.

7   Rhoda Estep identified a similar trend in media products (151–2; 154), and her research makes clear the reality that both the media and televisual fictions portray more female victims than male because within society women are more often victims of crime, aggression, and violence. In the Spanish context Paz de la Cuesta Aguado noted that greater numbers of women than men are victims of crime (1993: 13), and her observation has been repeated more recently by Horacio Roldán Barbero (166–7).

8   The passivity of the victim in genre fiction is a reflection of an apparent social reality in Spain and other national arenas. Roldán Barbero, a criminologist working at the University of Córdoba, repeats his perception of the female victim as 'sujeto pasivo' [a passive subject] (165; 166), and observes that criminology has traditionally been androcentric in that it has tended to focus far more on the delinquent (who is usually male) than on the victim (who is generally female) (165).

9   Some feminist scholars read (heterosexual) 'pornography' as the unremitting gendered violence to which women are routinely subjected. Jane Caputi, for example, uses the term 'the *pornography of everyday life*' with reference to 'mainstream images of gender dominance and subordination, exploitation and abuse, that proliferate throughout everyday culture', and within her study her aim is 'to highlight the function of pornography as a paradigm for the development of all manner of oppressive discourses' (58 [italics in original]). As discussed later in this chapter, Spanish feminist observers also draw attention to what they perceive as the continuous and unrelenting aggression at all levels of society to which women are subjected merely because of their sex.

10   Although I use the term 'gendered violence' I am cognizant that it can function to obscure the fact that it refers, specifically, to male violence directed against women. With reference to the Spanish context Miguel Lorente Acosta says:

> Al hablar [. . .] de violencia de género, en cierto modo estamos diluyendo la realidad y el significado (motivaciones y objetivos) de la agresión a la mujer en el mar de la violencia interpersonal. Como hemos indicado, se trata de la violencia llevada a cabo por el hombre (género masculino) sobre la mujer (género femenino) con el objetivo de perpetuar una serie de roles y estereotipos creados por el primero y asignados al segundo con el fin de continuar con la situación de desigualdad, inferioridad y sumisión que tiene la mujer en nuestra sociedad, y que es consustancial a los géneros. (166)

[When we talk [. . .] about gendered violence in a way we are
diminishing the reality and meaning (the motives and objectives) of assaults against women in the vast expanse of interper-
sonal violence. As we have noted, we are dealing with violence
carried out by men (male gender) against women (female
gender) with the aim of perpetuating a series of roles and
stereotypes created by the former and imposed upon the latter
in order to perpetuate the position of inequality, inferiority
and subjugation which is woman's lot in our society and which
is inseparable from gender itself.]

11   Although, as I detail later in this chapter, figures seem to suggest that
Spanish women are increasingly victims of specific gendered crimes
such as spouse or partner murder, 'domestic' violence, or rape, for
example, it is undoubtedly the case that such offences have always
occurred. It is likely, however, that the social and legal perception of
what constitutes a crime of 'gendered violence' in Spain has changed
very significantly over the past several decades and that women now
seem more willing to report cases because they refuse to accept as
normal or tolerable the violence to which they are subjected by men.

12   It should be noted that even though Falcón published this article
prior to the Madrid bombings of March 2004, she still asserts that
terrorism in Spain (i.e. ETA's activities) seems to be of far greater
concern to the media than violence against women.

13   Jesús Rodríguez also notes that the case of Ana Orantes had a much
wider effect on responses to violence against women in Spain: 'Tras
la muerte de Ana Orantes se crearon teléfonos de urgencia, casas de
acogida, servicios ambulatorios; se iniciaron programas de educación
no sexista en los colegios, y se proporcionó más información y mayor
asistencia médica y legal a las mujeres. Y un endurecimiento de las
leyes contra los maltratadores [. . .]' [Following the death of Ana
Orantes, emergency telephone help lines, women's refuges, and
specialist medical centres were established. Anti-sexist education
programmes were begun in schools, and more information and
better medical and legal provision was provided for women, with a
toughening of the law against the abusers [. . .]] (40).

14   For a particularly incisive discussion of the link between reality
television and gendered violence in Spain (albeit in a work of fiction)
see Andreu Martín and Verónica Vila-San-Juan (41–3).

15   This absence of journalistic concern for the issues underlying the
problem certainly seemed to be the case in two quality newspapers
during 2004. Throughout the spring of that year, *La Vanguardia* ran a
series entitled 'Vidas rotas' [Broken Lives], each article featuring a
brief life story of a woman who had been murdered by her husband,
partner, or ex during the past year. In April, the Sunday supplement
to *El País* included a four-page article containing details of the 60
women killed by a spouse or boyfriend since the previous April (*El
País Semanal* 04. 04. 04). Both pieces, however, were characterized by
their brevity, their focus on scandalous or unusual elements in each

case, and a nauseating pseudo-'concern' for the victim that aimed to titillate the reader but which detracted from the significance of the issue. My impression of these particular articles is similar to that I formed when reading many other items in the Spanish press reporting cases of violence against women, and this view has also been noted by Natalia Fernández Díaz (2003).

[16] Vázqez Montalbán's detective, Pepe Carvalho, discovers the woman's decomposing body in a very remote village in Thailand. She had travelled to the Orient in search of exoticism and adventure but 'going native' results in her death. While her corpse does not function as the archetypal symbolic dead female central to *noir* fictions, it is imbued with multiple levels of symbolic value, for it represents the European fear of decomposition, degradation and destruction of the self associated with the Orient in the Western imagination.

[17] In the concluding remarks to his study of US male-authored hard-boiled detective fiction and masculinity Forter states: 'I have argued that the crime novel is a place in our culture where a range of dominant fantasies about gender are at once hyperbolically elaborated and contested. Those fantasies are concerned above all with woman as threat to the bounded male self' (214). That threat has to be addressed and, in many cases, done away with. Chapter 2 of his monograph offers a succinct rationale for hard-boiled characters' victimization of the female, and he formulates an apologia for the mutilation, sexual assault, and killing of women founded in a Freudian reading of the significance of the female genitals (52–3).

[18] In an article for *El Temps*, Patricia Hart, the translator of Simó's novel, seems to suggest that the 'corpse of one's own' alluded to in the title that she gave to the translation is that of the protagonist's husband (1997: 81). From my reading of *Una ombra fosca, com un núvol de tempesta*, however, I would suggest that it is Sara's own corpse that is fundamental to any understanding of the text because her body – and particularly her dead body – is the only entity to which she can lay claim because her husband's control over her is absolute, both before and even after his death (an issue I analyse in Chapter 3 of this study). The translated title is also very clearly evocative of Woolf's *A Room of One's Own*. It thus functions to furnish ironic commentary on the subjugation and subordination Sara experienced while married.

[19] Similar scenes may also appear in the works of Anglophone writers such as Patricia Cornwell. This may be one of the reasons why feminist readers now reject the feminist credentials of such writers as Cornwell (personal communication from Carmel Shute, Melbourne Chapter, Sisters in Crime).

[20] In a fascinating twist to the closure of *Malpaís*, Sindo Roca discovers that Elda Meyers was not murdered and then burned; rather, one of the sculptress' female acquaintances suffered a fall that resulted in her death and Elda then set fire to her own home with the other woman's body inside in order to leave behind her old life and start

anew having assumed her friend's identity. The policeman does not glean this knowledge, however, until the very end of the events narrated in the novel, and by this textual point the reader may well have accepted the authorial strategy that de-sexualises the supposed victim. Furthermore, the *dénoument* does not, in my opinion, invalidate Soler Onís's device because as Elda herself points out to Sindo, she could indeed have been the victim. Commenting on the similarities between the dead woman and herself, she says: 'Nunca imaginé que pudiéramos ser tan parecidas. Ya ves, edad, estatura, ausencia de hijos, fumadoras arrepentidas . . . Lo demás no queda, ¿te has fijado? No dejan huella los viajes, ni los amores, ni los deseos, ni los baños en la playa cuando éramos adolescentes: el éxito o la dicha. Las ideas. Nada.' [I never imagined we could be so similar. Age, height, never having children, being repentant smokers, you know . . . Have you noticed that nothing else remains? Journeys, lovers, desires, swimming at the seaside when we were adolescents – none of them leaves a mark. Nor success nor happiness. Nor ideas. Nothing.] (171 [ellipsis in original]). Just as Simó's Sara can be read as a symbolic female victim of male violence against all women, so Soler Onís' corpse functions to remind her reader that in death women can become similar, and that such cadavers should be de-eroticised in literature.

21 Julia's home in central Madrid is, unusually, a detached house set in a garden filled with roses and other flowers. The property is thus hugely evocative of Miss Marple's abode. Similarly, just as Miss Marple is often portrayed sitting in her cottage waiting for those in some way involved in a crime to call in to see her, so Barbero's character sits and awaits visitors, venturing out occasionally with a specific purpose in mind, again as does Miss Marple when she wishes to seek out a particular clue or piece of information. And just as Christie's spinster sleuth resides in a tight-knit community, so does Julia, in the very middle of the urban sprawl. Where Barbero subverts the Miss Marple paradigm, however, is in affording vast amounts of textual space to her character's tumultuous inner thoughts, particularly her regret at having wasted so many chances in life.

22 For further discussion of the ways in which some male-authored crime and detective fictions punish the transgressive female with death, see, for example, Walton and Jones (192–3); Forter's *Murdering Masculinities* (2000); Young (97).

23 That the Spanish press often exculpates the male criminal in cases of gendered violence by offering up characteristics about him (e.g. that he takes drugs, is alcoholic, has a history of violence) in an attempt to 'explain' his actions is a central premise of Natalia Fernández Díaz's (2003) excellent study of the representation of sexual violence in the press in Spain.

24 In February 2004, a keyword search of the database of Madrid's Biblioteca Nacional [National Library] for the terms 'violencia' [violence] and 'España' [Spain] produced a list of over 100 works relevant to the theme. Of these, some 90% were recent texts on the

theme of gendered violence, a figure that reveals the extent of the scholarly, legal, and criminological response to the issue of violence against women.

[25]   That female 'liberation' leads to violence against women is a notion also espoused by the Spanish Catholic Church. In February 2004, the church published a lengthy tome on family issues, a central premise of which was that the 'revolución sexual' [sexual revolution] is a cause of domestic violence (Haro Tecglén 2004; *El País* 03. 02. 04; *El País* 04. 02. 04; *El País* 23. 04. 04).

[26]   Workplace harassment has recently become a major concern in Spain. Known as *mobbing*, the phenomenon has merited hundreds of studies by Spanish authors in the past few years. Many scholars and journalists have signalled that women are disproportionately the victim of bullying at work in Spain (see e.g. *El País* 10. 11. 02; *Diario Médico.com* 23. 05. 03; *El País* 28. 10. 03; *La Crónica de Guadalajara* 17. 03. 05). Harassment of women thus seems to be motivated by their sex – as well as by their status as vulnerable employees on low wages and non-permanent contracts, an issue flagged up in the early 1990s by de la Cuesta Aguado but which does not appear to have changed:

> Las mujeres pueden ser víctimas en su propio trabajo, bien a través del acoso sexual o bien por medio de la discriminación laboral. Las formas más habituales de acoso laboral son la mirada constante y atrevida, el manoseo, apretones o pellizcos, intimaciones sexuales, proposiciones etc. En cuanto a la otra faceta (discriminación laboral), las mujeres realizan los trabajos más ínfimos en relación con el varón y pese a que trabaja dos terceras partes de las horas laborales de todo el mundo, sólo gana una décima parte de los ingresos mundiales. (1993: 11)

> [Women can be victims at work either as a result of sexual harassment or as a result of workplace discrimination. The most usual forms of workplace harassment are continual blatant staring, being touched up, gropes or pinches, sexual innuendo, being propositioned, etc. As for work-based discrimination, women carry out the most menial tasks, and in spite of performing two-thirds of the world's working hours earn only 10% of the world's income.]

For a detailed overview of the increased awareness of gendered workplace harassment and the formulation of legal responses to it in Spain, see Valiente's fascinating study (1998).

[27]   Sally Munt notes that the return to Anglophone women's crime fiction of the vengeful female has recently put gendered revenge back on the agenda (204), while Josefina Ludmer – referring to Latin American writing – has also suggested that when real justice is not available to women they can resort to revenge to exercise their own form of it (157). Although their comments do not focus on Spain, the points they make are useful and valid when assessing Spanish women's crime narratives.

28 The only exception I have come across in my reading appears in a
    short story by Juana Salabert: 'Lenguaje de corazones dobles' [The
    Language of Duplicitous Hearts] (2000). Her tale is part of an
    anthology of stories by several authors and narrates the apparently
    senseless violence protagonized by a woman calling herself Helena
    Bas, a nurse who, in the company of her friends, murders an
    innocent bystander for kicks.

29 For a comprehensive study of this particular dramatic sub-genre see
    Stroud (1990).

30 Although the imprisonment of 'Tani' aroused journalistic and public
    support, this response does seem to have been prompted by know-
    ledge of the abuse to which she was subjected before she put an end
    to her husband's life. In a more recent – and equally high-profile –
    case a woman who killed her husband and daughter, was believed to
    have murdered her baby a decade and a half earlier, and who had
    tried to kill her teenaged son was treated harshly by the media and in
    public opinion. Francisca Ballesteros, known as the 'envenenadora
    de Melilla' [the Melilla poisoner] was sentenced to 84 years in jail.
    The press evinced no backing for her, possibly because she had
    apparently not suffered any form of abuse at her husband's hands
    and had taken a lover shortly before poisoning her spouse. Balles-
    teros, then, is the 'woman who step[s] beyond the boundary' of what
    Myers called 'appropriate gender roles and behavior' – and because
    of this the murders she committed could not be seen as justifiable
    and she did not attract media and public support (see *El Mundo* 23.
    09. 05; *El País* 23. 09. 05; *El País* 24. 09. 05).

31 The desire to protect the wealthy female may also partly (but not
    entirely) explain the response to Chelines' grandmother's murder of
    her husband in *Las niñas no hacen ruido cuando mueren*. In another
    text, Dulce Chacón's *Cielos de barro* [Skies of Clay] (2000), it appears
    that Aurora, a young woman who is a member of a landowning family
    from Extremadura, will escape punishment for murdering her father,
    and the narrative is structured in such a way as to suggest that social
    class will play a significant role in this travesty of justice. Chacón's text
    is an unusual detective novel from which the figure of the investigat-
    ing officer, his words, and thoughts are entirely absent. Within a
    narrative space shared between an omniscient narrator and the voice
    of an aged, illiterate potter, member of the province's poorest and
    most marginalized social group, the old man's self-reflexive discourse
    is privileged as his memories hold the key to solving the crime. The
    questions posed by the interviewing officer can only be guessed at
    from the old man's replies to them as they are not textualized. The
    sections of the novel that contain his answers are interspersed with
    those recounted by the unidentified omniscient narrator who,
    because of the knowledge he or she possesses, is clearly a member of
    the landed upper class. The crime investigated is the multiple
    murder of several members of a wealthy family, and although the
    reader is privy to the knowledge that the crime was committed by
    members of the family itself, the text's open ending hints that social

injustice, which has long prevailed in Extremadura and is catalogued in detail within the novel, will ensure that blame for the killings will be laid at the door of the potter's grandson, a disfigured illiterate.

[32]   Failure to describe the physical appearance of female investigators or female villains is a not uncommon feature of much crime fiction by contemporary Spanish women writers. This device serves to contest the primacy of the physical encountered in descriptions of characters such as the *femme fatale* typical of male-authored *noir* and detective novels.

[33]   A recent study by Catherine Scott-Clark and Adrian Levy concludes that the Germans removed the fabulous carved panels of the amber room and took them to Königsberg (later Kaliningrad) where they were burnt by Russian soldiers during the destruction of the city at the end of the war. Scott-Clark and Levy also claim that the Soviet government knew very soon after fighting ceased what had happened, but refused to make the information public as the theft of the amber served as a handle on the Germans to gain post-war financial reparation and exert a moral lever of sorts on the new Germany.

Chapter 3

The 'Crime' of National Repression: Crime Fictions by Catalan Women

Introduction

As both Patricia Hart and Joan Ramon Resina have pointed out, Catalonia was the first region of Spain to witness the emergence of a coherent and sustained engagement with crime and detective genres (Hart 1987: 51; Resina 1994: 119), not least because it experienced early on the capitalist industrialization often deemed essential for the birth of such literature (Resina ibid.).[1] Its geographical position facing away from Spain to the north of Europe where the earliest crime stories originated, and the receptiveness of an educated bourgeoisie to imported cultural models, perhaps also played key roles in this particular literary development, for as Daniele Conversi has noted, the region has traditionally absorbed many external cultural influences as well as movements of people (188).

The crime genre thus has a fairly long and illustrious history in Catalonia, and publication of fictions in Catalan during the dictatorship ensured the preservation and promotion of the language during the decades of linguistic and cultural suppression experienced in the Catalan linguistic area during the Franco era. At this time publishing in Catalan was severely curtailed (as indeed it was in all of Spain's languages other than Castilian, and even the latter underwent rigorous censorship). Throughout the years following the dictator's death, Catalan continued to be in some peril as a result of earlier policies imposed from Madrid by the regime and of many years of mass immigration by Castilian-speaking economic migrants encouraged to move to Barcelona. While the lengthy – although often endangered – history of publishing in Catalan is not in doubt, literary culture in Catalonia was traditionally an elite culture. During those periods of most significant threat to their linguistic integrity throughout the mid-twentieth century, however, Catalan writers began to seek a means of overcoming both this elitism and linguistic encroachment by Castilian. Detective genres were to prove an invaluable tool in their project to promote the reading and writing of their language.[2]

In the 1950s, Maria Aurèlia Capmany and fellow novelist Manuel de Pedrolo made concerted efforts to revive the fortunes of Catalan as a literary medium, despite the difficulties and even dangers that promotion of the language entailed at the time. They aimed to encourage the public to read in Catalan through the publication of popular genres, and part of their strategy initially involved the production of Catalan translations of novels in the French *Série Noir* and of key North American hard-boiled detective texts (Espelt 53–94). Although Hart observes that Pedrolo felt he had failed in the particular aim of encouraging other Catalan authors to write in popular genres (1987: 67), during the dictatorship he, as well as Capmany, published a number of critically acclaimed crime novels written in Catalan.

During the second period of immense popularity of this particular genre in Spain, from the late 1970s on, critics have remarked that in the country's non-Castilian speaking areas genre fiction written in the Catalan, Basque, or Galician languages, for example, was used to promote the national identities of those regions. The crime novelists Manuel Vázquez Montalbán and Jaume Fuster have noted the value of popular literature to aiding the development of a coherent Catalan national identity, and the importance mass culture played in linguistically and culturally assimilating working-class first- and second-generation immigrants to Catalonia (25). Àlex Broch has indicated the specific significance of the detective novel to a nationalist project based on the linguistic 'normalization' of Catalan (i.e. ensuring that the language was officially accepted and used once democracy was achieved post-1975), recalling that during the 1980s *La Negra*, the collection of crime novels in Catalan that he coordinated, attracted extensive attention from many quarters (1991: 11). And while writing in popular genres in Catalan promotes use of the language and cultural cohesion because of the market interest it elicits, in addition, female-authored novels – both in popular genres and those deemed more 'literary' – are 'productes que es venen molt bé' [products that sell very well], according to Martí-Olivella (202).[3]

Cultural cohesion founded on shared goals, mutual interests, and common identity traits is achieved not only through the medium of writing in Catalan, however, but also because a literary genre structured around crime can function to promote social unity. Both Stephen Knight (2) and Julian Symons (18–19) posit the yearning for such a social idyll as a primary motivator of readers of more traditional detective genres in particular, not least in their comforting return to 'order' with narrative closure that resolves the crime and thus confirms the status quo, but also because of the ways in which the genre bolsters established social structures. As David Lehman (187), and Ernest Mandel in his now seminal study *Delightful Murder* (1984), point out, however, very often the comforting group solidarity sought by the reader is merely nostalgia for times gone by when life was perceived to be easier and safer, and the community portrayed in fiction of this type is a desired, rather than an actual one. In *Imagining Crime* (1996), her study of criminology's resistance to feminism, Alison Young observes a similar situation in societal responses to real crime. She says that the members of a given social group tend to identify with the victim of criminal aggression because any one of them may become a victim him- or herself, although she goes on to argue that because cohesion formed around crime has shaky ideological foundations, the community arising from it is a construct derived from nostalgia (10):

> In criminal justice policy, in criminological theory and in the practices of criminal law can be found, first, an imagined community; second, an identifiable subject which represents a threat to the community; third, a desire to inflict violence upon that subject in the name of the community. (9)

In the case of many of the woman-authored Catalan crime fictions analysed in this chapter, illegal acts are perpetrated by the (Spanish) state or its militarized representatives, and Catalan national cohesion – however imagined, as Young and others propose – can thus be suggested textually through a fairly simple 'them' (the aggressors) and 'us' (the victims) structure which is often symbolized in violences perpetrated against the body of the female. Binary opposites of this sort, particularly in the guise of the 'good guy/bad guy' dichotomy, are of course one of the staples underpinning many crime sub-genres. The textual insistence on the primacy of notions of identity in this type of literature can also serve to highlight and interrogate this 'them and us' construction. Typically, of course, a crime text revolves around the attempts made to determine who committed the illegal act, and the central narrative question of '*who*dunit' functions not only to uncover the identity of the criminal, but also to discern *why* they 'dunit'. More generally, crime-related fiction makes constant use of identity-related themes and motifs like double agents, going undercover, assuming disguises, or changing appearance. Sally Munt has argued that one of the key aspects of crime novels as a genre, what she calls the 'driving mystery' of this multifarious literary form, is 'a search for identity – not just the murderer's, but by extension the reader's too' (207).

This may well account not only for the enduring popularity of this literary form but may also go some way to explaining the current interest in crime-related fiction in Catalonia and Spain among both producers and consumers of the genre. For this popular genre provides the ideal vehicle for safely exploring the dynamics of identity politics within a plurilingual and multicultural society while, particularly in the case of Catalonia, assisting the reader to an identification with traits of Catalan national and cultural identity. In many works by Catalan women writers the reconstructive technique typical of these particular genre fictions is deployed not only to probe the gendered and national identity of victim and criminal, but also to investigate the relationship between the national (Spanish) 'centre' and those 'nations within a nation' that have long been perceived as other to it, an enquiry in which female characters are inscribed with a symbolic value as repositories of or signifiers for nationhood. This technique produces and promotes a series of binary opposites in which, as noted above, one element is positioned as positive while the other is inevitably viewed as negative: Castilian-speaking Spain/ Catalonia, Madrid/Barcelona, Francoism/Republicanism as synonymous with the struggle for Catalan autonomy during several decades of the twentieth century.

The importance of national identity is also suggested through the choice of literary genre, for just like other crime authors in Spain and its constituent regions, Catalan women novelists write in imported genres. Since the inception of this type of literature in Catalonia they have published texts in the ratiocinative style popularized by Conan Doyle, the enigma sub-genre typical of British writers such as Christie, the hard-boiled cynical style born of the tumultuous 1930s in the United States, and later variants such as the political thriller. Authors from other areas, and especially those who write in Castilian, have tended to adopt wholesale many features of these sub-genres from overseas, applying their generic principles to the socio-political reality of the Spain in which they were writing. In the case of women from Catalonia, however, the situation is complicated by the double bind of gender marginalization and membership of a cultural collective that long constituted the 'periphery' of a nation that until relatively recently was highly politically centralized. The foundation of their crime fictions is thus a sub-genre that was developed far from the geographical space in which they write, and which articulated and interrogated a set of socio-economic and political concerns that may initially appear to have little relevance to issues of primary interest to the female Catalan novelist.[4] Writers then transmute and transpose those textual and ideological elements of the imported style into Catalan, and deploy them to consider their own concerns, a process that in another context has been called 'transcultural reinscription'.

The term was originally coined by Marsha Kinder in her study of the fruitfully symbiotic relationship between Spanish and Hollywood cinemas. In her work, she examines how film directors in Spain have imported conventions borrowed from other cinematic cultures and creatively reworked these for their own aesthetic and political purposes. She defines the notion as 'the ideological reinscription of conventions that are borrowed from other cultures and set in conflict with each other, a process of hybridization that is capable of carving out a new aesthetic language' (11), a description that suggests that the cultural interplay and exchange she identifies can be applicable not only to cinema, but also to literature – and specifically to the crime fictions by female Catalan novelists analysed in this chapter.

Women were among the first authors in Catalonia to write in the genre, and their history of publishing crime fictions spans seventy years. Some of the region's best-known women of letters have penned novels or stories that conform – sometimes very closely, at times rather more loosely – to the parameters for this sort of literature. Their texts are usually written in Catalan, occasionally with later translations into Spanish, and in some cases they have been translated into other European languages as well. However, where crime narratives by women from Castilian-speaking parts of Spain have tended to focus on the links between gender and crime and have explored the value of the various crime sub-genres for articulation of a feminist or female-centred worldview, texts by their Catalan counterparts have included an interrogation of issues of national identity in addition to a consideration of questions of gender, both topics of particular concern in the context of Catalonia, for as Kathleen McNerney and Cristina Enríquez de Salamanca (1994) have pointed out, by virtue of their sex and their national origin, Catalan women belong to a 'double minority'.

In this chapter, then, I want to analyse a number of crime novels by female Catalan writers in order to show how they use this type of literature to explore the link between violence against women and violence against Catalonia. All of the works analysed in this chapter were first published in Catalan, and while some are by well-known, established authors who have long been active on Catalonia's literary scene, others are by newcomers. What all the texts have in common, however, is the authorial insistence on the use of the Catalan linguistic area (or a country or region that is Catalonia 'in disguise') as a setting for these tales, and the primacy of Catalan issues within them. While most of the texts studied were published during the late twentieth- and early twenty-first century, I also want to look at a small number of fictions by earlier writers in order to show how the use of the genre to foreground Catalan nationalist concerns was established very early on in Catalonia. I shall also discuss how, within their narrative, the selected women authors ponder female right of access to nationhood and national identity, specifically through the revision of female character types traditionally associated with the various crime sub-genres, and through a re-writing of numerous tenets of this type of literature, particularly, but not exclusively, the spy thriller's foundation in national and international politics. While some of the concerns evinced by the authors analysed reflect those of Castilian-speaking writers surveyed in the first two chapters, a number of issues that preoccupy the Catalans are very different, engaging as they do with the politics of nation as well as the politics of gender.

The Catalan critic, Patrícia Gabancho, asserted that during the Transition politics of any hue or conviction, whether gendered or nationalist, did not figure prominently in women's writing from Catalonia. In her study of many of the region's leading twentieth-century female authors, she claims that 'No és sorprendent, doncs, que la presència del món exterior – la política, les relacions socials i de poder – [. . .] també aparegui molt de trascantó i gairebé com a element intrús en aquestes obres [. . .] La militància política és vista como una pèrdua de temps, i massa masculina' [It's therefore not surprising that the presence of the outside world – politics, social and power relations – [. . .] also figure only very briefly and often as an intrusive element in these works [. . .] Political militancy is seen as a waste of time, and too masculine] (73–4). Gabancho's view, however, has been implicitly contested by many scholars, particularly with regard to the most eminent Catalan women authors – some of whom have also penned crime fictions. Resina draws attention to the extensive body of critical material that reads Mercè Rodoreda's texts as feminist writing (1987: 226), while Ramón Buckley reminds us of the undeniable engagement with feminist politics apparent from Montserrat Roig's fiction, and points to the link between her feminism and the class struggle (130). Stewart King also notes the increasing critical awareness of the Catalanist political issues that underpin Roig's fiction (1998: 37), and his paper draws a tentative, if apparently unintended, parallel between the problematics of nation and gender apparent from a reading of her work, as does Maria-Lourdes Möller-Soler's study of Catalan women's theatre. Irene Boada, in both an article and her book, which was developed from her thesis, has linked sex and nation in Catalonia through a feminist-postcolonial reading of a number of short-story writers.

Despite the scholarly commentary and analysis that the interstices between gender and nation in Catalonia have aroused among academics like those cited above, they have not been a frequent theme in criticism. Josep-Anton Fernàndez attributes this absence of gendered nationalist literary scholarship to the perceived incompatibility of questions of gender or sexuality and the status of Catalan literature as a national cultural product: 'If

Catalan Studies largely ignores gender and sexuality, it is to a great extent because the historicist paradigm around which it is methodologically structured depends heavily on the concept of national literature' (1). The junction between these two political concerns does come to the fore in Catalan women's fiction – as I noted above with reference to a number of scholars, and it is also apparent from a reading of the type of crime fictions analysed in this study. These are literary formulae that have furnished Catalonia's female authors (as well as those from other places) with a textual space within which, subject to revision and rewriting, the interrelation between the issues can be examined. As I pointed out in Chapter 2, crime and detective literature is extremely useful to the woman author who wants to write about her victimization because, quite simply, these are genres founded in crime and violence. Female writers from Catalonia, then, deploy them to articulate the aggression they experience not only as women, but also as Catalans, a point to which I shall return throughout this chapter.

Mercè Rodoreda's *Crim* [Crime] (1936) – the first crime novel by a Catalan woman writer – was strongly influenced by the unabashedly bourgeois British enigma-style novel (as epitomized in Christie or Allingham) complete with its comfortable country house setting, its nostalgic yearning for the days of yore when social structures founded in class were unshakable, and its middle-class self-congratulatory introspection. Rodoreda's text, however, was considerably more irreverent than those of the British writers she emulated, and *Crim* proved to be the ideal vehicle for the author's tongue-in-cheek commentary on the Catalan bourgeoisie. Some twenty years later, during the 1950s, Maria Aurèlia Capmany would use the framework of the North American hard-boiled style – itself an eminently political sub-genre – to produce highly politically engaged texts structured to elicit readerly attention for the plight of her homeland under the Franco regime, although with an eye for the censor's pencil the identity of Catalonia was veiled behind that of other real or fictional small nations.[5] By the 1980s, the political changes wrought by the Transition to democracy ensured that genre literatures would prove to be the literary phenomenon of the decade in Catalonia (Broch 1991: 119). Not only would male Catalonia-based crime writers such as Andreu Martín, Jaume Fuster, or Manuel Vázquez Montalbán (who published in Castilian) achieve prominence, however. Female novelists – some of whom wrote in Catalan while others published in Castilian – occupied a place at the very forefront of this boom in the production and consumption of crime fictions in Catalonia because this was one of the genres which would now make possible the textual convergence of gendered and national themes central to the concerns of Catalan women writers. Since the 1980s, then, women authors have added gender to the earlier meshing of national and literary considerations, and they use crime fictions to probe the links between gender, nation, the structuring of national identity, and access to citizenship of Spain and Catalonia. Clear parallels between Catalonia and the female body are frequent in their novels and stories, and their gendered and nationalist preoccupations are textualized through the medium of a number of devices inherent to the crime sub-genres.

The victim is of course central to a very significant number of crime fictions, for upon his or her body or property is visited violence perpetrated by a more powerful individual or social group, and aggression may culminate in death or permanent bodily or psychological marking, as discussed in Chapter 2. Similarly to the texts examined in the previous chapter, victims in the novels to be analysed here are more often than not female, and their bodies are subjected to brutally hostile acts committed by men, by the forces of 'law and order' ordained by the dictatorship under which they live, or by representatives of the patriarchal system perpetuated by the Franco regime. Violence against women is not a particularly new topic in Catalan women's writing, for as Kathleen McNerney points out, it has underscored the non-genre fictions of a number of the region's female authors, particularly since the 1970s (1988: 2). Where many crime novels are innovative in this respect, however, is in their linking of gendered and nationally oriented aggression. For example, in positioning the female body as the victimized object of murder, rape, or other physical violence in crime narratives, Catalan women writers highlight how their fellow countrywomen are victims of a two-pronged socio-political and cultural marginalization based not only on their sex but also on their identity as Catalans. Psychological battery and gendered silencing are contrasted with the dictatorship's attempts at the cultural and linguistic annulment of Catalonia following the Francoist victory in 1939. Many of these fictions, while penned during the 1980s and

1990s, make extensive reference to, or are set during, the Civil War and the Franco regime – in far more overt terms than earlier examples of the genre had done.[6] These particular periods of Spain's recent past are recalled with specific reference to Catalonia, especially the often very violent repression to which the region was subjected as a possible separate national entity during the dictatorship. In many texts the aggressions against Catalan culture, political self-determination, and language perpetrated by the forces of the regime are clearly and overtly paralleled with sexual violence against the female body, the subjugation of women, and the denial of access to full citizenship or to the power bases of the nation they experienced at the time, all themes I shall analyse in detail in this chapter.

The narrative function of women within these texts is not only that of victim, however, for they also act as sleuths and fulfil a number of significant social roles. At first glance, many of these female characters may appear to conform to models for 'woman-hood' peddled in crime stories of the type popular from the 1930s on, particularly in Britain – the amateur investigator, the comfortably off housewife, the eccentric artist or writer and, at the other end of the social spectrum, the 'unfortunate' poor woman who exists to service the wealthy both domestically and sometimes sexually. While Catalonia's women detective writers undoubtedly reproduced many tenets of this type of literature, including norms for characterization, the value of the 'cosy' or 'enigma' sub-genre to the expression of a feminist or female politics should not be overlooked. Glover has pointed out that 'its focus upon domestic crime also feminized detective fiction' (71), and many critics have signalled its feminist potential. Cora Kaplan ponders the possibilities for disrupting established bourgeois norms inherent in a figure like Christie's Miss Marple (18), and Marty Knepper (1983) and Michele Slung (1988) structure a coherent case for Agatha Christie as a feminist writer whose female characters revealed her to be profoundly preoccupied with the limited roles afforded women in the contemporary milieu. Furthermore, as Patricia Craig and Mary Cadogan repeatedly remind their readers in *The Lady Investigates* (1981), British and US crime fictions contemporaneous with the early Christie con-tained just as many competent, articulate, daring female sleuths as inept bumblers whose main objective in life was submission to a male within the context of marriage. In the final section of this chapter, I shall analyse how in a number of recent crime fictions Catalan women writers reproduce the kind of characters formerly found in 'Christie-esque' style novels, and I want to show how the authors revise the significance of these figures in order to imbue them with specifically Catalan traits.

In fact, the Catalan writers whose novels will be analysed here position their female characters in such a way as to reveal that despite their apparent conformity to traditional gendered stereotypes typical of the 'cosy' British crime novel, they actually embody powerfully contestatory traits, much as some critics claim Christie's women protagonists often do. Importantly, many of these characteristics are founded in tenets of Catalan national identity. In showing how the female can not only personify but also uphold ideals of Catalanness, the novelists on the one hand confirm their engagement with several norms of the crime genres, while on the other using this particular type of literature to contest the masculine bias inherent in nationalist activity that is a cornerstone of the thriller in particular, as I show in the penultimate section of this chapter. Female genre writers from Catalonia confront and overturn this virilist leaning which, in the case of Catalonia (as in other national arenas), features a male controlled nationalist movement within which women can often encounter difficulties locating themselves and their aspirations as the 'other' sex. As McNerney has remarked, 'women who try to espouse both Catalanism and feminism often run into difficulties' (15), a view reproduced in the fictions of many recent Catalan women writers (not only of crime narratives) who ponder the complexity of attempting to exteriorize both a national and a gendered politics.

The 'double bind' of being female and Catalan is particularly apparent in more recent Catalan women's crime fictions. Isabel Olesti's *El marit invisible*, a family saga constructed around a murder, makes explicit the parallel subjugation of women, of the poor, and of the politically marginalized and dispossessed in Catalonia during the Franco regime. Margarida Aritzeta's *El verí* – a contemporary 'country house' style mystery – explores at length the position of women during the long decades of the dictatorship. The text posits the female as the standard-bearer of a Catalan national identity based on a regional tradition that contests attempts at Spanish cultural assimilation of Catalonia, and empowers the female while asserting Catalanness. The notion of the female as the embodiment of Catalanness is also advanced in

El crim d'una nit d'estiu [Crime on a Summer's Night], published in 1981 by the prolific novelist Núria Mínguez whose crime narratives are gentle, 'enigma' type texts reminiscent of their British antecedents from the 1930s and more recent Anglophone fictions in the same mould.

Two female-authored spy thrillers also make clear the parallel situations of women and Catalonia, and also essay possible female functions in the Catalan nationalist movement. Assumpció Maresma's *El complot dels anells* [The Conspiracy of the Rings] (1988) is based on Francesc Bellmunt's controversial film of the same name, and Anna Grau's *El dia que va morir el president* [The Day the President Died] (1999) is a humorous take on the political thriller and spy novel on which both she and Maresma draw heavily. Maria-Antònia Oliver's Lònia Guiu series also foregrounds gender and national issues. Her detective's importance as a feminist figure was discussed in Chapter 1, but here aspects of her status as a product of the Catalan linguistic area, particularly as it relates to, and is reflected in, issues of global politics, will be addressed briefly. Gendered features of Isabel-Clara Simó's *Una ombra fosca, com un núvol de tempesta* and Assumpta Margenat's *Escapa't d'Andorra*– both of which were analysed in Chapter 2 – will also be assessed here with some reference to nationalist issues, for while both texts are set in Catalan-speaking areas and were written in that language, gender issues within them take narrative primacy over national themes.

The novels by Aritzeta, Mínguez, Simó, and Olesti (discussed in Chapter 2), investigate either a murder or an attempted homicide, the motivations for which lie in the victims' pasts and in the recent history of Spain, while Margenat's fiction tells the tale of a female-engineered robbery. Aritzeta's *El verí* recounts the discovery by her relatives of the body of 'la tieta boja' (6), the mad aunt who had been kept locked in the attic of her family's ancestral *masia* [farmhouse] in rural Catalonia for many years. A detailed reconstruction of her youth spent between the stultifying Spain of the early Franco years and a more liberal, artistic southern France, offers up clues to her poisoning as an old woman. Her life story also places in sharp relief the restrictions imposed on women during the period, and establishes a contrastive parallel between the Spain of the dictatorship and its democratic northern neighbour, a technique which clearly has as its primary aim the negative portrayal of Spain. The novel reproduces many of the essential elements of the 'country house' type of murder mystery. Events unfold among the members of Catalonia's wealthy land-owning class and within the confines of a large comfortable house which is nonetheless very isolated. Suspects are few, and are drawn from the dead woman's immediate family and their very reduced social circle, and the mystery is discussed and pondered in the kitchen of the house, thus evoking Poirot's technique of uniting all suspects in a single room to reveal to them the results of his investigations – albeit with an ironic 'female' twist as the kitchen has traditionally been gendered as a female space.

As with *El verí*, Mínguez's *El crim d'una nit d'estiu* adheres to the norms of the 'country house' setting. Similarly to Aritzeta's novel, possible suspects for the multiple murder attempts against Valentí, a wealthy Catalan businessman, are restricted to members of his immediate circle. Once again, the uncovering of Valentí's youth in Catalonia before the Civil War, his years in exile in South America, and the motivations for his return to his homeland after an absence of forty years will be essential to identifying the author of the criminal attempts against his life. This mystery is solved by his sister Esperança, who, as I shall show later on in this chapter, is positioned by Mínguez as embodying all the positive features the novelist associates with Catalan national identity.

Simó's *Una ombra fosca, com un núvol de tempesta* touches on the themes of female subjugation and incarceration, and thwarted motherhood – which is also explored by Aritzeta in *El verí*. Protagonized by Sara, a lonely and unhappy Barcelona housewife, Simó's novel considers the boredom and frustration experienced by many Spanish women during the Franco period. Her activities and movement are controlled by her husband, a mean, unpleasant, and impotent tyrant whose sexual insufficiency inevitably means that the couple have no children, a source of great sadness for Sara. Following her husband's disappearance and murder Sara discovers that he had been involved in illegal international business wheeling and dealing for many years. Her investigation of the events surrounding his death take her outside her home and beyond the restrictions of the role of housewife that had been her lot for many years. During the course of her enquiries into her late husband's nefarious commercial affairs, Sara operates in a manner that generally avoids confrontation or aggression, much as might a latter day Miss Marple.[7] When she finally decides to confront the director of a business with which her husband had been involved in arms trafficking, she is murdered in the street by a professional hit man.

Olesti's *El marit invisible* opens with the return to contemporary Barcelona of the male narrator after a long self-imposed exile in Morocco. The discovery of his mother's body in her dirty, unkempt apartment in the working-class area of El Clot sets in motion a train of reminiscences that will eventually clarify the crime by shedding light on the victim's and the murderer's pasts. Necessarily, then, the narrative delves into the sad and sordid history of a woman and her family who lived the aftermath of the Civil War. Their tale is one of restrictions and limitations imposed by the Franco regime. It is the evocation of these experiences, articulated in the histories of female characters, that function to foreground issues relating to national identities, as well as to poverty and socio-political exclusion and marginalization and its gendering in the Catalan context.

A possible crime is also at the centre of both *El complot dels anells* and *El dia que va morir el president*, and in both of these espionage thrillers the mystery focuses on the death in suspicious circumstances of the President of the *Generalitat* [the autonomous government of Catalonia]. Given the significance to Catalan autonomy and self-governance of this particular political leader and the legislative body he heads, issues of nationality, citizenship, and centre versus periphery are inevitably raised in the two novels. The specific theme of Catalan national identity in conflict with Spanish nationalism is highlighted in *El dia que va morir el president*, Grau's highly comical spoof on the spy thriller. (Grau's text, and Maresma's *El complot dels anells* will be analysed in the penultimate section of this chapter.)

What all of the novels chosen for study here have in common is their original publication in Catalan. While the junction of gender and nation is a pre-eminent consideration in many crime and detective fictions by women writers from Catalonia, their engagement with nationalist politics as evinced by their writing in, and discussion within their texts of, the Catalan language is also evident. Catalan is central not only to Catalonia's national identity but also to its nation-building project, and Kathryn Woolard has identified it as 'a prime symbolic reserve of Catalan nationalism' (1). The importance for Catalans of their language is also noted by Clare Mar-Molinero who calls it a 'highly successful and visible badge of [. . .] identity' (47), while Geraldine Nichols claims that in Catalonia 'la lengua ha sido siempre la seña de identidad por antonomasia' [the language has always been the badge of identity *par excellence*] (1989: 15), a significance acknowledged officially in the 1998 law on Catalonia's linguistic policy which stated that:

> La llengua catalana és un element fonamental de la formació i la personalitat nacional de Catalunya, un instrument bàsic de comunicació, d'integració i de cohesió social dels ciutadans i ciutadanes [. . .] A més ha estat el testimoni de fidelitat del poble català envers la seva terra y la seva cultura específica. (Cited in Mar-Molinero 166)

> [The Catalan language is a fundamental element of the formation and the national character of Catalonia, a basic instrument of communication, integration and social cohesion for its citizens, male and female [. . .] Furthermore, it has been the evidence of the loyalty of the Catalan people towards their land and their particular culture.]

In penning literature in Catalan, women writers from the Catalan linguistic area clearly participate fully in the use and promotion of their language. They thus ensure a continuation of a tradition, identified by Conversi, characterized by an unfailing engagement with, and use of, the language in their writings by Catalan intellectuals as a badge of their nationalist engagement over very many decades (184). With specific reference to the region's women writers Irene Boada-Montagut has observed that 'the mere fact of choosing the officially rejected Catalan language in which to write, instead of the powerful and fashionable Spanish, meant and still means strong commitment to a form of nationalism' (109).[8]

In many of the texts studied here, female characters are often shown to be advocates and supporters of the language and of the culture and traditions it transmits and perpetuates. Perhaps the most powerful example of this stance is manifested by the protagonist's mother in *El dia que va morir el president*:

> Quan algú li parlava en castellà, la mare s'ofenia. O sigui que es va passar tota la vida molt i molt ofesa. Va començar ofenent-se amb les monges del col·legi, va seguir amb els funcionaris de Correus, guàrdies civils i taxistes, després amb el de l'estanc i amb el farmacèutic [. . .] La meva mare sospitava que Franco en persona havia anat a Andalusia a treure gitanos de sota les pedres, i a pagar-los un per un perquè agafessin tots alhora el tren fins al

nostre barri, amb la missió específica d'atracar-la a ella quan tornés de plaça, i d'infligir-li humiliacions lingüístiques fins a fer-la petar boja. La mare intentava defensar-se del complot del barri escoltant discos de Joan Capri i llegint les obres completes de Folch i Torres. (48–9)[9]

[When anybody spoke to her in Castilian, my mother felt offended. So she spent the whole of her life feeling very, very offended. She started off feeling offended with the nuns at school, then with post office employees, Civil Guards and taxi drivers, then with the tobacconist and the pharmacist [. . .] My mother suspected that Franco himself had gone to Andalusia to fetch gypsies from every nook and cranny, and had paid them individually to take the train all together to our neighbourhood with the specific aim of mugging her on her way home from shopping and inflicting linguistic humiliations on her to drive her mad. My mother tried to defend herself against the neighbourhood conspiracy by listening to records by Joan Capri and reading the complete works of Folch i Torres.]

The mother's view of the assault on her linguistic identity, although highly colourful and therefore amusing, is nonetheless an articulation of a real concern for the massive regime-sponsored immigration into Catalonia from Castilian-speaking areas of Spain that occurred during the latter years of the Franco period, and the curtailment, and at times prohibition, of educational and cultural endeavour in Catalan, did indeed compromise the continued existence of a distinct identity (see Balcells, chs 14, 15). Each of the figures incapable of addressing the mother in her native tongue represents a distinct group: the nuns are members of the Catholic Church that colluded with the Franco regime to ensure its perpetuation (and as educators they were in a prime position to do so);[10] the post office employees are civil servants working in a nationwide Spanish institution in which the use of Castilian was obligatory; the Civil Guards are symbolic of the strong arm of the centralized state which reached over each of its constituent parts and, as Shafir notes, would have policed the use of Catalan in public spaces (62); and the taxi drivers are representative of the vast numbers of unskilled workers from other parts of Spain who flooded into Catalonia during the decades following the Civil War. Grau's character attempts to flee the invading linguistic infidels by immersing herself in song and literature in Catalan. Despite being a Catalan, the mother is a member of the 'double minority' identified by McNerney and Enríquez de Salamanca. She is also part of a linguistic and cultural minority in her neighbourhood given the vast numbers of Castilian speakers who surround her, who are clearly symbolic of the hegemony of the central government in Madrid during the dictatorship in particular, and because she is a woman she is repeatedly robbed by the Andalusian gypsies who live locally. Her doubly peripheralized status means that as a Catalan she encounters no opportunity for expression of a national identity through language, and that as a woman her personal security is compromised, a situation which reflects the use of force by the regime.

The politics of language and its link to nation and national identity is explored further in *El dia que va morir el president* through the use of Castilian and Catalan by different figures. Most characters use Catalan as their medium of expression, but there are important exceptions, notably the Civil Guard and the ministers from Madrid who are central to the political conspiracy to discover who killed the president and place their own candidate in office – all of whom use ludicrous variants of Castilian and have ridiculous regional accents. A similar pattern emerges in *El marit invisible*, a text in which Castilian is very rarely used, but is the language of the police force, a group made up of men from other parts of Spain who have been brought to Catalonia to oversee and control the region. Clearly, then, Castilian is the language of the oppressor, of linguistic and, by extension, physical violence, imposition, and brutality. As Milton Azevedo has noted in his study of code-switching in a number of Catalan novels written between the 1950s and 1980s, 'the switch to Spanish [in dialogue] connotes violence and deflects to this language (and by implication the political regime it represents) the negative traits evoked by the brutality of the characters speaking it' (229).

Further examples of Castilian as a control mechanism are also to be found in *El marit invisible*. Within the text, Spanish is spoken by the psychiatrists employed at the clinic where the narrator's sister is interned – where clearly control by the 'sane' deriving from the linguistic centre is exerted over the 'mad' or 'unruly' on the periphery; by a bizarre evangelical preacher who uses Castilian to impose on the narrator's family the ideological straitjacket of fundamentalist Christianity; and by the police. It is no coincidence that medics, preachers, and police officers are all male, while a significant percentage of psychiatric patients, members of the evangelical congregation, and those who suffer most at the hands of the police in the novel, are female. Linguistic control and violence thus assume a gendered overtone, reminding us once again of the double marginalization that the victims, as women and Catalans, experience. In Mínguez's *El crim d'una nit d'estiu* the condemnatory tone evinced towards the central government and its policies apparent in other texts studied here is absent, but even within this far more traditional, enigma-style mystery story, Castilian is used only by an indigenous South American with no knowledge of Catalan, and his every utterance is absurd in the extreme, founded as it is in the esoteric and other-worldly. Mínguez thus appears to signal that she does not consider Castilian to be a valid vehicle for the expression of the emotional, economic, or cultural identity of the Catalans, which within her narrative, is conveyed only in Catalan. Furthermore, the textualization of an indigenous Latin American as the sole speaker of Spanish within the novel could perhaps be read as an authorial reminder of the linguistic (and other) colonization by the Spanish not only of the Americas – but also of Catalonia.

Gender and linguistic issues are linked in other ways, too. If, as Mar-Molinero asserts, 'the role of language is central to the sense of national identity [in Catalonia]' (47), and the Catalan language is the primary tool for expression of that identity and its attendant cultural manifestations, then because women are transmitters of linguistic norms in their functions as mothers, and are also traditionally the principal caretakers of the domestic arena occupied by the family, they can play a key role in preserving linguistic identity and promoting a national consciousness.[11] Anthias and Yuval-Davis situate women as the 'ideological reproducers' within a community based on shared ethnicity, and note that they 'transmit the rich heritage of ethnic symbols and ways of life to the other members of the ethnic group, especially the young' (9). In the specific case of Catalonia, the anthropologist Oriol Pi-Sunyer has pointed out that particularly during the post-war decades the family was essential to the preservation of the Catalan national identity, as it was within the home that individuals could speak Catalan without fear of reprisals, learn the oral lore of the region through songs and sayings, and read in Catalan, as many families preserved books in the language dating from before the Civil War (130).

The use and perpetuation of the Catalan language by female characters in the woman-authored crime and detective fiction analysed here is important for many reasons. Martí-Olivella has pointed out that 'la dona ha estat tradicionalment "muda", que no ha existit com a subjecte historic amb veu pròpia' [women have traditionally been 'silenced' and have not existed as a historical subject with their own voice] (204) (and this situation has prevailed not only in Catalonia but in most human societies). If women use the national language, then, this move can help them to overcome gendered silencing, as well as promoting Catalanness in an alternative way to that practised by Catalan nationalists who work in the public, political arena – and most of whom are men (a point to which I shall return later). Furthermore, depicting female characters who deploy and promote the Catalan language from within the home can also be read as an eminently contestatory strategy in view of the ways it revises earlier, dictatorship patterns of linking language, gender, and (Spanish) nationalism. As Carbayo-Abengózar (2001) shows, the Franco regime used Castilian to encourage women to engage in and enjoy the function of mother and wife – and this mechanism was integral to its plan to promote 'Spanishness' across the land. Female figures in many Catalan crime novels subvert this paradigm, however, by promoting their *own* national language and culture from within the domestic space. The periphery thus triumphs linguistically (and culturally) over the centre. What is more, the strategy deployed by Catalan women writers revalorizes and legitimizes the domestic environment vis-à-vis the public, political arena. No longer is the Catalan language 'condemnada al ghetto de l'ús domestic' [condemned to the ghetto of domestic use] as Charlon (1993: 55) says it was during many decades, but, as McNerney and Enríquez de Salamanca remind us, it also functions to imbue both the language and the arena in which it is spoken and transmitted with new, powerful meanings:

> The private domestic space defines political community, in contrast to Castilian, the language of the superimposed public space. These differences do not necessarily imply hierarchical placement (i.e. Castilian would be the language for important matters, while Catalan, Galician, and Basque would be relegated to trivia); rather, they involve a politicisation of things feminine and domestic. For cultural and political minorities, domestic affairs, on impact with public affairs, acquire connotations they do not bear in the

'normal' order of things in modern societies. Domestic space becomes that of resistance. (7)

In the final section of this chapter, then, I shall return to this issue and analyse closely how a number of the writers chosen for study reveal the value of promoting Catalan language and culture from within the home.

Early Catalan Women Detective Writers: Mercè Rodoreda and Maria Aurèlia Capmany

I want now to return to some of the earliest women producers of Catalan crime fiction: Mercè Rodoreda, who, during the 1930s, was associated with brilliant avant-garde groups (see Nichols 1986: 405), and Maria Aurèlia Capmany. Rodoreda would achieve international acclaim for novels such as *La Plaça del Diamant* [translated into English as *The Time of the Doves*] (1962) and her narrative is now considered part of the contemporary Catalan canon, but her only crime fiction, *Crim*, had appeared in 1936. Some years after the publication of this early work she renounced it, despite the light-hearted and humorous description of herself she appended to it by way of a preface, which seemed to suggest an authorial pleasure with the volume. The playful tone of her introductory remarks continues throughout the book which, as Resina (1994) has amply shown, is a parody of British detective precursors, particularly stories dating from the 'golden age' of British crime fiction when authors such as Christie were at the peak of their creative talent. It is this interaction with the Anglophone 'cosy' crime novel that suggests *Crim* could profitably be read with reference to the dynamics of the process labelled by Kinder as 'transcultural reinscription', mentioned in the Introduction to this chapter.

Crim reproduces many of the textual elements that underpin the enigma-style mysteries that were popular in Britain at the time Rodoreda published her only crime narrative. Despite the distinctly Catalan-sounding names of many of its multiple protagonists the novel replicates the *haute-bourgeois* world characteristic of Christie or Allingham. Characters are also stock types: a moustachioed, pipe-smoking detective much given to pondering small issues in detail and whose name, Flac [Skinny], is as evocative as that of the Belgian Poirot;[12] exotic foreign characters whose presence and actions function as an ironic and amusing comment on the xenophobia and racism of British detective texts of the period;[13] and a pseudo-British aristocrat known as Lady Body (a name which clearly alludes to the usual generic protagonization of a corpse, ironically in this case as this is the one essential element of the detective tale missing from Rodoreda's text). Not only is a 'body on the carpet' (or, indeed, draped across some item of furniture), absent from *Crim*; despite the novel's evocative title, it fails to feature a real crime at all.

The title, then, functions to signal the status of the work as a construct, as a contrivance designed to draw attention to its own literary artificiality, and to point up its parodic intention. This aim is developed and perpetuated in the many textual allusions to character types and characterization devices in other literary genres such as the romance, chivalrous novels, or religious texts, and also in the way *Crim* flags up the use of certain types of language culled from its British detective precursors. Rodoreda's concern with the issues of form that underpin an imported literary sub-genre can be read as a shrewd commentary on Catalonia's place in relation to the world and to the rest of Spain at the time the novel was written. As Resina summarizes:

> Because the Catalan bourgeoisie entertained a parodic relation to its counterpart in advanced capitalist states, where it had long appropriated the state apparatuses, its historical frivolity could be brought to consciousness by an easy maneuver. Literalizing the parody, Rodoreda places that bourgeoisie in the midst of an ideological form corresponding to its assumed historical status. (1994: 133)

The confluence of generic and national considerations that was the hallmark of Rodoreda's only foray into detective fiction would also characterize the crime fiction of Maria Aurèlia Capmany, another of Catalonia's best known writers, and a member of its cultural elite. Her first detective text drew heavily on the North American hard-boiled model that she had promoted in translation. Ironically entitled *Traduït de l'americà* [Translated from the American] (1959), it thus clearly signalled the source of its influences. Significantly, however, when the novel was reissued in 1980, it was with the revised title of *Vés-te'n, ianqui! o, si voleu traduït de l'americà* [Yankie Go Home! or, If You Wish, Translated

From The American]. This device was almost certainly a means of drawing attention to the text's political content and intentions, rather than simply to its literary parodic qualities, a perceptual shift facilitated by the death of Franco and the increasing liberalization of Spain. Under the regime's stifling censorship laws the transcultural reinscription of this particular imported literary form proved a useful means of discussing taboo political issues, particularly life in a totalitarian state and the relationship with Spain.[14]

Although the novel does read as if it had been translated from English – another form of transcultural reinscription – in terms of plot, characters, and location, it would not have been difficult for the Catalans, whom censorship had trained to read between the lines, to understand Capmany's reasons for setting the work in Albania. As Guillem-Jordi Graells has commented, 'el que hi ha de voluntat paral·lelística Albània-Catalunya, dos països petits i riberencs de la Mediterrània, desconeguts i en una situació política precària, és prou evident' [the fact that there is an intention to draw a parallel between Albania and Catalonia, two small countries on the shores of the Mediterranean, unknown and in a precarious political situation, is quite obvious] (cited in Espelt 87).[15] Capmany thus draws her reader's attention to the value of aspects of this literary genre for articulating a specific political and cultural agenda, far from the context in which the hard-boiled crime novel first appeared. Indeed, with specific reference to Capmany, Anne Charlon has noted that 'en el camp de la literatura policíaca la novel·lista examina les possibilitats que ofereix el gènere per a analitzar i desemmascarar les mentides oficials en un país on impera la censura' [in the field of detective fiction the novelist examines the possibilities offered by the genre to analyse and uncover official lies in a country where censorship prevails] (1993: 44).

The Albania portrayed in *Traduït de l'americà* is a police state in which individual action is regulated and group activities are restricted, a state of affairs that to Catalans living under a totalitarian regime would have proved very familiar. All meetings within the text, whether between only two people such as the detective and informant, or between small groups of people, always take place in hidden venues – from private homes to hotel rooms, from a tavern to a forest – a situation clearly evocative of the control of gatherings and groupings enforced across the whole of

Spain by the Franco regime. The only get-together that is inter-
rupted and terminated by state forces in the novel, however, is an
evening of cultural activities dedicated to promoting and preserving Albanian musical and literary traditions. Such action by the
state's enforcers of a spurious 'law and order' would have evoked
for the Catalan reader the realities of his or her own situation in
which use of the Catalan language was seriously circumscribed,
and cultural expression such as publishing in the language was
curtailed during most of the Franco regime. In this episode
Capmany also offers a commentary on the portrayal of the police
in detective fiction. For in keeping with her 'translation from the
American', she is transposing the corruption and heavy-
handedness that characterize the police in the US hard-boiled
sub-genre to the police in her Albania-Catalonia.

Further control mechanisms, particularly of a gendered
nature, are enforced by the local oligarch and power-broker, the
dangerous Dr Variboba whose spectacular rise to fame had
ensured his position as the local political strongman. This feature,
together with his omnipotence, would have positioned him as a
hugely suggestive figure for the Catalan reader of the novel, the
analogy with Franco being more than implicit. The women over
whom the mysterious Variboba – and, by extension, the state –
exercise control hail from all levels of society. There are those
who, like May/Serafina – a childlike waif, tavern keeper's wife and
informant – are poor and marginalized, and those such as
Variboba's own wife who, despite her wealth and singular efforts
to free herself from gendered societal constraints, is also circumscribed by social rules. Thus, whether existing on the margins of
society as a member of a criminal group, or inhabiting the
apparently privileged space of the nation's elite and functioning
within the text as an alluring *femme fatale*, women in Capmany's
'Albania' are subjugated and controlled physically, economically,
and intellectually, and serve primarily as the sexual objects of
men. Female Catalan readers of her novel would have encountered no difficulties in identifying their own situation as a gender
'minority' within a national minority mirrored in that of the
female characters in the text.

In Capmany's tale, considerable emphasis is placed on the
portrayal of militaristic states that deploy their might for imperialist ends as illegitimate and invalid. The novelist also textualizes
the rejection of the USA and all it stands for, specifically through

the permanent move to Albania by Thomas Compton-Bates, North American heir to a multi-million-dollar fortune, and the individual for whom the novel's protagonist, the private detective Marc, searches Tirana. A parallel with Catalonia's situation is evoked in the extensive passages within the text that consider the attempts at imperial control of Albania by the Ottomans, the Italians, the Soviets, and, latterly, US capitalism and political meddling. Indeed, the revised title of the novel, *Vés-te'n, ianqui!*, is a clear message to imperialists – actual or intended – to refrain from attempting to impose their own political and cultural models on the country, much as Catalonia wished to shake off what was often posited as the imperialist attitude of Spain's central government towards the region. The Albanians in Capmany's story take delight in the use of their language as a medium for cultural expression and in the continued buoyancy of a national cultural identity in spite of the presence of waves of invaders with imperialist intentions. Similarly, the Catalan reader of the novel, identifying with the fictional characters, might feel pride at ongoing attempts to preserve the national culture despite the efforts of the Franco machinery to curtail it, and realize that immersion in what Catalan cultural products were available would function as a means of rebutting central government's aim of 'castilianizing' all the Spanish territory.

Traduït de l'americà ostensibly recounts the search by a Chicago-based PI for a young North American who has disappeared in Tirana. Marc, the detective, wanders aimlessly around the Albanian capital, is shot at by an unknown assailant, is initially invited to gatherings in the most select social circles and then inexplicably shunned, and is portrayed as the mouse in a cat-and-mouse game within the context of a political situation that remains at best unclear. This structure is repeated almost verbatim in a later novel by Capmany, *El jaqué de la democràcia* [The Morning Coat of Democracy] (1972) in which another North American detective, Malhakias Ryt of Chicago's Gold Shell Agency, is called to Balvacària, a small, coastal nation in Europe, by Jeroni Corona, the local patriarch, who fears for his life.

The first part of the novel recounts the relationship between the narrator, a Catalan woman called Maria Aurèlia, and a North American friend, Greg, who is preparing a doctoral thesis on the posthumous [sic], unfinished, and unpublished last work of a US novelist called Dennyson Heath. Greg believes that Salona, the capital of Balvacària in Heath's detective text, is in fact Barcelona, and over the course of a number of years he travels to the Catalan city in a bid to prove his supposition. His trips cease with the passage of time, but he continues to send Maria Aurèlia photo-copies of fragments of Heath's novel and asks her to visit certain parts of Barcelona in order to ascertain whether the geography of the real metropolis is replicated in that of the city in the book.

The second section of Capmany's novel is narrated by the fictional Maria Aurèlia, and incorporates verbatim the segments of Heath's alleged text that had appeared in the first part of the narrative. Maria Aurèlia's tale commences with the detective's arrival in Salona. Ryt wanders around the city and becomes caught up in the violent activities of a number of vicious gangs representing conflicting political interests, from trade unions, to the ruling elite, to the official forces of law enforcement who, as in *Traduït de l'americà*, are as brutal and corrupt as all other groups. None of the occurrences in which Ryt is involved appear to be entirely comprehensible, either to the PI himself or the reader of the novel: individuals are assassinated, repression is routine, conflicting interests lie at the heart of the various security forces, a night-time curfew is strictly enforced, individual and group activities are controlled and policed, political meetings stir up hatred against unidentified groups, gangs of thugs rule the streets, and shady secret police remove dissidents swiftly and silently – elements clearly evocative of the North American hard-boiled novel on which Capmany founds her detective fictions.

Although the text generated by the fictional Maria Aurèlia is set firmly in the imaginary Balvacària, the description of Salona, its streets and squares, its port area and adjacent red light district, the disparities that exist between the poverty of the port city and the wealth of its hillside suburbs, and even the name of its prison, all clearly suggest it to be Barcelona. Furthermore, Salona is an important port and large industrial centre and, despite the existence of an official capital city inland, is the de facto eco-nomic centre of Balvacària, just as Barcelona has long been a rival 'capital' to Madrid. Indeed, critics have confirmed Salona's basis in Barcelona. Àlex Broch has noted that it is in *El jaqué de la democràcia* where Capmany's knowledge of the geography of Barcelona is most apparent (1993: 21), even though the author describes 'Salona' within its pages. Its agitated political scene and routine repression by the police and other armed forces also evoke periods of the Catalan city's turbulent twentieth-century history, as Anne Charlon comments:

> Els personatges s'inspiran en la realitat històrica (atemptats organitzats contra els sindicalistes pels patrons i contra els patrons pels anarquistes, o de vegades pels propis patrons, com fou el cas Barret). Les aliances, divisions entre els grups i les declaracions de certs líders de la novel·la recorden homes com Lerroux, Prat de la Riba, etc. (1993: 54)[16]

> [The characters are inspired in historical fact – organized attempts on the lives of the trade unionists by the bosses, and on the bosses by the Anarchists, or sometimes on the bosses by themselves, as in the Barret case. The allegiances and divisions between the groups, and the declarations by certain leaders in the novel recall men like Lerroux, Prat de la Riba, etc.]

Despite the fictional (and the real) Maria Aurèlia's careful siting in Salona of the events recounted in the novel, it is clear that Greg's surmise as to the identity of the city portrayed in Heath's unfinished novel is the Barcelona of the 1900s to 1930s, a period that also informs Eduardo Mendoza's *La verdad sobre el caso Savolta* (1973). Both texts evoke the social turmoil and upheaval that generated extreme violence in Catalonia during the early twentieth century, and through the medium of multiple unsolved crimes and mysteries posit the prevailing uncertainty and insecurity experienced by the Catalans at the time.

In *El jaqué de la democràcia* the figure of the national patriarch, Jeroni Corona can be read as another of Capmany's textual configurations of Franco. Corona's murder at the hands of an unknown assailant, despite official protestations that the death was the result of natural causes, is clearly the projection of a wish on the part of an author who was still writing under the political and cultural controls imposed by the regime and upheld by state forces and the censor. The parallel between Balvacària and Catalonia is further made explicit by the fictional area's eventual secession from the larger nation of which it was part, another event that can perhaps be read as a projection of the Catalan novelist's desires. And the imperialist antagonists of the fictional country, in the guise of the ominously named Central Power electricity generating concern, are eventually ousted when workers take over the power station. For a Catalan reader, then, Capmany's message of possible independence from Spain for

Catalonia, and the destruction of a foreign (Spanish) 'central power' (the Madrid government), would have been more than clear. Once again, transcultural reinscription – the use of an imported genre and its style and content – functions to allow a Catalan woman author to deploy detective fiction to articulate the reality of her homeland. She hides its true identity behind that of an imaginary nation, a process made much easier by the use of the hard-boiled sub-genre, which was not widely engaged upon by writers (of either sex) from Catalonia (or elsewhere in Spain) at the time Capmany published *El jaqué de la democràcia* – perhaps helpful in evading the ever-vigilant censor.

Re-writing the Espionage Thriller: Anna Grau and Assumpta Maresma

More recently, questions of gender and nation have been explored through the format of the spy thriller or espionage novel by Anna Grau and Assumpta Maresma. This section will focus on their works, *El dia que va morir el president* and *El complot dels anells* respectively. I want to show how, while acknowledging the primacy of the political within this type of thriller, these two authors significantly revise important elements of the sub-genre – particularly with regard to the political legitimacy of central and regional governments. Through a reading of key scholars whose work focuses on gender and nationality, I also want to address the gender stereotypes and their relation to nationhood usually encountered in this type of fiction inasmuch as its norms have been established primarily in the Anglophone world.

National identity, and how it pertains to gender, is a principal concern articulated in many Catalan female crime fictions from the 1980s and 1990s. From the 1970s women across Spain were afforded legal equality with men, a right denied them during the dictatorship; and their participation in the workforce and in the political, educational, and social arenas expanded – as I noted in Chapter 1. Despite these gains, however, the move from dictatorship to democracy did not bring with it real gendered parity. This scenario is not unsurprising for, as Jan Pettman has observed, in some post-dictatorial societies 'democratisation and liberalisation appear to mean masculism' (140). With specific reference to nations recently freed from 'imperial control' (among which

Catalonia post-1975 may be included according to Boada-Montagut [2003]), numerous scholars including Cynthia Enloe (62) and Rick Wilford (3–4) have pointed out that women are often denied any participation in state apparatuses, in spite of often having played an important role in the anti-imperial struggle. In the Catalan context, the contributors to Capmany's edited volume *Dona i societat a la Catalunya actual* writing in 1978, shortly after Franco's death, all noted, inter alia, that in contemporary Catalonia women did not enjoy equal opportunities with male citizens. Since 1975, political protagonization has also been largely male. This reality is perhaps unsurprising, for Umut Özkırımlı points out that '[n]ationalism has been generally regarded as a male phenomenon' (204), and Daniele Conversi recalls that historically all of the principal actors on the stage of Catalan nationalism have been male (214).[17] Kathleen McNerney has also noted, somewhat caustically, that 'the Catalanist movement is dominated by men, and not particularly enlightened ones at that' (15). More recently, in an echo of McNerney's assertion, Irene Boada-Montagut has claimed that the Catalan nationalist movement 'has turned out to be a patriarchal discourse with a tendency to marginalize women' (109).[18]

These observations are significant for they highlight the male bias of Catalan nationalism, which in turn is both a product and reflection of a gendered partiality in issues pertaining to statehood and citizenship in multiple – if not most – national arenas. Indeed, in her oft-cited *Bananas, Beaches and Bases: Making Feminist Sense of International Politics*, Cynthia Enloe confirms this gender slant and posits nationalisms as originating in 'masculinized memory, masculinized humiliation and masculinized hope' (44). Benedict Anderson also recalls the imaginary or illusory nature of the nation and its origins, defining nation as 'an imagined political community' (15). Anderson's seminal study of nationalism might also be read as something of an – inadvertent – precursor of the gendering of the concept as summarized by Enloe, for he describes this fiction of cohesion as a 'horizontal comradeship', a '*fraternity*' (16 [my italics]), thus implicitly excluding the female. In a more recent text John Hutchinson and Anthony D. Smith also masculinize nationalism, stating, quite without irony, that

Nationalism was, first of all, a doctrine of popular freedom and sovereignty. The people must be liberated – that is, free from any external constraint; they must determine their own destiny and be *masters* in their own house; they must control their own resources; they must obey only their own 'inner' voice. But that entailed *fraternity*. (4 [my italics])

Anne McClintock has pointed out that even writers like Frantz Fanon – usually more than aware of the stratification of access to the privileges that nationality and citizenship can confer – at times posit nations as wholly and solely male (1993: 62). She also says that 'Despite nationalisms' ideological investment in the idea of popular *unity*, nations have historically amounted to the sanctioned institutionalization of gender *difference*. No nation in the world gives women and men the same access to the rights and resources of the nation-state' (1993: 61 [italics in original]).

Her own observations, and those of others, can be seen as foundational to more recent feminist scholarship on gender and citizenship, a concept which Ruth Lister interprets as essentially 'membership of a community' (3). When that community (usually a nation) is predicated on gender imbalances, however, then the female citizen may be an oxymoron (8). As Floya Anthias and Nira Yuval-Davis observe, citizenship is certainly not gender-neutral, for it constitutes males and females very differently (6), while Lister notes that 'Behind the cloak of gender-neutrality that embraces the idea [of citizenship] there lurks [. . .] a definitely male citizen and it is his interests and concerns that have traditionally dictated the agenda' (3).

The gendering of nation and of the right of access to national identity, and to citizenship or membership of a national collective, can be further complicated by questions of ethnicity – issues which have arisen as a result of the ethnic multiplicity of contemporary nations, despite the recent trend in Europe towards the splintering along ethno-religious lines of former monolithic nation-states. Although Spain continues to function as a state governed from the centre, it is a state made up of several nations which are predicated along divergent linguistic and cultural lines, and each of which enjoys a not inconsiderable degree of autonomy.[19] Within this 'greater Spain', so to speak, and in each of its constituent autonomous communities, there exists legal provision for equality of access to citizenship, and of participation in decisions affecting the make-up of the nation, the way it is run, and the meaning of national identity – all regardless of sex. In Spain, however, as in other national contexts discussed by Enloe, McClintock, and the other scholars cited above, women do not have full and unhindered access to citizenship, nor to participation in what constitutes the nation on multiple levels – despite the existence of the sort of legal provision I have already outlined, an issue to which I shall return later.

The exclusion of the female from nation-building endeavour, or real citizenship, is also usually a staple of the spy thriller or espionage novel, founded as this type of literature is in the exaltation of the male and *his* defence of his nation or national space in the face of a threat often embodied as female. Grau and Maresma engage with these notions and question the privileging of male action and the male worldview that typically underpins this sort of fiction. They prefer to place their countrywomen at the forefront of the nationalist groups they depict, and quizzically interrogate the traditional portrayal of the female character in the espionage thriller in particular, as a sexual plaything of the male spy (an element very often replicated in the hard-boiled thriller, too, with reference to the male investigator). An innovative feature of their fictions thus lies in the reconfiguration of gender stereotypes usually encountered in this type of narrative. Their strategy is important because they textually re-inscribe and apportion new roles to women within a sub-genre constructed on 'the denigration of domesticity [and] lack of interest in women' (Thompson 86) and in which, according to Josée Dupuy, the only female characters portrayed are 'algunas mujeres entradas en carnes, que pronto desaparecen' [a few women with voluptuous figures who soon disappear] (cited in Veraldi 175). Although 'mujeres entradas en carnes' appear in thrillers by Catalan women authors, they are positioned to contest the lack of female agency and the objectification of the female body that has been a constant of the genre. Instead they deploy their sexuality autonomously while simultaneously revelling in many of the activities formerly engaged in by the male hero of the espionage thriller, including the casual sexual use of members of the opposite sex.

El complot dels anells is protagonized by Mike O'Brian, an intrepid journalist from the United States who is a tough action hero, in true James Bond style. Like Bond, he is also attractive to women, proving to be particularly successful with Catalan women who appreciate his support of the Catalanist cause. Despite his initial siting as the archetypal thriller hero, however, it is the female character Muriel who is shown to be the most staunch supporter and promoter of Catalan nationalism. In the novel, O'Brian maintains a highly erotic relationship with Muriel, an activist with the FAP (Front d'Alliberament Patriòtic [Patriotic Liberation Front]), a fictional group whose aim is Catalan independence from Spain. Her dedication is made evident at the very end of the novel when she turns herself into a suicide bomber to kill Joan Giralt. He was a politician who had been her lover, but had betrayed the cause of independence for Catalonia both by ending the power of the FAP when he ordered the killing of its leader, Muriel's father, and by obeying commands from central government in an attempt to secure his own political future.

The parallel figure in Grau's text is Glòria, a Valencian beauty who, despite her somewhat caricatured portrayal within the context of what is essentially a humorous novel, is nonetheless a rabid defender of an independent Catalan homeland and a unique Catalan identity expressed through the Catalan language. Significantly, although she might initially seem to be part of a 'triple minority', in that as a Valencian woman she is not only at two removes from the political centre of Spain but is also at a further remove from Barcelona and the heartland of the Catalan linguistic area (already geographically marginal to the centre of Spain), neither her regional origins nor her sex impede her status as an ardent, politically aware activist who embodies all of the prerequisite qualities for a Catalan – none of which is evinced by her male co-religionists.[20] She is the undisputed leader of a clandestine Catalan separatist group calling itself the Almogàvers, a name derived from that of a fourteenth-century group of mercenaries who conquered extensive territories throughout the Mediterranean for Catalonia, and therefore evocative of the region's glorious medieval past when it was not only politically, militarily, and culturally independent, but also exercised power well beyond its modern-day borders.

In both texts, then, women are positioned at the forefront of the fight for Catalan independence: Muriel is willing to pay the ultimate price for her beliefs, and Glòria heads a group of which she is the only female member. Her fellow male independence seekers are portrayed as lazy and ineffectual. They lie around reading pornographic magazines, smoking cannabis, and eating doughnuts while their intrepid leader, sporting panties made from the Catalan flag, fearlessly pursues their goals, thus revealing herself to be the most ardent Catalan nationalist of them all. In keeping with the highly sexualized portrayal of the female in the spy thriller observed by critics such as Michael Denning (107–13) and Jerry Palmer (29–39), and also with the image of the sexually predatory murderous female terrorist posited in Matías Antolín's recent *Mujeres de ETA* [ETA Women] (2002), both Glòria and Muriel also function within the respective novels as the archetypal *femme fatale* who deploys her sexuality in the service of political beliefs. Muriel seduces O'Brian to keep him from meddling in affairs that may compromise FAP's success, and Glòria has sex with the male protagonist of *El dia que va morir el president* in order to later use him as a spokesman to proclaim independence from Spain.

While this type of sexualization of the female in the context of the spy thriller treads the ideologically questionable ground of her objectification for male voyeuristic consumption – as Denning reminds us (109–13) – in the case of the Catalan woman-authored novels studied here, it is important to note that neither Muriel nor Glòria are ordered to have sex by the male controllers of an organization for which they work, as is the norm in the spy thriller in particular, but that they deploy their seduction techniques independently and of their own volition. In fact they use men not only to further their own political agenda, but also to achieve their own sexual satisfaction. In these Catalan texts women are not used by men either in a sexual way, or to promote any nationalist project; rather, the women use men. Furthermore, the male nation-building imperative on which the spy thriller is erected is interrogated and deconstructed, as is female access to political activism and decision-making processes. Importantly, because both women assume full agency and are the leaders of the groups to which they belong, their authors turn upside down the norm identified by Anthias and Yuval-Davis: that in ethnic and nationalist struggles women function in 'a supportive and nurtur-ing relation to men' (10). The positioning of Glòria and Muriel as Catalan freedom fighters might also be read as an ironic com-ment on women's more usual political participation. As Lister notes, female political endeavour is infrequently 'mainstream', as women tend to operate in more informal political structures (10).

Grau and Maresma offer a parody of this more usual reality by portraying characters whose 'informal' politics have terrorist underpinnings.

However, these two authors do not only invert the more usual portrayal and function of the female within the thriller; they also ensure that male stereotypes are reversed and subjected to scrutiny. The protagonist of *El dia que va morir el president* is an impotent, inept young journalist who is catapulted to fame because he was the last person to see the murdered Catalan president alive. This fortuitous occurrence unleashes a bizarre sequence of events during which the young man, now perceived by most political groups as some sort of hero and the lynchpin of Catalonia's political future, is pursued across Barcelona by several police forces, local and national politicians, Glòria's unruly gang of dope-smoking Catalan freedom fighters, and varied picturesque characters who function within the narrative to symbolically represent actual interest groups in the contemporary Catalan political arena. His social, political, and sexual ineptitude position him in direct contrast to Glòria, the flag-waving nationalist with whom he will eventually fall in love.

Where she is fearless and unafraid, this nameless young journalist dreads meetings with the editor of the newspaper on which he works because his superior assaults him physically and verbally. He is terrified by his encounters with the various groups who chase him across his home city, and cowers in fear during a bizarre attack by Spanish politicians who throw hand grenades shaped like mobile telephones, although in such situations Glòria is in her element and responds in kind to the aggressors.[21] Despite his rejection of violence and his quest for a peaceful existence, however, he is ironically positioned by Grau as what might be termed an 'anti-Catalan', a point to which I shall return later. Furthermore, because of his pacifism he is clearly a parody of the action hero protagonist of the conventional spy thriller.

The traditional primacy of the masculine in the spy thriller is recalled by Jon Thompson who identifies the sub-genre as 'the continuation of the masculinist adventure tradition' protagonized by a heroic individual (86) 'without personal history' (103) who leads a 'life of action' (86) or, as Palmer describes him, 'the hero: alone, sexy, competitive' (24). Grau's eternally terrified male protagonist fails miserably to qualify for his role as macho thriller hero, for he shuns excitement, is reluctant to leave his home city, is encumbered with an excessive amount of emotional baggage contributed to by a rabid Catalan nationalist mother, a Socialist activist father, and a delinquent older brother. Moreover, in addition to being sexually inexperienced he is impotent, clearly a far cry from the erotic prowess of the likes of James Bond. In fact, where Glòria is sexually aggressive, 'alone, sexy [and] competitive' as Palmer says of the central (male) character in the espionage thriller, the hapless young man in Grau's text seems drawn from what R. Gordon Kelly calls 'the Buchanesque formula – the convention of the innocent caught up in intrigue and espionage' (89) in which the political and social *ingénu* is manipulated with ease by his opponents (94). Or as Lehman summarizes, the kind of fictions identified by Kelly are texts about 'ordinary chaps thrust willy-nilly into extraordinary circumstances' (192).

In *Fiction, Crime, and Empire*, Thompson highlights the foundation of the espionage thriller in the overtly political. He repeatedly flags up the intricate meshing of generic strategies and nationalistic political concerns within this particular sub-genre and observes that, like many other sorts of crime fiction, this particular formula is British, its roots lying in late nineteenth-century bourgeois perceptions of empire. He goes on to assert that

> The espionage novel emerged out of this culture of imperialism, for the general subject of all modern espionage novels, then as now, is the threat posed to a nation by a foreign power or conspiracy, whether external or internal. The modern spy novel, that is, takes imperialism, with its attendant systems of domination and political intrigue, as its necessary precondition. (85)

Despite its origins outside Catalonia and even beyond the borders of Spain, the spy thriller, or what Thompson calls 'the espionage novel', suggests itself as an ideal medium for an investigation of Catalonia's positioning within a state that for a long time sought to impose centralized socio-cultural and linguistic norms on the Catalan-speaking areas in a somewhat 'imperialistic' fashion, according to Boada-Montagut (2003). Grau and Maresma in fact generate a number of important contestatory strategies that subvert and revise some central tenets of the sub-genre in this regard. For example, within this type of literature the political centre (which has structured itself as the legitimate political hub, and perpetuates this vision of itself in its quest to retain legitimacy) posits the political periphery as the menace, the danger to its 'legitimate' siting as a political nucleus. Catalan women writers of the spy thriller invert this model, suggesting, of course, that in the case of Catalonia the threat of conspiracy and intrigue originates from the Madrid government, Spain's self-constructed centre.

It is just such concerns that furnish the foundation stone for Maresma's *El complot dels anells*, for within the novel although the Catalan separatist – the *internal* conspirator – is potentially a danger to Castilian, centralized hegemony, so the Spanish state is posited as a threat to Catalanism. A far darker tale than *El dia que va morir el president*, Maresma's novel recounts the visit to Catalonia by television reporter Mike O'Brian to cover the Barcelona Olympic Games, and deals extensively with that particular sporting event as a possible space and vehicle for expression of demands for a fully independent Catalan-speaking region. The protagonist, a sworn defender of a distinct Catalan national identity, ensures that he promotes the nationalist cause in the reports he prepares for consumption by a US television audience that is clearly assumed to be ignorant of the fact that a place called Catalonia even exists. He is heavily involved in local political activities much in the manner of a secret agent, and has to contend with tough characters sent by the CIA to oversee the games, and ensure that they are not used by the Catalans to promote their own agenda – evidence of a US neo-imperialism that echoes Spain's attempts to commandeer the games to its own propagandistic ends (see Hargreaves 2000).

Maresma's novel explores the possibilities for expression of nationalist sentiments inherent in the Olympic Games held in Barcelona in 1992. As Hargreaves (ch. 3) has pointed out, despite the internationalism of the Games, they also offer extensive opportunities for articulation of national identities, and in this regard those that took place in Barcelona were no exception. Catalan nationalists feared that the event would be taken over and controlled by central government, while politicians in Madrid were nervous lest the occasion be used by the Catalans to promote separatism, or that it generate conflict between the political centre and periphery (Hargreaves 60). While the violent takeover of the Olympic village, FAP infiltration of the police force, and hostage-taking by Catalan terrorists central to *El complot dels anells* did not actually occur, Maresma's novel nonetheless serves as a literary reminder of the symbolic significance of the Olympic Games to the project of nation-building and national expression.[22]

The failure of the fictional FAP's attempt at an armed assault of the Olympic Games, the loss of its leader and its most dynamic female activist, and the Almogàvers' unsuccessful bid in *El dia que va morir el president* to claim Catalan independence, also function to highlight characteristics of Catalonia's political reality. Díez Medrano observes that Catalan nationalism has always been moderate (152) and that separatist parties have enjoyed little support there (171–2). This may be because, as Shafir posits, Catalans are in the main happy with regional autonomy (68), and their political self-confidence has led them to largely reject violence and extremism of the type experienced in the Basque Country, for example (Hargreaves 33). Indeed, although Díez Medrano claims that 'contrary to popular perceptions [. . .] Catalonia has a long history of violent separatist organizations', he does go on to note that they lacked the manpower, organizational capabilities, and public support enjoyed by ETA (169), and they were never considered particularly newsworthy as they targeted buildings in their attacks and purposefully avoided taking human lives (185). Indeed, nationalist endeavour need not always be manifested in violent activity, for although both Özkırımlı (2000) and Smith (2001) note in the early pages of their respective studies that nationalism was long associated with civil strife and armed struggle, Smith's definition of the term as '[a]n ideological movement for attaining and maintaining autonomy, unity and identity for a population which some of its members deem to constitute an actual or potential nation' (9) does not include mention of violent extremism, but it is clearly highly suggestive of the form of nationalism that is more usually associated with Catalonia.

It is perhaps in response to this rather lacklustre and unexciting recent history of Catalan separatist militancy that Grau – ironically – and Maresma – provocatively – offer up exaggerated portrayals of fictional organizations with the aim of eliciting greater readerly interest and commenting humorously on the absence of an ETA-type organization in the Catalan linguistic area. More importantly, though, we might also construe the failure to achieve Catalan independence by the two fictional groups portrayed within the novels, as a reaffirmation by Grau and Maresma of the confidence Catalonia has in its position within contemporary Spain. Philip Spencer and Howard Wollman have the following to say about this siting:

> One of the most cited examples of successful self-government short of independence in recent years has been that of Catalonia [. . .] Here, under the leadership of Pujol, head of the Catalan autonomous government since 1980, regional autonomy based on the Spanish constitution of 1978 has been pushed forward a long way. Distinctive language, media and cultural policies and relations with the wider European Union [have] made Catalonia seem almost a separate state. Yet despite occasional flirting with the idea of independence, Pujol has used nationalist rhetoric to assert greater autonomy against but within the Spanish state [. . .] Unequivocal support for outright independence seems low, with only 10 per cent of the Catalan vote going to the main (left) pro-independence party, the ERC. (177)

Manuel Castells quotes Pujol's statement that 'Catalunya is a nation without a state. We belong to the Spanish state, but we do not have secessionist ambitions' (43), while Michael Keating (1996; 1997) flags up the increasing flexibility of Catalan political leaders to Catalonia's stance vis-à-vis independence and autonomy and its position within an increasingly globalized international political environment.

My point, then, is that in revealing within their espionage thrillers that the fight for Catalan independence fails, Grau and Maresma are in fact perhaps flagging up that, at the time they were writing, this 'failure' was really no such thing because Catalonia was not actively seeking – nor did it need – to be a *state* separate from the Spanish state because it is so sure of its contemporary positioning as a nation within Spain and, perhaps more importantly, within Europe. In one of the seminal works on nationalism, Smith reminds us that a nation is 'a named human community occupying a homeland, and having common myths and a shared history, a common public culture, a single economy and common rights and duties for all members' (13) – a characterization that substantially develops Anderson's description of 'nation' cited earlier. While in the case of Catalonia Smith's definition might be minimally problematized by the presence within its borders of speakers of Castilian and other languages (a point to which I return in the next section), Catalan politicians have introduced educational and cultural policies aimed at inducing the kind of cohesion Smith identifies. Smith also points out that 'it is not necessary [. . .] for a nation to possess a sovereign state of its own, but only to have an aspiration for a measure of autonomy coupled with the physical occupation of its homeland' (12) – so, just as Pujol noted (see the above quotation), Catalonia is not a state but it is a nation (see also Guibernau 2000 and McRoberts 2001, both of whom tease out this classification of Catalonia).[23] Perhaps Grau and Maresma are reminding us – tongue in cheek – of these complicated realities. However, while independence and statehood might not be deemed really necessary in fictions such as these – and others –, preserving Catalan identity is, and it is to this issue that I shall turn in the next section.

Gender and Nation

Catalans perceive their national character to be founded on four principal virtues which Flaquer and Giner identify as '*continuïtat* (working steadfastly over the long term to achieve objectives), *mesura* (taking a measured, balanced view of things), *ironia* (an ironic outlook on life), and *seny* (a traditional attitude characterized by good, practical commonsense)' (Flaquer i Giner 1991*a*, 1991*b* cited in Hargreaves 22). Who is Catalan, however, is an issue that has caused some polemic. Jordi Pujol, the long-time president of Catalonia, has observed: 'Our central problem is immigration and, hence, integration. The basic objective is to build up a community valid for all Catalans. And I would add that by Catalan I mean everybody who lives and works in Catalonia, and who makes Catalonia his/her own home and country, with which he/she incorporates and identifies' (cited in Conversi 195). Despite Conversi's insistence on the assimilationist or inclusivist bent of Catalan nationalism (185–9), Hargreaves counters his assertion, saying that this civic model of nation and national identity promoted by the Catalan government is in fact an attempt to paper over the cracks in its policy of cultural assimilation which cannot disguise a reality of considerable ethnic divisions between Catalans and immigrants from other parts of Spain, and their children (35). Josep Llobera (1990) has noted that, given the complexities of Catalan nationalism, neither the civic nor the ethnic model pertains in a clear-cut way, but Catalan scholars like Josep Termes certainly consider perceived ethnic traits to be fundamental to a national identity that is compromised by the presence of 'non-native' Catalans and is in danger 'de despersonalitzar-se, de desintegrar-se i de convertir-se en un híbrid, en un ésser estrany que no és ni carn ni peix' [of becoming depersonalized, of disintegrating, and of turning into a hybrid, a strange thing that is neither fish nor fowl] (113–14). For many Catalans, then, it would seem that despite the assertions of politicians like Pujol, being Catalan entails speaking Catalan as a first language, coming from a family that has its roots in Catalonia and participates in and perpetuates Catalan culture, and also having a Catalan name and surnames.

The Catalan of the sort identified by Termes is also deemed to be economically successful, on an individual as well as a national level, and a very significant percentage of professional and managerial posts in Catalonia are held by Catalans rather than by immigrants from other parts of Spain (Shafir 72 *et seq.*), a situation that perhaps accounts for the perception of Catalonia as a bourgeois nation (Hargreaves 23). Indeed, writing in the early 1980s, Susan DiGiacomo even went so far as to claim that '[g]enerally speaking, to be Catalan is to be middle-class; to be non-Catalan is to be working-class' (73).

Numerous female Catalan crime authors flag up and comment on these ethnic-based class differences within their fictions and, as I shall discuss later in this section, they also explore at length the kind of personality traits supposedly possessed by their country-folk as propounded by Flaquer and Giner. Although I would not go so far as to assert that the crime novel is necessarily more suited to the articulation of issues of class and ethnicity than any other sort of literature, it is the case that because different crime sub-genres tend to feature characters from very specific social backgrounds (e.g. the enigma style novel is set among the bourgeoisie while the investigator in the *noir* thriller often moves through the criminal underworld), crime writing does function well as a narrative space in which to present these concerns. Within the novels I want to look at in this section, issues of class are very often analysed through the lens of gender, too.

One text in which class and ethnic difference is made clear is Isabel-Clara Simó's *Una ombra fosca, com un núvol de tempesta.* Sara's husband, Oscar, buys a house on a middle-class estate on the outskirts of Barcelona, and the couple initially live in harmony with their *petit bourgeois* neighbours, all of whom are Catalan

speaking with Catalan names and surnames. As the neighbourhood becomes unattractive due to the unbearable stench generated by nearby industry, however, the middle-class Catalans all
leave the area and are replaced by working-class families from
other parts of Spain who speak only Castilian, and with whom
Sara has nothing in common culturally or linguistically. It is the
women of the new community who seem to Sara to be promoting
and perpetuating both the cultural and linguistic identity of
working-class, Castilian-speaking Spain:

> Així començà l'éxode. Anaren marxant, un rere l'altre. La felicitat
> havia durat poc més d'un any. 'La Carrasqueta' es devaluà, es
> vengueren les cases a baix preu, s'omplí de famílies que ... [. . .]
> les famílies modestes que vingueren a viure-hi tenien costums
> estranys a la Sara. Les dones sortien al carrer amb la bata de buata
> i rul·los al cap. Es cridaven de casa a casa, per la finestra, en un
> castellà fet de ganivets i d'agulles, amb erres estirades i
> allargassades com una serra. No era cap esnob, la Sara, i ara! Però
> eren gent diferent. Una gent que no convidaries a berenar a casa.
> (20–1 [first ellipsis in original])

> [So the exodus began. They all moved away one after the other.
> Sara's happiness had lasted only a little more than a year. At 'The
> Oaks' property values went down, the houses were sold cheaply,
> and the place filled up with families that ... [. . .] the modest
> families that moved in later had customs that were strange to Sara.
> The women went out into the street in their bathrobes and curlers.
> They called from house to house out of the windows, and they
> spoke Spanish, a Spanish made of knives and needles, with rolling
> r's that went on and on like the teeth of a saw. Sara was no snob, no
> sir! But these people were different. They were people you
> wouldn't invite to your house. (*A Corpse of One's Own* 14–15 [first
> ellipsis in original])]

Because Sara is not a particularly educated woman nor, at the
beginning of the narrative, is she overly perceptive of the subtleties and nuances of her environment, Simó uses her character as a
mouthpiece to replicate the somewhat straightforward (and
apparently widely held) view of the ethnic and class makeup of
Catalonia, of the type propounded by DiGiacomo. Simó's intention, then, is to draw attention to the unsophisticated nature of
such a stance, one with which other scholars, such as Conversi,
clearly do not agree:

this is only a rough generalisation and we cannot speak of class as coterminous with ethnicity, particularly in more recent years. In fact, some Catalans are likely to be found at the bottom of the social ladder too. On the other side, there are immigrants who have succeeded in reaching the highest ranks of class stratification, thanks to a relatively diffuse social mobility. (212)

In view of this assertion it is worth remembering that despite the take on the issue evinced by Simó's Sarah, the family portrayed in Olesti's *El marit invisible*, although culturally and linguistically Catalan, is very poor and exists on the very edges of society – and it is the many aspects of this poverty which can ultimately be read as being responsible for the crime featured in the novel. Similarly, Grau deploys the humour that characterizes *El dia que va morir el president* to reveal that her protagonist also realizes that he is not well off as a middle-class Catalan should 'ideally' be.

Indeed, that the perceived link between Catalan identity and wealth is not always indissoluble is ironically highlighted in the words of Grau's protagonist: 'A casa érem pobres però catalans, i aquesta resultava la pitjor combinació possible. Perquè no érem ni carn ni peix' [Our family was poor but Catalan, and that was the worst combination possible. Because we were neither fish nor fowl] (48). Not only does the nameless character fail to conform to the notion of the Catalan as staidly prosperous, however; he is also too simple to be ironic, too uninformed or unversed in the ways of the world to exercise any commonsense, and his sudden involvement in political events far beyond his ken impedes him from exercising the *mesura* he should manifest as a Catalan. Nor is he professionally or economically successful, because despite his status as a Catalan born of Catalan parents, he occupies a post as a junior reporter, earns very little, and exists in a precarious limbo as a temporary employee whose contract is never formalized. His failure to conform to the Catalan stereotype is compounded by the location of his family's residence in La Trinitat in one of the 'worker tenements' identified by Shafir (72) in which few (if any) Catalans live, and described by Kathryn Woolard as comprising 'row after row of grimy cement-block apartment structures' (31).[24] Termes asserts that such neighbourhoods are 'guetos tancats' [closed ghettos] (114) in which incomers from other parts of Spain and, more recently, immigrants from Sub-Saharan Africa and the Maghreb, experience profound difficulties in

adapting to the language and socio-political and cultural traditions of Catalonia because they have no contact with Catalans
(115). What is clear, then, is that although a character such as
Grau's protagonist might be expected by virtue of his sex and
ethno-national origin to occupy a place at the heart of all that is
Catalonia in economic, socio-cultural, and national terms, despite
his apparent 'qualifications' (that is, his status as a male and a
Catalan) he does not. Grau thus uses her humorous spy thriller to
complicate and interrogate assumptions about the gendering of
nationality and citizenship in even more ways than those signalled
in the previous section.

Within a significant number of the novels selected for study in
this chapter the preservation and promotion of a Catalan heritage
that would overcome the cultural and linguistic 'hybridization'
identified by scholars such as Termes is shown to be the domain
of the female, particularly the mother. This process of conserving
and transmitting 'Catalanness' is clear from the example cited
earlier of the mother figure in *El dia que va morir el president* –
however ironic Grau's commentary may have been. It is much
more apparent, however, in *El verí, El crim d'una nit d'estiu*, and *El
marit invisible*, because these novels, in keeping with a norm
established in the traditional 'country house' type of mystery
story, are all set in enclosed domestic spaces presided over by
women: a typical Catalan farmhouse, a small holiday development, and a Barcelona apartment, respectively. In Aritzeta's tale it
is within the spatial enclosure of the *masia* that traditional Catalan
values are observed and reproduced by Constança Maduell, the
matriarch of a sizeable extended family. She ensures that Catalan
is always spoken in her home, preserves furniture and portraits
that have long been family heirlooms, and proscribes her son's
choice of partner lest the girl fail to perpetuate the Catalan and
family traditions which she herself observes. By these (albeit
draconian) means she thus ensures transmission to her children
of a particular set of national values. A similar pattern emerges in
Mínguez's novel in which Esperança – clearly the 'hope' for the
future of Catalanness – speaks only Catalan to her children and
encourages in them a value system founded on the character
traits Catalans perceive as the cornerstone not only of their
national identity, but also of the prosperity and economic and
cultural buoyancy of Catalonia. These two characters, then, promote what Walker Connor (1994) has called in the context of

Catalonia 'ethno-nationalism', which Smith summarizes as 'a psychological bond of ancestral relatedness, stemming ultimately from kinship sentiments' (15).

Both Esperança and Constança also embody the traits of *continuïtat, mesura, ironia,* and *seny* that Flaquer and Giner allege to be the prime virtues of the Catalan. Ironically, while their husbands are portrayed as inept business failures, it is the hard work and business sense of the two women that ensure their families' continued economic well-being, in addition to contributing to the perceived affluence of Catalonia. Significantly, the textual invalidation of the business*man* from the Catalan linguistic area, long presumed to be a lynchpin of the regional economy, is also perpetuated in *Escapa't d'Andorra* and *Una ombra fosca, com un núvol de tempesta* – if we understand that male Catalans who engage in illegal business deals do not uphold nor promulgate the norms on which many aspects of Catalan national identity are believed to be constructed, while women can and do promote them to successful ends. It is the foundation of these novels in crime, then, that facilitates the project of Mínguez, Margenat, and Simó to reveal the nefarious business dealings of their male characters. This narrative strategy echoes that evinced by many of the writers' male contemporaries who published *novela negra* in Castilian and Catalan which uncovered the fraud and corruption that seemingly abounded in the Spain of the Transition to democracy and the *desencanto.*

Although the protagonist of Assumpta Margenat's *Escapa't d'Andorra* is female, the unrelentingly mind-numbing world of the Andorran tax-free shopping zone in which she works is owned and controlled by men. Despite their business acumen, however, they exhibit none of the positive traits usually associated with the Catalan according to Flaquer and Giner; instead they resort to highly dubious business practices that often verge on the illegal, and are exploitative in the extreme. Coll, a supermarket owner, smuggles duty free whiskey across the border from Andorra (part of the Catalan linguistic area and the only state where Catalan is the official language) into Spain in order to supply bars in Barcelona, sexually harasses his younger female staff and lacks respect for other employees; he also skims off cash from each day's takings in order to launder it through Spanish bank accounts. Likewise, Tarratts, the bank manager, is involved in shady financial schemes, and Andreu, owner of the Principality's largest building firm, is known to have links to the local mafia, contacts that ensure continued business and economic success.

In Isabel-Clara Simó's *Una ombra fosca, com un núvol de tempesta* the protagonist, Sara, discovers that her husband, far from being the mild insurance agent she had always believed him to be, is involved in an international arms trafficking gang supplying weapons to third-world regimes who use them against their own people. His fabulous – if secret – wealth has thus been generated using business practices that stand in direct contrast to the traditional perception of Catalan commercial behaviour, and in opposition to the methods deployed by female characters in novels by Simó and other Catalan women authors. Indeed, when Sara decides to enter the world of business, she does so by establishing a small knitting-wool shop that she will run in accordance with traditional Catalan capitalist and commercial mores.

Women who write crime fiction in Catalan thus position many of their female characters as embodying the traits of what some scholars see as the Catalan character, and these women protagonists also engage in activities that mark them out as Catalan. In many ways, then, the junction of these particular facets of their personalities and their role as perpetuator and disseminator of the Catalan language and Catalan culture suggest that they could be read as contemporary textualisations of *La Ben Plantada* [literally 'the well planted'], Catalonia's female allegory of nation. *La Ben Plantada* is an interesting figure who on the one hand unites traditional views of the female as wife and mother, but on the other upholds and promotes Catalan identity, and apparently functions with some considerable degree of autonomy. The character was the creation of Eugeni d'Ors, eminent Catalan author and founder of the *Noucentisme* [New Century] movement,[25] and Boada-Montagut summarizes the figure's portrayal as that of 'a good-looking woman, the virgin Teresa and a well-planted tree' (2003: 109–10). Cristina Dupláa, who has analysed the *Ben Plantada* in a number of publications, has commented on her 'valor metafórico de "mujer-madre" y de "mujer patria": es, pues, la "madre de todos los catalanes" y el mito de la "nacionalidad catalana"' ['metaphorical value as the "woman as mother" and the "woman as homeland"; she is, therefore, the "mother of all Catalans" and the myth of "Catalan nationality"'] (1988*a*: 3–4). In a later article, Dupláa developed and defined her observations, and noted that 'hay una doble función en este personaje: la mujer como transmisora de la raza, en términos biológicos, y la mujer como portadora de la esencia de una cultura, en términos ideológicos' [this figure embodies a dual function: that of the female as the transmitter of racial identity in biological terms, and the female as the bearer of what is fundamental to a culture in ideological terms] (2002: 25). On the one hand, then, in Dupláa's reading the *Ben Plantada* has a significant domestic role, but on the other seems to fulfil an important socio-political function and is presented by d'Ors 'como ser voluntarioso y partícipe de un proyecto colectivo' [as a headstrong being who participates in a collective project] (2002: 24), suggesting autonomy and independence of action beyond the confines of the domestic arena.

In view of the two rather distinct sides to this character I would posit that Mínguez's Esperança and Aritzeta's Constança in particular can be read as possible renderings of the *Ben Plantada*. While both women are mothers, wives, and homemakers who work to instil in their children an understanding of what it means to be a Catalan, each also directs a commercial undertaking which helps to underpin Catalonia economically as a nation. Business acumen and the generation of wealth of the sort that characterize these two women are key to the Catalans' beliefs about who they are and others' perception of them. Much of the region's wealth has traditionally been generated by precisely the type of enterprise headed by Mínguez's and Aritzeta's characters: a flourishing family agricultural concern, and a family-run construction business, respectively. Typically, however, such concerns have been owned and run by men. Esperança and Constança can thus be read not only as revealing both sides of the *Ben Plantada* of whom they are so suggestive, but as contesting the gendered skewing towards the male of nation and citizenship – an issue with which Mínguez and Aritzeta take issue, as I discuss below. Esperança enters the 'male' world of building and makes a success of the enterprise where her husband had failed. Constança, in running single-handedly the extensive lands surrounding her *masia*, and ensuring they return excellent profits,[26] inverts and contests the *dret pairal* [right of male primogeniture] which has traditionally been the backbone of rural Catalonia, converting it instead into a '*dret mairal*' [right of female primongeniture].[27]

Thus the female figures at the narrative centre of *El crim d'una nit d'estiu* and *El verí* in particular can, in my opinion, usefully be read as the embodiment of the *Ben Plantada*, personifying as they do everything that is deemed to be positive in the Catalan character and functioning as allegories for their nation. And although neither Mínguez nor Aritzeta names the *Ben Plantada* in their fictions, an analysis of their protagonists through this particular lens is particularly fruitful. Furthermore, their authorial strategy in this regard also functions to highlight the problematics of allegorizing the nation as female – an issue upon which a number of feminist scholars have commented – and to negate many assumptions about the gendering of relationships to nation. Anthias and Yuval-Davis suggest that women often function as the 'actual symbolic figuration' of the cultural and ideological traditions underpinning a nation (9) – a stance that is indeed replicated in the fictions by Mínguez and Aritzeta studied here. However, in *Monuments and Maidens. The Allegory of the Female Form*, Marina Warner notes that '[a]lthough the absence of female symbols and a preponderance of male in a society frequently indicates a corresponding depreciation of women as a group and as individuals, the presence of female symbolism does not guarantee the opposite' (xx). With reference to the Catalonia shown in the two crime novels under analysis, however, the authors make some interesting points in this regard. First of all, despite 'the presence of female symbolism' in Catalonia in the form of the *Ben Plantada*, women within the Catalan society portrayed in the texts are revealed to be dynamic citizens who in fact, as I mentioned earlier, seem to be more truly Catalan than their male consorts. Within the texts studied, Catalan females are only subjected to what Warner calls 'depreciation [. . .] as a group and as individuals' during the Francoist dictatorship, a period during which Catalonia enjoyed no autonomy at all.

In fact, then, although Lois West observes that despite the nation being gendered as female, as *la patrie*, it is 'constructed and perpetuated as discourses and struggles between men as "fraternity"' (xvi); and although Anne McClintock claims that 'women are typically construed as the symbolic bearers of the nation, but are denied any direct relation to national agency' (1993: 62), Mínguez and Aritzeta use their female characters to dispute this claim. Esperança and Constança are indeed rendered symbolically as the Catalan nation, but there can be no doubt that in later adulthood they have full access to its cultural capital as well as to a certain power gained through their financial savvy. These two authors thus energetically revise assertions of the sort proffered by Pettman who concludes that 'Women [. . .] are commonly constructed as the symbolic form of the nation whereas men are invariably represented as its chief agents and, with statehood achieved, emerge as its major beneficiaries' (49). In this way, then, Catalan women who write crime fictions in the 'cosy' or 'country house' enigma style revise their female characters' link to nation and citizenship as skilfully as do the authors of spy thrillers of the sort analysed in the previous section.

The obverse of the Catalan female as allegory of Catalonia is the Spanish woman as representative or symbolic of the Spanish nation, a positioning replete with negative connotations as is clear from Grau's *El dia que va morir el president*. Unfortunately for the novel's hapless protagonist his girlfriend, Lola, is a member of the immigrant group that his mother so despises, who perpetually made her life a misery with their insistence on speaking Castilian and their attempts to rob her. Lola's very name conjures up a quintessential Spanishness and evokes the flamenco dancing and other 'typical Spanish' elements of the notion of a unified Spain promoted by Franco.[28] Lola is portrayed by Grau as embodying an equally nauseating and negative set of allegedly Spanish attributes, which are positioned in direct contrast to the characteristics the Catalans perceive in themselves. Thus, Lola has disgusting eating habits, is dirty, allows her bra strap to hang out of her top (long before this became a fashion), and never wears any underwear under her very short skirts. Significantly, despite being a sexualized figure, she is unable to seduce the narrator who finds he is impotent unless making love to a Catalan girl. Symbolically rendered in the figure of Lola, then, is the emasculation of Catalonia by a rather sordid Spain peopled by unappetizing individuals. Grau's ludic engagement with many elements of the thriller permits a parodic siting of Lola as the very antithesis of the *femme fatale*. Despite her very evident sexual desire, attempts to eroticize her body by wearing few and revealing garments, showing her underwear, and her exposing herself each time she sits down in her short skirt, she is very definitely not sexy or alluring. Once again, and in keeping with Grau's revision of the spy novel format, the centre endangers the periphery, rather than the other way round as is usual in this particular sub-genre; Lola's squalid, dirty Spanishness emasculates Catalanness.

If, within Grau's text it is the male protagonist who is cowed by his Spanish girlfriend, by his boss, by the police, and just about everybody else he meets, female scholars have signalled that throughout the history of Catalonia it is women who have been subjugated. Indeed, observers have attempted to establish parallels between the situation of women and that of Catalonia and have tended to focus on common experiences of subjugation. Writing in 1990, Anne Charlon posited that '[l]a situació de les dones i la de les nacions històriques evolucionen paral·lelament; de fet són la mateixa època i els mateixos règims que han tingut en compte o han ridiculitzat les reivindicacions tant d'un grup com de l'altre' [[t]he situation of women and of the historic nations of Spain have evolved in tandem;[29] in fact, the same period or the same political regimes have either taken into account or ridiculed the demands of both groups] (1990: 13). With specific reference to Catalan women writers, Nichols offers a personal note which functions as a precursor of McNerney's and Enríquez de Salamanca's work on double minorities cited earlier:

> no pude menos que relacionar la situación cultural de esas naciones tan largamente subordinadas al poder central a la de otras minorías o marginados – grupos mudos – que había conocido en mis lecturas teóricas. Se me ocurrió que en el caso de estas escritoras de origen catalán podría tratarse de una doble marginación – como mujeres y como catalanas. (1989: 13)

> [I couldn't help linking the cultural situation of those nations that had been subjugated to a central power for such a long time to that of other minorities or marginalized people, silenced groups that I had learnt about in my theoretical readings. It occurred to me that in the case of these women writers of Catalan origin it could be a case of double marginalization, as both women and Catalans.]

Her point is in turn echoed by Shaudin Melgar-Foraster who observes that during the Franco period, the regime's 'ataque a la lengua catalana' [attack on the Catalan language] was paralleled by 'una política de gran dureza contra la mujer' [a very harsh policy towards women] (155). Indeed, novelists and other women of letters have themselves signalled the nature of the similarities. Maria Aurèlia Capmany made the point in her contribution to *Dona i societat a la Catalunya actual* [Woman and Society in Contemporary Catalonia]. From her perspective 1939, the year of the Francoist victory in the Civil War, was 'l'any de la derrota' [the year of the defeat] for Catalan women on two counts – of sex and nationality, and she goes on to draw direct parallels between the disastrous consequences of the Franco regime for the project of socio-economic and political development in Catalonia and the cause of women's social participation (1978: 8–9). More recently, Maria-Antònia Oliver has also indicated the parallels she perceives to exist between the status of women and that of the Catalan linguistic area, a situation which in her particular case is prob-lematized even further by the fact that as a Mallorcan she is spatially and linguistically marginalized to a further degree. Kathleen McNerney notes that the novelist

> came to feminism and Catalanism through a need to relate directly to the world [. . .] These are two parallel lines for her, and she sees the search for identity in colonized people as a necessary starting point for rebelling against the oppressor and redefining the self. Even though men and Spain may not think they are oppressing anyone, the struggle to avoid being defined as the other by the one is paramount. (1988: 15)

I have already discussed how, in Grau's *El dia que va morir el president*, the protagonist's mother is subjected to verbal and physical violence on account both of her sex and of her Catalan origins. This double victimization is also made clear in two other of the novels selected for analysis: Margarida Aritzeta's *El verí*, and Isabel Olesti's *El marit invisible*. Olesti's text tells the tale of three generations of Catalans who exist at the very margins of society, outside the formal economy, and well beyond the parameters of established 'moral' behaviour dictated by the Francoist regime in collusion with the Catholic church or as constructed by the Catalan and Spanish bourgeoisies. The situation endured by the narrator's mother in particular reveals how those triply marginal-ized – by their sex, their Catalan nationality, and their poverty – were consequently triply victimized by the dictatorship. The mur-dered mother is posited as a tragic symbol for her nation, and she and her family are representative of the group that lost the Civil War and suffered the consequences.

The illegitimate daughter of a Catalan mother and a Moroccan smuggler, the narrator's mother works from home as a hair-dresser and rarely ventures outside her squalid, malodorous, fly-infested apartment which is also *interior* [facing onto an inner patio or air shaft], and thus enjoys no sun, little natural light, and no view out onto the wider world. It is within this 'prison' that she is symbolically incarcerated for many years, just as many of the defeated were jailed when hostilities officially ceased at the end of the war. Her position as one of the 'losers', and the specific gendering of her situation, are confirmed early on in the novel during an episode at the local cinema during which she passively acquiesces to sexual harassment from an unknown man sitting next to her, while watching on the newsreel 'una escena familiar de la Carmen Polo guarnint un dels salons del Pardo amb boles de Nadal' [a family scene with Carmen Polo [Franco's wife] decorating one of the drawing rooms at the Pardo Palace [Franco's official residence] with Christmas baubles] (14). The juxtaposition of the happy family scene with the sordid encounter in the movie theatre highlights the socio-economic gulf between the victorious (the Castilian-speaking Spanish Nationalists) and the defeated (Republicans, Catalan nationalists, Anarchists, and others) that resulted from the devastating events of 1936–9. That women were doubly the 'losers' is apparent from the sexual aggression to which the protagonist's mother is subjected in this episode, a theme developed throughout the novel in the context of her relationship with a policeman.

A constant and threatening presence throughout the work, the police are symbolic of the repression the regime enforced on the populace by means of uniformed agents and other institutions.[30] Even as a child the sight of a policeman inspires mistrust, embarrassment and fear in the male narrator. His reaction is born of witnessing his mother and her policeman lover engaged in a sex act during which his mother is tied up while her partner penetrates her with his regulation pistol. Symbolized in this action, the literal screwing of one of the 'losers' by a uniformed representative of the 'winning' side, is the metaphorical screwing of the defeated by a regime which implacably sought out and punished those who had actively supported the Republicans or the Catalan nationalists prior to and during hostilities. The mother's health, and thus the possibility of her distancing herself from her oppressors (her lover or the police sergeant who would later replace him in her bed), are seriously undermined by the repeated illegal, botched abortions she undergoes, and which are once again symbolically representative of her position as a loser twice (or thrice) over – as a woman but also as a member of a social group marginalized because of its national identity and former political allegiances.

In her gloss of Cynthia Enloe, Catherine Hall observes the 'strategic importance of women's sexuality, together with their reproductive and child-rearing roles, in emerging nationalisms, and [. . .] the control which nation-states attempt to exert over their women and girls in their efforts to protect, revive and create nations' (51). This scenario describes very well the situation in Spain following the Civil War, a Spain in which there emerged a regime-sponsored 'Spanish' nationalism which used Castilian as its tool and which aimed to annul the incipient nationalisms in other areas that had flourished before the conflict began. Within this Spain, Franco obliged women to occupy a role at the centre of the domestic arena, and to perform the function of mother which would ensure a populous Spain boasting forty million inhabitants – a figure achieved only recently. Women who had many children were fêted by the regime and often awarded medals and prizes, and a high birth rate was assured (particularly among the poor) by means of the criminalization of abortion and contraception, as well as social and political pressure to conform. Despite the dictatorship's alleged reverence for the figure of the mother, however, within *El marit invisible* the female body is used and abused sexually by representatives of the Spanish state, a situation that once again highlights the parallel subjugations of Catalonia and of women. What is more, given that abortion was illegal during the Franco years, the narrator's mother is forced to the 'crime' of abortion by the men who impregnate her and who are the self same officials charged with upholding the laws that the central government imposed on the whole of Spain, thus revealing the hypocrisy and often tragic consequences of its gendered policies. It is also clear that a woman who, like Olesti's character, aborted frequently was denied the possibility of becoming a mother many times over by the contradictions inherent in the regime's policy of encouraging the very poor to have large families which they could not possibly hope to feed or educate.

In keeping with the negative portrayal of the family, the narrator's father is shown to be a violent, brutish man whose death is mourned by nobody, particularly his wife who then conducts affairs with numerous married men. What is more, the narrator's grandmother has illegitimate children by two different men: blond twin boys who are the fruit of one night of summer passion with a passing member of one of the International Brigades during the Civil War, and a daughter (the narrator's mother) who is the result of the grandmother's long liaison with the Moroccan smuggler turned construction worker. And although the narrator and his sister – who becomes progressively madder and evinces ever more bizarre behaviours – are born to a legally married couple, his brother Albert is the offspring of his mother's affair with a police officer, as are various aborted foetuses, one of which is kept in a jar of formaldehyde in the mother's bedroom. The family at the centre of *El marit invisible* is thus very different from the stable, bourgeois or working-class nuclear units or extended families portrayed in other fictions studied here. But inasmuch as it is through the family that the history of Catalonia and the region's relationship to central government are reviewed, Olesti's novel subscribes to a particular norm. The technique of presenting Catalan history through the family saga is not at all uncommon, particularly in popular genres in Catalonia, as Hugh O'Donnell (2002) has noted with particular reference to the soap opera. Catalan literature has also produced important texts which review the region's history through the eyes of several generations of a family, such as Ignacio Agustí's tetralogy, Monsterrat Roig's trilogy, and Terenci Moix's *El dia que va morir Marilyn* [The Day Marilyn Died]. As the cover blurb of *El marit invisible* suggests, the novel is not only a mystery but also offers a panorama of Catalonia's recent past: 'es pot llegir com una novel·la de misteri però també com un gran fresc de tota una època' [it can be read as a mystery novel but also as a vast fresco of a whole era].

The key events of this era were, of course, the Civil War and the subsequent dictatorship, and it is clear from Olesti's positioning of the narrator's mother that one of the main aims of her text is to uncover the crimes perpetrated upon the female body during the decades from the 1930s. In *El marit invisible* and also in Aritzeta's *El verí*, female characters' past of victimhood at the hands of the patriarchal system during the period mentioned holds extensive clues to their positioning as homicide victims in the narrative present – the late twentieth century. In both texts the victim is the 'disposable female' identified by Linda Barnes as a norm in male-authored crime fiction in particular, and mentioned earlier in this study. As discussed in Chapter 2, crime literature furnishes an ideal forum for discussion of the structuring and function of the victim (see, e.g. Resina 1997: ch. 3) and particular opportunities for an interrogation of the gendering of victimization when the target of aggression is female. Many crime sub-genres also permit the minute review and reconstruction of the past that can throw up not only clues to a crime, but also expose social attitudes which police gendered behaviours – and this is certainly the case in *El verí* and *El marit invisible.*

The female victim in *El verí* is Caterina, the 'mad' aunt who is found poisoned in a locked room after being incarcerated in the attic of the family's *masia* for decades. She and her sister, the matriarch Constança, grew up in a Catalonia subjugated and controlled by the Franco regime that imposed on its wealthiest region the kind of grey uniformity that characterized the whole of post-Civil War Spain: 'Tot era trist en els anys i el país de la seva infantesa, des de les cares de les persones [. . .] fins als colors i les formes dels vestits [. . .] També eren grises i sense gràcia les converses, i no menys grisos els somnis i els desigs' [Everything was gloomy in the years and the country of their childhood, from people's faces [. . .] to the colours and styles of their clothes [. . .] Conversations were also grey and lacking wit, and no less grey were dreams and desires] (95). Within the novel, this portrait of Spain is positioned in contrast to France during the same period, a country described as politically and culturally liberal where personal and artistic expression could be given free reign.

While the Catalan nation and Catalan culture were proscribed by dictatorial decree, during the same period strict models of gendered behaviour were rigorously propagated, thus subjecting Caterina and Constança to a double discourse of control, as women and as Catalans:

> elles havien après a comportar-se d'acord amb les conveniències d'un món on les dones i les criatures eren éssers silenciosos i invisibles, a mostrar-se per fora com unes senyoretes serenes i immutables encara que la processó els anés per dintre. A no protestar. A no cridar. Ni riure. Ni plorar. A no ser sinó una ombra que es movia sense molestar ni fer-se evident. (95–6)

> [They had learned to behave according to the conventions of a world in which women and children were silent and invisible beings, to outwardly appear to be serene and immutable young ladies even though they were being eaten up inside. They learned

not to complain. Nor shout. Nor laugh. Nor cry. To be nothing more than a shadow that moved without bothering anybody or being visible.]

Any woman who stepped outside the tightly controlled boundaries of this 'ideal' of Spanish womanhood – which also clearly prevailed in Catalonia – paid a heavy price. Thus, Caterina's 'punishment' for moving to France to live in a dancing school, travel extensively, and bear a child outside marriage was imprisonment and, later, death by poisoning.[31] She is not just a victim of strychnine, but, as the closure of the novel makes clear, of a regime that destroyed women's lives and their right of access to cultural and personal development.

Another life that was changed irrevocably by the Civil War and subsequent political upheaval was that of the narrator's grandmother in *El marit invisible*. '[U]na republicana convençuda' [a committed Republican] (18), she was obliged to flee Catalonia when the fighting ceased at the end of the war in order to avoid being shot or imprisoned by the Nationalists, for having assisted Republican soldiers during the conflict. Self-exiled to Morocco, she suffered endless humiliation at the hands of Moroccan men but, more particularly, abuse by French and Spanish police stationed in the country. She could find no home other than a brothel where, although not employed as a prostitute, she was witness to the never-ending degradation of the sex workers who also resided there, women whose sense of sisterhood in some ways managed to compensate them for their situation. The grandmother later returned to Barcelona with her illegitimate daughter, born and raised within the walls of the bordello. This female figure, then, embodies the trials faced by those who saw in the Republic opportunities for personal and Catalan emancipation and advancement, and who paid for their beliefs with geographical exile, removal from their families and communities, and subsequent relegation to an economic, educational, social and cultural underclass, if indeed they ever returned to Spain.

While Olesti uses her re-writing of the crime novel to foreground her concerns about the predicament of the poor Catalan woman, she deploys her male characters within *El marit invisible* to comment critically on the brand of masculinity conventionally featured in the hard-boiled crime genre, which is characteristic of Spain's *novela negra* and even some recent male-authored police procedurals (Lorenzo Silva's series can be considered a case in point). Generally speaking, the kinds of male figures who would traditionally be at the centre of the action in the crime genre are sidelined in this text, and more marginal masculinities are featured: it is revealed, for instance, that the narrator is homosexual. Crucially, too, although the novel's title seems to suggest that a man will constitute the central interest of the story, this is another of Olesti's ironic touches, for the narrator explains that his mother's 'invisible husband', the ideal man with whom she falls in love and to whom she remains faithful until her death, is none other than the film star, Tyrone Power, playing the role of Zorro. The supposed key male protagonist is thus nothing more than an illusion, a mere trick of the light, a strategy that again underscore's Olesti's questioning of the traditional siting of the tough, macho male at the centre of this type of genre fiction.

It is not only in the interrogation of the textual function of the male hero, or inviting readerly reflection on how crime is constituted and gendered in such activities as abortion, however, that make clear how Olesti pushes at the boundaries of this type of literature. *El marit invisible* also reviews and rewrites many other standard elements of the crime genre. In places it is reminiscent of Latin American Magical Realism, as Olesti constructs a curious world of strange coincidences and marvellous happenings, recounting whimsical tales of women who levitate at will and of an apartment inhabited by the whistling spirits of the dead. She also challenges one of the key conventions of the crime genre, albeit one often re-written by female authors, for although the central mystery at the core of the novel is finally solved, there is no neat resolution, since the narrator makes it plain that he has no intention of telling the police what he knows, leaving the guilty party unpunished. In addition, the myriad smaller mysteries which litter the pages of the novel remain unsolved. Many enigmatic episodes are left as tantalizing loose threads in a murder mystery that resists the closure that the genre normally demands. Thus, the true identity of the narrator's grandfather cannot be established; the reason why a neighbour commits suicide is never explained; and the purpose of the bizarre telephone call that sends the narrator's family on a wild goose chase to claim a non-existent competition prize remains unclear.

The family's mad dash around Barcelona to find their prize is, surprisingly in a novel apparently founded in both physical and social stasis and stagnation, just one of a number of expeditions, journeys, and voyages undertaken by the characters, a strategy that evokes the movement through the city characteristic of the hard-boiled genre. Although within the text the grandmother's relocation to Morocco is enforced – as a consequence of her support of the Republicans during the Civil War – not all movement beyond Catalonia within this novel and others studied here is shown as negative. Indeed, the narrator of *El marit invisible* repeats his grandmother's journey to Tangiers many years later, but this time it is a freely chosen odyssey of self-discovery rather than an imposed flight into political exile. His voyage allows him to move beyond the stultifying atmosphere of El Clot. This was something his mother had never been able or willing to do, obsessively attached as she was to the claustrophobic family apartment. Even as her home became plagued by flies – symbolic evidence of the stagnation in which she lives – and her own mother's decaying body filled the house with the stench of death, she refused to move on. However much many female Catalan writers of crime fictions champion and promote Catalan nationhood and identity, an inward-looking, static Catalanness, one which demonstrates a tendency towards fossilization, is ultimately self-destructive, as Olesti makes clear.

The cultural theorist Stuart Hall has argued that –

> We need to situate the debates about identity within all those historically specific developments and practices which have disturbed the relatively 'settled' character of many populations and cultures, above all in relation to the processes of globalization [. . .] and the processes of forced and 'free' migration which have become a global phenomenon of the so-called 'post-colonial' world. (4)

He later sums up his notion about what identity is by stating that it should be about 'not the so-called return to roots but a coming-to-terms-with our "routes"' (ibid.). It is exactly this position that Olesti assumes in her novel, since the personal stories narrated therein show the positive benefits of the movement of individuals out of and into Catalonia. At the same time, they also emphasize the negative effects of remaining anchored to particular places or of becoming overly attached to tradition.

Journeys beyond the borders of Catalonia are also key to the detective activity of Lònia Guiu in Maria-Antònia Oliver's series of novels analysed in Chapter 1. Drawing heavily on the generic conventions deployed by North American writers such as Paretsky, Oliver's stories are another clear example of Marsha Kinder's concept of transcultural reinscription. One of the things that transcultural reinscription does is to inflect the global with a local accent – clear in the case of Oliver's Majorcan flavouring of a literary sub-genre from outside Majorca, Catalonia, or even Spain – a strategy Featherstone and Lash (1995) have termed glocalization. Guiu's wanderlust and the cases that she takes on give the series a sense of displacement from Spain or Catalonia. Scales of geographical space are often made to seem unimportant: dividing lines between 'home' and 'away', between the local and global become blurred, neatly illustrated by the fact that in *Antípodes*, the second book in the series, when travelling from Majorca to Australia Lònia considers that she is merely leaving one island for another. The crimes she investigates can also be described as glocalized: they are carried out via global networks, making use of the free flow of capital, goods, and people, or exploiting such phenomena as tourism or economic migration. Crucially, however, they are also shown to impact most acutely at the local level. Ultimately, all the victims of the globally-oriented crimes with which Lònia comes into contact originate from, or have close links to, Majorca. Oliver's strategy thus not only highlights female victimization and criminal abuse beyond the borders of her detective's home territory as well as within it, but also reveals Catalonia's place at the very centre of an increasingly globalized universe, while at the same time showing that the region – and specifically Lònia's native island – can retain important symbols of and pointers to a separate regional identity.

Writing in the early 1990s about what he saw to be the key developments in narrative, Homi Bhabha commented that 'the margins of the nation displace the centre; the peoples of the periphery return to rewrite the history and fiction of the metropolis' (7). Although he was referring on that occasion to literature written in English, his words also summarize the processes described and considered by authors analysed in this chapter. Women, formerly resident at the periphery of society, have moved centre stage to articulate not only their own history but also that of the other peoples of Catalonia. To do so they have chosen a literary genre formerly considered to exist at the margins of culture but which has now fully entered the main-stream. And they have shown that Catalonia is no longer peripheral to Spain, and much less to the rest of the world, and that they may legitimately interrogate the crimes visited on their region and on the bodies of its inhabitants by other individuals, but specifically by the Spanish state and its representatives. They can thus literally 'write the wrongs' historically suffered by their countrywomen as women and as Catalans.

NOTES

1   Within Spain the earliest writers of crime fictions, such as Emilia Pardo Bazán, published in Castilian. The point I wish to make here, however, is that Catalonia is the first part of Spain to develop a sustained engagement with this sort of literature, particularly one that was overtly politicized, as I shall discuss later in this chapter.

2   Interestingly, Kathryn Crameri considers a tension to exist between the Catalanist mission promulgated in literature and the novel as a genre, observing that 'since 1975 Catalanists are now having to project their nation-building message to a much wider and more diverse audience [. . .] The novel does not lend itself particularly well to this, as in its "high culture" form it is above all a genre of complexity and depth of thought' (9). As discussed here, however, popular types of the novel have proved singularly successful in ensuring that a broad-based readership access texts in Catalan about Catalan topics.

3   Martí-Olivella does point out, however, that there exists an inherent contradiction between the marketing and popularity among readers of female-authored novels, and what he sees as the 'buidor crítica' [critical vacuum] that surrounds them and the '"guetoïzació", la reducció a un espai cultural marginal quant a la cultura oficial' ['ghettoisation', the reduction to a marginal cultural space with relation to official culture] (202) to which they are subjected.

4   The early capitalist development of Catalonia and its cultural and economic association with the rest of Europe mentioned at the beginning of this chapter would, however, induce some novelists to use imported detective genre models to investigate Catalan reality. I discuss the specific cases of Mercè Rodoreda and Maria Aurèlia Capmany in the next section.

5   During the 1950s and 1960s, Maria Aurèlia Capmany was one of only a very small handful of Catalan novelists producing crime narratives – other eminent contributors to detective fiction included Rafael Tasis and Manuel de Pedrolo – but she was the only female author writing in the genre in Catalonia. Although both her detective novels (as well as the earlier *Crim* by Rodoreda) are significant because of the way in which they foregrounded Catalan nationalist issues, they did not serve to herald a boom in detective writing by Catalan women because, as

Àlex Broch notes, any nascent Catalan crime genre had to confront multiple difficulties to its very existence. At the very root of the problem was the absence, during the Franco regime, of the socio-cultural development necessary for the genre to flourish:

> A la societat catalana, aquesta evolució li fou, lògicament, negada. I li ho va ser per les raons que hem dit i que, sense pretendre fer ara una anàlisi sociològica de la qüestió, hem vinculat a factors externs o exògens al mateix fet literari: la visió essencialista i transcendentalista del fenomen literari – posició nacionalista –, el fet de tenir-lo per subgènere d'evasió – posició de l'esquerra – i que la societat industrial fos en harmonia aparent – ideología franquista. A aquests factors externs cal afegir els específicament literaris. En primer lloc, és prou clar que encara no hi havia, ni encara no hi ha, una tradició literari del gènere dins la literatura catalana. En segon lloc, hi havia problemes tècnics d'escissió lingüística i del paper dels serveis d'ordre de l'Estat al si de la societat catalana. S'havia de fer parlar català a la policia, o inventar-se els *perdiguers* o *privats* catalans en una societat on les llicències professionals eren del toto controlades i limitades. Així és que l'escriptor s'enfrontava amb una manca de tradició, però també amb problems de versemblança literària pel que fa a un element clau com el de la llengua. (1991: 118)

> [Catalan society was understandably denied this development. And it was for the reasons I have mentioned and which, without aiming to carry out a sociological analysis of the issue, I have linked to external factors or those exogenous to literature: the nationalist position evident in an essentialist and transcendental view of literature; the leftist position which held it [crime fiction] to be a sub-genre and escapist fiction; and the Francoist view that industrial society lived in apparent harmony. In addition to these external factors should be added the specifically literary ones. In the first place, it is clear that a tradition of the genre in Catalan literature never existed and still does not exist. Secondly, there existed the technical problem of a schism between language and the role of the [Spanish] state forces of law and order working in Catalonia. It would have been neces-sary to make the police speak Catalan, or invent some Catalan sleuths or PI's in a society in which professional licences were strictly controlled and limited. The writer was thus faced with a lack of tradition, but also with questions of literary credibility, for which language was a key element.]

6   The concern with the past evinced in a considerable number of very contemporary detective novels by Catalan women reflects a tendency in 'post-postmodern' Spanish literature identified by Gonzalo Nava-jas. He claims that in a new type of Spanish fiction '[e]l pasado existe pero no hay con él una relación unívoca, como ocurría con [. . .] la ficción anterior. La nueva estética recupera el pasado pero lo hace de

modo subjetivo filtrando la objetividad de la reflexión histórica a través de la mirada personal' [[t]he past exists but there is no single relationship to it as there was [. . .] in earlier fiction. The new aesthetic recovers the past but it does so in a subjective way, filtering the objectivity of reflection on history through the personal gaze] (1996: 28). Within his study he pays particular attention to how this changing view of the past has underpinned the revisions of crime and detective genres that have characterized the literary scene in Spain over the past couple of decades.

7   This parallel was developed in a co-authored paper with Anne M. White, 'Investigating Fictions of Identity: Contemporary Catalan Crime Fiction by Women' (223–4).

8   Some critics do contend, however, that nationalist sentiment is not the only reason writers choose to publish in Catalan. Stewart King, for example, notes that the suppression of Catalan during the Franco regime, and even personal factors such as the death of a Catalan-speaking mother, can contribute to writers' decisions to pen novels, non-fiction, and journalistic pieces in Catalan or Castilian (2005: 53–4).

9   Joan Capri was the artistic name of the Catalan actor Joan Camprubí i Alemany who began his career in 1955. He was particularly famous for his comic roles and for his monologues which parodied popular forms of speech. These latter were made available on record from 1961 and were best-sellers in Catalonia. Folch i Torres was an eminent early to mid-twentieth-century Catalan writer who in the main published children's literature. Capri and Folch i Torres are thus clearly used here by Grau with profoundly ironic and humorous intent, for the Catalan culture the mother attempts to preserve and which she uses to maintain her 'Catalanness' are far from being Catalonia's great works of literature or music.

10   Although the Catholic Church was generally a key supporter of the dictatorship, in Catalonia a number of Catalan bishops played an important function in expressing anti-Franco sentiments.

11   The foundational text of the Catalan *Renaixença* [the 'Renaissance' of Catalan culture and language during the late nineteenth century], Aribau's 'Oda a la pàtria' [Ode to the Fatherland] refers to learning Catalan 'quan del mugró matern la dolça llet bevia' [when from the maternal breast sweet milk was drunk] (vv. 34).

12   Stephen Knight notes of Poirot that '[a]s a Belgian he combines the French-speaking tradition of close detective analysis with the contemporary idea of Belgium as a 'brave little' country. Even his name suggests a redirection of male heroism. By implication he is a Hercules who is also something of a "poirot", a buffoon' (108). In Rodoreda's novel, Flac's surname is also redolent with overtones of the sort of masculine inadequacy personified in Christie's character. It suggests he is a pale copy, a skinnier and physically weaker version of the effete investigator in vogue in British detective fiction of the 1930s, a notion ironically compounded in his false moustache.

13   In the British novels, which *Crim* parodies, foreigners were usually portrayed as being of questionable moral conduct, and villains were

often of non-British origin. Colin Watson has observed that such texts were packed with despicable and evil-intentioned foreigners, while even writers of more sedate detective stories devoted some of their talents to remarkably splenetic portraiture of characters with dark complexions or guttural accents. Foreign was synonymous with criminal in nine novels out of ten, and the conclusion is that most people found this perfectly natural (123).

[14] Although she does not use the term 'transcultural reinscription', Maria Alessandra Giovannini nonetheless flags up the status of Capmany's first detective novel as a product of just such a trend:

> més enllà del fet que la novel·la *Traduït de l'americà* es presenti com un diari escrit pel protagonista *ianqui* que no sabem com va ser traduït ni si va ser publicat ni en quina llengua, el títol de l'obra també suggereix la deliberada voluntat de l'autora de *traduir* a la seva llengua, de trasposar a la literature feta en el seu país un model cultural estranger. (58 [italics in original])

> [quite apart from the fact that *Traduït de l'americà* is presented as the diary of its 'Yankie' protagonist and we have no idea how it was translated, nor if it was published, nor in which language, the title of the novel also suggests the deliberate desire on the part of the author to *translate* a foreign cultural model into her own language, to transpose that model into the literature written in her own country.]

[15] Giovannini notes that in *Vès-te'n ianqui* Albania is a *metaphor* for Catalonia, while in *El jaqué de la democràcia* Balvacària is the *pseudonym* of Catalonia (59).

[16] The Barret case is a reference to the murder in 1918 of Josep Albert Barret Moner, a wealthy Catalan industrialist. He was killed by German spies because his company manufactured weapons which were sold to the French during WW I. For a reading of the fictionalization of the case with specific reference to Eduardo Mendoza's *La verdad sobre el caso Savolta*, see Eduardo Ruiz's article.

[17] In addition to Jordi Pujol, the undisputed lead player on the Catalan political scene both before and since autonomy, Conversi mentions the early twentieth-century Catalan nationalists Antoni Rovira i Virgili, Francesc Pi i Margall, Enric Prat de la Riba, and Valentí Almirall (214), all of whom were male.

[18] Although scholars have noted a relative absence of women from the contemporary Catalan political scene, Mercedes Ugalde claims that Catalan women were organized into Catalanist political groups from the late nineteenth century (237). Joana Luna and Elisenda Macià's article on Catholic Catalan women's political groupings also notes that during the early years of the twentieth century, female members of the region's social elite formed such organizations with the aim of educating women (228). They also conducted philanthropic work among the poor, especially children (228) and prostitutes and 'fallen' women (229). In a rather unique gesture, they also set up sports clubs which promoted a progressive political mentality and

Catalan nationalism (238), and from the 1910s onwards helped working-class women to form trade unions to represent specifically female labour areas (231–2). Mary Nash observes that during the Second Republic and the Civil War Catalan women were politically active. She asserts that Catalan nationalism was the most important route to female political mobilization (248), while during the war large numbers of women were affiliated to Anarchist and anti-fascist groups (257). Both before and after the Civil War Catalan women were also involved in the Sección Femenina [The Female Division], an organization established by José Primo de Rivera, the founder of the Falange, Spain's fascist movement (Riera 139 *et seq.*). According to Ignasi Riera, right-wing Catalans actively promoted the Sección Femenina (146). It does appear to be the case, however, that this intense political activity by women, organized as it was along gender lines, did not lead to protagonization for women on the nationalist or national political scenes.

[19] Article 2 of the Constitution of 1978 states that 'the constitution is based on the indissoluble unity of the Spanish Nation, the common and indivisible fatherland – *Patria* – of all Spaniards, and recognizes and guarantees the right to self-government of the nationalities and regions of which it is composed and solidarity among them all' (cited in Arbós 146).

[20] Glòria's origin is significant in that historically Valencia has not considered itself part of a Catalan nation. Mar-Molinero claims that the Valencians 'have felt themselves separate from Catalonia for many centuries' (47), and now their region constitutes a separate and distinct autonomous community. During the early nineteenth century the *Blasquistas* – a Spanish nationalist group who took their name from the novelist Blasco Ibáñez – in collaboration with Valencian agrarian elites originated a discourse founded in the rejection of Catalonia's alleged 'imperialist' designs on Valencia which led to anti-Catalan sentiments among large sectors of the population (Smith and Mar-Molinero 14–15). More recently, intellectuals such as Joan Fuster, have promoted pan-Catalan nationalism, although this particular scholar was subjected to physical violence, bomb attacks, and verbal abuse as a response to his views (Cultiaux 139). Catalan intellectuals, however, have not rejected the possibility that Valencia may yet become fully incorporated into a possible Catalan nation. Josep Termes, for example, expresses just such an aspiration:

> El model de Països Catalans ha passat de ser un model encunyat al Principat, portat per un motor que era Barcelona, a un model en què el País Valencià ja juga un paper decisiu. Ara hi ha la possibilitat, nova, d'establir un eix Barcelona–València, on dos capitals de cultura impulsen el projecte nacional, donant-li unes perspectives més favorables per a un future no necessàriament llunyà. (122–3)

> [The model of a Catalan homeland has gone from being a model based solely on the Principality, powered by Barcelona

as its motor, to being a model in which Valencia now plays a decisive role. We now have the new possibility of establishing a Barcelona–Valencia axis in which two cultural capitals drive the national project, imbuing it with a more favourable outlook for a future that is not necessarily far off.]

Glòria repeatedly refers to her origins in humorous and ironic terms, thus flagging up the often tortured relationship between Valencia and Catalonia.

21 Significantly, the male protagonist of *El dia que va morir el president* is nameless, a technique which suggests an annulment of the male and his significance in relation to nation and national endeavour, a stance reinforced by the siting of the character as marginal to questions of nation because he evinces not the least interest in the subject. The failure to name the male character could also be read as a ploy aimed at undermining the traditional primacy of male naming within the espionage thriller tradition where entire series carry the name of the 'hero' – Fleming's Bond or Le Carré's Smiley, for example.

22 The events recounted in the novel are also a clear echo of those that occurred at the Munich Olympics in 1972.

23 The use of the term 'nation' to describe Catalonia was one of the major sticking points in passing the *Estatut d'autonomia de Catalunya 2006* [The 2006 Catalan Autonomy Charter] proposed by the Catalan autonomous government through the Spanish parliament. The Charter suggested a greater degree of autonomy for Catalonia in a number of political and legal areas, and for an increased percentage of revenues from taxation to remain in Catalonia rather than being channelled to Madrid. The debate about the Charter raged on in Spanish political circles during late 2005 and early 2006 until the document was eventually ratified in March 2006 pending passage through the Senate and a referendum in Catalonia in the summer of the same year. Writing in the *Observer*, Giles Tremlett noted that the Charter, '[i]n a roundabout way [. . .] also refers to Catalonia as "a nation"' (Tremlett 2006).

24 Within the context of contemporary crime fiction written in Catalonia an excellent description of this type of poor quality housing on the outskirts of Barcelona is that of (the fictional) San Magín in Manuel Vázquez Montalbán's *Los Mares del Sur* (1981).

25 Alan Yates translates *Noucentisme* as 'the movement of the 1900s, of the new century' (258). It was a cultural tendency that influenced all forms of artistic activity in Catalonia from 1908 to 1923. D'Ors used the term to designate the new 'spirit' in Catalan art he saw from the beginning of the twentieth century.

26 Hargreaves explains that the *mas* was the traditional economic and family unit of rural Catalan society and was founded in patriarchal law and traditions (20). The house itself is also of significance, for as Dupláa notes,

'la casa p[ai]ral' és el lloc on es nodreix l'esperit de les ensenyances que generació darrera generació es transmeten

> per via oral de pares a fills. La metàfora de la 'casa' com a
> sinònim de 'regió' comporta que els membres de la família
> siguin els membres de la regionalitat i, per tant, els defensors
> de la catalanitat entesa com a concepció de vida. (1988*b*: 176)
>
> [The 'family house' is the place where the spirit of those
> teachings that are passed verbally from father to son, genera-
> tion after generation, are nurtured. The 'house' as metaphor
> for the 'region' means that the members of the family are
> members of the regional group, and are therefore the defend-
> ers of Catalanism as a way of life.]

27   Interestingly, Catalan customary institutions in the nineteenth century did sometimes allow for a woman to inherit. Known as the
pubilla, Stephen Jacobson describes such a woman as 'the eldest
female who inherited the estate when no male heir was alive or
deemed worthy' (341 [my italics]).

28   Her name can also be read as a reference to Lola Flores (1923–95),
an Andalusian singer, dancer, and actress also known as 'Lola de
España' [Lola of Spain] who was immensely popular during the
dictatorship and afterwards.

29   'The "historic regions" (Catalonia, the Basque provinces and Galicia)
were [. . .] regions which had had Statutes of Autonomy in the past
[i.e. prior to the Francoist dictatorship]' (Rodgers 38).

30   This negative portrayal of the police as inept, violent, stupid, and
dangerous to the citizenry is a constant of the *novela negra*, although
such a stance revises substantially norms for the genre established in
many Anglophone texts in which the police do tend to be the force of
'law and order' – certainly in more traditional genres and the police
procedural. Olesti published *El marit invisible* in 1999, by which time
the 'classic' *novela negra* of the Transition was no longer the primary
crime sub-genre appearing in Spain and the police procedural and the
police television series – and, hence, the police themselves – had
become 'normalized' within the country, particularly in the works of
such authors as Alicia Giménez-Bartlett and Lorenzo Silva (whose
works do, however, perpetuate the stereotype of the rather sexist male
police officer). Olesti's novel, however, is set during the Franco period,
a time of significant repressive activity by the police, and it is for this
reason that she portrays the force in a negative way.

31   Caterina's imprisonment, as I noted in Chapter 2, was not imposed
by the regime or its agents, but by her family, operating in collusion
with the dictatorship to uphold its 'moral' stance. Similarly, as I
pointed out earlier, within *El marit invisible* the narrator's mother is
also symbolically incarcerated, 'imprisoning' herself in her apartment. Aritzeta and Olesti thus offer an interesting revision of one of
the standard tenets of some of the crime sub-genres in which –
traditionally – it is the *perpetrator* of a crime who is locked away with
the successful resolution of the narrative enigma. In the two novels
studied here it is the *victim* – of gendered and national circumstances
– who is interned.

Conclusion

In *Killing Carmens: Women's Crime Fiction from Spain*, I have shown how selected female authors who write in the crime and detective sub-genres use this type of literature to articulate numerous concerns about the role and status of women in contemporary Spanish society, and I also consider some older fictions dating from the middle decades of the last century with the same aim. While the texts chosen for analysis represent only a fraction of the many hundreds of crime narratives by women writers in Spain to have appeared in print since Emilia Pardo Bazán first published her crime short stories and novella in the early twentieth century, they evince an extensive range of thematic concerns and author-ial consideration of generic norms, and were published in both Castilian and Catalan. They can thus be considered eminently representative of the broader currents both within the develop-ment of the crime genre in Spain in general, and women's engagement upon it, in particular.

Crime literature by women from Spain does not exist in a vacuum outside of, and separate from, either the wider crime fiction scene – which in this national context is an exceptionally vibrant one, as I pointed out in my Introduction – nor the broader panorama of female writing, which also seems to have been especially buoyant during the last couple of decades or so. I thus read the texts I analyse within this study as an integral and important part of both of these narrative currents in order to situate them generically and thematically. On the other hand, however, I point out in each chapter that the crime genre can function in very particular ways to credibly – and enjoyably – foreground and deliberate on a range of topics pertaining to women's experience of life in twentieth- and twenty-first-century Spain in both urban and rural areas, among several social classes, and in regions where Castilian or another language is spoken.

Thus, because – as I note throughout each chapter – the various crime sub-genres are founded primarily in violence and aggression, but also in the characterization of protagonists and other figures according to fairly rigid gendered, class, and ethno-national paradigms, this particular sort of literature can function very effectively to textualize matters such as violence against women and female responses to (male) aggression. This pattern assumes additional significances when the woman victim is of a different ethnic, racial, or national origin from her abuser – a notion I develop in Chapter 3. So, because violence of some sort is at the very centre of this sort of narrative, the reader *expects* to confront a crime or aggression, thus facilitating greatly the writer's task of foregrounding, for example, the murder, rape, or battery of a woman character. Other cultural products highlight these issues too, of course. The past decade or so in Spain has witnessed the publication and production of a significant number of novels, plays, cinema and television films and documentaries, and autobiographies which focus on the specific problem of 'domestic' violence (against women) in contemporary Spanish society. As I make clear throughout this book, however, it is the perceived inflexibility and intractability of the norms that apparently undergird the respective crime sub-genres that attract female authors – both in Spain and elsewhere – to revise, re-write, and subvert them to their own (gendered) ends, sometimes humorously, sometimes ironically, and often playfully, but always with fairly serious intent. Thus, where Dulce Chacón's 1996 novel *Algún amor que no mate* [A Love That Does Not Kill] or Icíar Bollaín's highly successful film, *Te doy mis ojos* [Take My Eyes] (2003) – neither of which belongs to the crime genre – are rightly considered as important cultural responses to the issue of violence against women in the home, they do not offer up the kind of revisionary paradigms (of the female husband-killer, the woman robber, or the female sleuth, for example) that crime narratives by Spanish women authors do. As I argue throughout this study, it is precisely figures of this kind who embody the sort of female agency that furnishes the (female) reader with the visions of empowerment that may be absent from other narrative forms. Yet at the same time, as I show in each chapter, they are uniquely well placed to comment on a vast range of gendered issues from within the narratives they protagonize. Given, then, that crime and detective fictions sell well and are often energetically promoted by publishers, booksellers, and the organizers of literary and cultural events, novels and anthologies of short stories of the sort analysed in this study may function within contemporary Spain both to promote awareness of problems such as violence against women, and to suggest possible responses to this gendered victimization, to a broad-based readership.

Works Cited

Alborch, Carmen. *Malas. Rivalidad y complicidad entre mujeres*. Madrid: Aguilar, 2002.

Altable Vicario, Charo. '¿Qué educación queremos para el siglo XXI?' *Quin feminisme per al segle XXI?* Coord. Pilar Blasco. Valencia: Esquerra Unida del País Valencià, 2000. 31–3.

Álvarez, Blanca. *La soledad del monstruo*. Madrid: Grupo Libro 88, 1991.

—— *Las niñas no hacen ruido cuando mueren*. Premià de Mar: El Clavell, 1998.

Amorós, Celia. 'Algunos aspectos de la evolución ideológica del feminismo en España'. *La mujer española: de la tradición a la modernidad*. Eds. Concha Borreguero et al. Madrid: Tecnos, 1986. 41–54.

—— *Tiempo de feminismo. Sobre feminismo, proyecto ilustrado y postmodernidad*. Madrid: Cátedra, 1997.

Anderson, Benedict. *Imagined Communities: Reflections on the Origin and Spread of Nationalism*. London: Verso, 1983.

Andrews, Margaret and Anny Brooksbank Jones. 'Re-registering Spanish Feminisms'. *Spanish Cultural Studies*. Eds. Barry Jordan and Rikki Morgan-Tamosunas. London: Arnold, 2000. 233–40.

Anthias, Floya and Nira Yuval-Davis. 'Introduction'. *Woman-Nation-State*. Eds. Nira Yuval-Davis and Floya Anthias. London: Macmillan, 1989. 1–15.

Antolín, Matías. *Mujeres de ETA. Piel de serpiente*. Madrid: Temas de Hoy, 2002.

Arbós, Xavier. 'Central Versus Peripheral Nationalism in Building Democracy: The Case of Spain'. *Canadian Review of Studies in Nationalism* 14, 1 (1987): 143–60.

Aritzeta, Margarida. *El cau del llop*. Barcelona: La Magrana, 1992.

—— *El verí*. Valls: Edicions Cossetània, 2002.

Asensi, Matilde. *El salón de ámbar*. Barcelona: Plaza y Janés, 1999.

—— *Iacobus*. Barcelona: Plaza y Janés, 2000.

—— *El último catón*. Barcelona: Plaza y Janés, 2001.

—— *El origen perdido*. Barcelona: Planeta, 2003.

—— *Todo bajo el cielo*. Barcelona: Planeta, 2006.

Azevedo, Milton. 'Code-Switching in Catalan Literature'. *Antípodas* 5 (1993): 223–32.

Bados Ciria, Concepción. 'Espacio y representación en la novela negra española. Barcelona en *Tatuaje* y *Estudio en lila*'. *Iris* (1995): 7–23.

Balcells, Albert. *Catalan Nationalism. Past and Present.* Ed. and Intro. Geoffrey J. Walker. Trans. Jacqueline Hall. Basingstoke: Macmillan, 1996.

Barbero, Teresa. *Planta baja.* Madrid: Libertarias, 1998.

Bardsley, Barney. *Flowers in Hell. An Investigation into Women and Crime.* London and New York: Pandora, 1987.

Bhabha, Homi K. 'Introduction'. *The Nation and Narration.* Ed. Homi K. Bhabha. London: Routledge, 1990. 1–7.

Bird, Delys and Brenda Walker. 'Introduction'. *Killing Women. Rewriting Detective Fiction.* Ed. Delys Bird. Sydney: Angus and Robertson, 1993. 1–60.

Boada, Irene. 'Nacionalisme i llengua en el conte contemporani català i irlandès: Algunes perspectives feministes i postcolonials'. *Journal of Catalan Studies: Revista Internacional de Catalanística* 2 (1999): np. http://www.uoc.es/jocs/.

Boada-Montagut, Irene. *Women Write Back. Irish and Catalan Short Stories in Colonial Context.* Dublin: Irish Academic Press, 2003.

BOE 313 (29. 12. 04): 42166–42197. 'Ley Orgánica 1/2004, de 28 de diciembre, de Medidas de Protección Integral contra la Violencia de Género'.

Broch, Àlex. *Literatura catalana dels anys vuitanta.* Barcelona: Edicions 62, 1991.

—— 'Maria Aurèlia Capmany i Montserrat Roig o el temps com a memòria col·lectiva'. *Catalan Review* 7, 3 (1993): 21–37.

—— 'M. Antònia Oliver'. *Catalan Writing* 13 (1995): 55–60.

Brooks, Ann. *Postfeminisms. Feminism, Cultural Theory and Cultural Forms.* London: Routledge, 1997.

Brooksbank Jones, Anny. *Women in Contemporary Spain.* Manchester: Manchester University Press, 1997.

Brown, Joan L. 'Women Writers of Spain: An Historical Perspective'. *Women Writers of Contemporary Spain. Exiles in the Homeland.* Ed. Joan L. Brown. Newark: University of Delaware Press, 1991. 13–25.

Brownmiller, Susan. *Against our Will: Men, Women and Rape.* New York: Simon and Schuster, 1975.

Buckley, Ramón. 'Montserrat Roig: The Dialectics of Castration'. *Catalan Review* 7, 2 (1993): 129–36.

Buffery, Helena and Deborah Parsons. 'Undressing Barcelona'. *Perversas y divinas. La representación de la mujer en las literaturas hispánicas: el fin de siglo y/o el fin de milenio actual.* Eds. Carme Riera, Meri Torras and Isabel Clúa. Valencia: eXCultura, 2002. Vol. II, 425–31.

Campillo, Neus. 'Quin feminisme per al segle XXI?' *Quin feminisme per al segle XXI?* Coord. Pilar Blasco. Valencia: Esquerra Unida del País Valencià, 2000. 49–55.

Canteras Murillo, Andrés. *Delincuencia femenina en España.* Madrid: Ministerio de Justicia, 1990.

Capmany, Maria Aurèlia. *Traduït de l'americà.* Barcelona: Alberti, 1959.

—— *El jaqué de la democracia.* Barcelona: Nova Terra, 1972.

—— 'El feminisme, ara'. *Dona i societat a la Catalunya actual.* Eds. Maria Aurèlia Capmany et al. Barcelona: Edicions 62, 1978. 5–28.

—— *Vés-te'n ianqui! o, si voleu, tradüit de l'americà.* Barcelona: Laia, 1980.

Caputi, Jane. 'The Pornography of Everyday Life'. *Mediated Women. Representations in Popular Culture.* Ed. Marian Meyers. Creskill: Hampton, 1999. 57–79.

Carbayo-Abengózar, Mercedes. 'Feminism in Spain. A History of Love and Hate'. *Women in Contemporary Culture. Roles and Identities in France and Spain.* Ed. Lesley Twomey. Bristol: Intellect, 2000. 111–25.

—— 'Shaping women: national identity through the use of language in Franco's Spain'. *Nations and Nationalism* 7, 1 (2001): 75–92.

Carr, Helen. 'Introduction: Genre and Women's Writing in the Postmodern World'. *From My Guy to Sci-Fi: Genre and Women's Writing in the Postmodern World.* Ed. Helen Carr. London: Pandora, 1989. 3–14.

Castells, Manuel. *The Power of Identity.* Oxford: Blackwell, 1997.

Cavadas, María José. 'Día de caza'. *República de las Letras* 47 (1996): 101–4.

Cervera, Montserrat et al. 'Reflexiones sobre el movimiento feminista de los años 80–90'. *Mientras Tanto* 48 (1992): 33–49.

Chacón, Dulce. *Cielos de barro.* Barcelona: Planeta, 2000.

Charlon, Anne. *La condició de la dona en la narrativa femenina catalana (1900–1983).* Trad. Pilar Canal. Barcelona: Edicions 62, 1990.

—— 'Dona, catalana, i a més novel·lista'. *Catalan Review* 7, 2 (1993): 41–56.

Ciplijauskaité, Biruté. *La novela femenina contemporánea (1970–1985). Hacia una tipología de la narración en primera persona.* Barcelona: Anthropos, 1988.

Clemente Díaz, Miguel. *Delincuencia femenina: un enfoque psicosocial.* Madrid: UNED, 1987.

Clover, Carol J. *Men, Women and Chain Saws: Gender in the Modern Horror Film.* London: BFI, 1992.

Cole, Cathy. *Private Dicks and Feisty Chicks. An Interrogation of Crime Fiction.* Fremantle: Curtin University Books, 2004.

Collins, Jacky and Shelley Godsland (eds.). *Mujeres malas: Women's Crime Fiction from Spain.* Manchester: Manchester Metropolitan University Press, 2005.

Colmeiro, José F. *La novela policiaca española: teoría e historia crítica.* Barcelona: Anthropos, 1994.

Connor, Walker. *Ethno-Nationalism: The Quest for Understanding.* Princeton: Princeton University Press, 1994.

Conversi, Daniele. *The Basques, the Catalans and Spain. Alternative Routes to Nationalist Mobilisation.* London: Hurst and Co., 1997.

Coward, Rosalind and Linda Semple. 'Tracking Down the Past: Women and Detective Fiction'. *From My Guy to Sci-Fi: Genre and Women's Writing in the Postmodern World.* Ed. Helen Carr. London: Pandora, 1989. 39–57.

Craig, Patricia and Mary Cadogan. *The Lady Investigates. Women Detectives and Spies in Fiction.* London: Victor Gollancz, 1981.

Crameri, Kathryn. *Language, the Novelist and National Identity in Post-Franco Catalonia.* Oxford: European Humanities Research Centre, 2000.

Cranny-Francis, Anne. 'Gender and Genre: Feminist Re-Writings of Detective Fiction'. *Women's Studies International Forum* 11:1 (1988): 69–84.

—— *Feminist Fiction. Feminist Uses of Generic Fiction.* Cambridge: Polity, 1990.

La Crónica de Guadalajara. 'El *mobbing* no está tan lejos como parece'. (17. 03. 05): np.

Cruz, Jacqueline and Barbara Zecchi. 'Más que evolución, involución: a modo de prólogo'. *La mujer en la España actual. ¿Evolución o involución?* Eds. Jacqueline Cruz and Barbara Zecchi. Barcelona: Icaria, 2004. 7–24.

Cuesta Aguado, Paz de la. 'Victimología y victimología femenina: las carencias del sistema'. *Victimología femenina: asignaturas pendientes para una nueva ciencia.* Actas 14º Curso de Verano San Roque, 12–31 julio 1993. Ed. Paz de la Cuesta Aguado. Cádiz: Universidad de Cádiz, 1993. 7–18.

Cultiaux, Yolande. 'The Shaping of a Nation: Catalan History and Historicity in Post-Franco Spain'. *Modern Roots. Studies of National Identity.* Eds. Alain Dieckhoff and Natividad Gutiérrez. Aldershot: Ashgate, 2001.

Davies, Catherine. *Contemporary Feminist Fiction in Spain. The Work of Montserrat Roig and Rosa Montero.* Oxford: Berg, 1994.

Denfeld, Rene. *The New Victorians. A Young Woman's Challenge to the Old Feminist Order.* New York: Time Warner, 1995.

Denning, Michael. *Cover Stories. Narrative and Ideology in the British Spy Thriller.* London: Routledge and Kegan Paul, 1987.

Diario Médico.com. 'Más de 2 millones de españoles sufre maltrato psicológico en el trabajo, lo que supone el 15% de los empleados en activo'. (23. 05. 03): np.

Díez Medrano, Juan. *Divided Nations. Class, Politics, and Nationalism in the Basque Country and Catalonia.* Ithaca: Cornell University Press, 1995.

DiGiacomo, Susan M. 'Images of Class and Ethnicity in Catalan Politics 1977–1980'. *Conflict in Catalonia: Images of an Urban Society.* Ed. Gary W. McDonogh. Gainesville: University Presses of Florida, 1986. 72–92.

Dilley, Kimberly J. Busybodies, *Meddlers, and Snoops. The Female Hero in Contemporary Women's Mysteries.* Westport, Conn.: Greenwood, 1998.

Dove, George. *The Police Procedural.* Bowling Green: Bowling Green Popular Press, 1982.

Dunant, Sarah. 'Body Language: a Study of Death and Gender in Crime Fiction'. *The Art of Detective Fiction.* Eds. Warren Chernaik, Martin Swales and Robert Vilain. Basingstoke: Macmillan, 2000. 10–20.

Dupláa, Cristina. '*La Ben Plantada*' o la construcción mítica de la nacionalidad catalana. Ph.D. Thesis, University of Minnesota, 1987. Ann Arbor: UMI Dissertation Information Service, 1988*a*.

—— 'Les dones i el pensament conservador català contemporani'. *Més enllà del silenci: les dones a la història de Catalunya.* Ed. Mary Nash. Barcelona: Generalitat de Catalunya, 1988*b*. 173–89.

—— 'La Ben Plantada: una propuesta ideológica orsiana'. *Perversas y divinas. La representación de la mujer en las literaturas hispánicas: el fin de siglo y/o el fin de milenio actual.* Eds. Carme Riera, Meri Torras and Isabel Clúa. Valencia: eXCultura, 2002. Vol. I, 21–7.

Edgar, Andrew and Peter Sedgwick (eds.). *Key Concepts in Cultural Theory.* London: Routledge, 1999.

Enloe, Cynthia. *Bananas, Beaches and Bases: Making Feminist Sense of International Politics.* Berkeley: University of California Press, 1989.

Espelt, Ramon. *Ficció criminal a Barcelona (1950–1963).* Barcelona: Laertes, 1998.

Estep, Rhoda. 'Women's Roles in Crime as Depicted by Television and Newspapers'. *Journal of Popular Culture* 16, 3 (1982): 151–6.

Etxebarria, Lucía. *Nosotras que no somos como las demás.* Barcelona: Debolsillo, 2000 [1999].

Falcón, Lidia. *Mujer y sociedad. Análisis de un fenómeno reaccionario.* Barcelona: Fontanella, 1969.

—— *Violencia contra la mujer.* Madrid: Vindicación Feminista, 1991.

—— *Asesinando el pasado.* Madrid: Vindicación Feminista/Kira Edit, 1997.

—— *Los nuevos mitos del feminismo.* Madrid: Vindicación Feminista, 2000.

—— 'Violent Democracy'. *Journal of Spanish Cultural Studies* 3, 1 (2002): 15–28.

—— *Las nuevas españolas. Lo que las hijas han ganado y perdido respecto a sus madres.* Madrid: La Esfera de los Libros, 2004.

Faludi, Susan. *Backlash. The Undeclared War Against Women.* London: Chatto and Windus, 1992.

—— 'Postfeminism'. *Routledge International Encyclopedia of Women.* Eds. Cheris Kramarae and Dale Spender. New York: Routledge, 2000. Vol. 3. 1646–48.

Featherstone, Mike and Scott Lash. 'Globalization, Modernity, and the Spatialization of Social Theory: an Introduction'. *Global Modernities.* Eds. Mike Featherstone, Scott Lash and Roland Robertson. London: Sage, 1995. 1–24.

Fernàndez, Josep-Anton. *Another Country. Sexuality and National Identity in Catalan Gay Fiction.* London: MHRA, Leeds: Maney, 2000.

Fernández Díaz, Natalia. *La violencia sexual y su representación en la prensa.* Barcelona: Anthropos, 2003.

Fernández Morales, Marta. *Los malos tratos a escena. El teatro como herramienta en la lucha contra la violencia de género.* Oviedo: KRK, 2002.

Flaquer, Lluís and Salvador Giner. *El debat de la cultura catalana.* Barcelona: Centre d'Estudis de Temes Contemporanis, 1991*a*.

—— *La cultura catalana: propostres teòriques i metodològiques.* Barcelona: Centre d'Estudis de Temes Contemporanis, 1991*b*.

Folguera, Pilar. 'De la Transición política a la democracia. La evolución del feminismo en España durante el período 1975–1988'. *El feminismo en España. Dos siglos de historia.* Comp. Pilar Folguera. Madrid: Pablo Iglesias, 1988. 111–31.

—— 'El franquismo. El retorno a la esfera privada (1939–1975)'. *Historia de las mujeres en España.* Ed. Elisa Garrido. Madrid: Síntesis, 1997. 527–48.

Forter, Greg. *Murdering Masculinities. Fantasies of Gender and Violence in the American Crime Novel.* New York and London: New York University Press, 2000.

Freixas, Laura. *Literatura y mujeres. Escritoras, público y crítica en la España actual.* Barcelona: Destino, 2000

Fritz, Kathlyn Ann and Natalie Kaufman Hevener. 'An Unsuitable Job for a Woman: Female Protagonists in the Detective Novel'. *International Journal of Women's Studies* 2, 2 (1979): 105–28.

Gabancho, Patrícia. *La rateta encara escombra l'escaleta. Cop d'ull a l'actual literatura catalana de dona.* Barcelona: Edicions 62, 1982.

Gamble, Sarah (ed.). *The Routledge Companion to Feminism and Postfeminism.* London: Routledge, 2001 [1998].

Gamman, Lorraine. 'Watching the Detectives. The Enigma of the Female Gaze'. *The Female Gaze. Women as Viewers of Popular Culture.* Eds. Lorraine Gamman and Margaret Marshment. London: Women's Press, 1994 [1988]. 8–26.

Garrido, Elisa. 'Democracia y cambio social. De la democracia representativa a la democracia paritaria (1975–1996)'. *Historia de las mujeres en España.* Ed. Elisa Garrido. Madrid: Síntesis, 1997. 549–71.

Gil Ruiz, Juana María. *Las políticas de igualdad en España: avances y retrocesos.* Granada: Universidad de Granada, 1996.

Giménez-Bartlett, Alicia. *Ritos de muerte.* Barcelona: Grijalbo, 1996.

—— *Día de perros.* Barcelona: Grijalbo, 1997.

—— 'Muerte en el gimnasio'. *Historias de detectives.* Ed. Ángeles Encinar. Barcelona: Lumen, 1998. 199–224.

—— 'Modelados en barro'. *Damas del crimen.* Barcelona: Comunicación y Publicaciones, 1998. 7–28.

—— *Mensajeros de la oscuridad.* Barcelona: Plaza y Janés, 1999.

—— *El misterio de los sexos.* Barcelona: Debolsillo, 2000*a*.

—— *Muertos de papel.* Barcelona: Plaza y Janés, 2000*b*.

—— 'Sin teorizar'. *El País* (29. 10. 00): np. 2000*c*.

—— *Serpientes en el paraíso.* Barcelona: Planeta, 2002.

—— 'La voz de la sangre'. *Doce cuentos cruentos.* Madrid: Suma de Letras, 2002. 18–68.

—— *Un barco cargado de arroz.* Barcelona: Planeta, 2004.

Giovannini, Maria Alessandra. 'La novel·la policíaca en la reescriptura de Maria Aurèlia Capmany'. *Maria Aurèlia Capmany: l'afirmació en la paraula.* Eds. Montserrat Palau and Raül-David Martínez Gili. Barcelona: Edicions Cossetània, 2002. 57–65.

Giralt, Alicia. *Innovaciones y tradiciones en la novelística de Lourdes Ortiz.* Madrid: Pliegos, 2001.

Glover, David. 'The Stuff Dreams Are Made Of: Masculinity, Femininity and the Thriller'. *Gender, Genre and Narrative Pleasure.* Ed. Derek Longhurst. London: Unwin Hyman, 1989. 67–83.

Godard, Barbara. 'Sleuthing: Feminists Re/writing the Detective Novel'. *Signature: Journal of Theory and Canadian Literature* 1 (1989): 45–70.

Godsland, Shelley. 'Maria-Antònia Oliver: la reescritura femenina/ feminista de la novela negra'. *Bulletin of Hispanic Studies* 79, 3 (2002*a*): 337–52.

—— 'Re-writing Eve: contesting the female function in original sin through gendered deviance in women's crime fiction from Spain'. *Revista Monográfica* XVIII (2002*b*): 161–75.

—— and Anne M. White. 'Investigating Fictions of Identity: Contemporary Catalan Crime Fiction by Women'. *Crime Scenes. Detective Narratives in European Culture since 1945*. Eds. Anne Mullen and Emer O'Beirne. Amsterdam: Rodopi, 2000. 219–27.

Grado, Mercedes de. 'Encrucijada del feminismo español: disyuntiva entre igualdad y diferencia'. *La mujer en la España actual. ¿Evolución o involución?* Eds. Jacqueline Cruz and Barbara Zecchi. Barcelona: Icaria, 2004. 25–58.

Grau, Anna. *El dia que va morir el president*. Barcelona: Empúries, 1999.

Griffin, Susan. 'Rape: The All-American Crime'. *Ramparts* 10, 3 (1971): 26–35.

Gubern, Román. 'Prólogo'. *La novela criminal*. Ed. Román Gubern. Barcelona: Tusquets, 1970.

Guibernau, Montserrat. 'Nationalism and Intellectuals in Nations without States: the Catalan Case'. *Political Studies* 48 (2000): 989–1005.

Hall, Catherine. 'Gender, Nations and Nationalisms'. *People, Nation and State. The Meaning of Ethnicity and Nationalism*. Eds. Robert Mortimer with Robert Fine. London and New York: I. B. Tauris, 1999. 45–55.

Hall, Stuart. 'Introduction: Who needs identity?' *Questions of Cultural Identity*. Eds. Stuart Hall and Paul du Gay. London: Sage, 1996. 1–17.

Hargreaves, John. *Freedom for Catalonia? Catalan Nationalism, Spanish Identity and the Barcelona Olympic Games*. Cambridge: Cambridge University Press, 2000.

Haro Tecglén, Eduardo. 'El sexo y el obispo'. *El País* (04. 02. 04): 61.

Hart, Patricia. *The Spanish Sleuth: The Detective in Spanish Fiction*. Cranbury, NJ and London: Associated University Presses, 1987.

—— 'Quan les dones investiguen'. *El Temps* (10. 03. 97): 80–1.

—— 'Introduction'. *Blue Roses for a Dead . . . Lady?* Maria-Antònia Oliver. Trans. Kathleen McNerney. New Orleans: University Press of the South, 1998. vii–xiv.

Heilbrun, Carolyn. 'Keynote Address: Gender and Detective Fiction'. *The Sleuth and the Scholar. Origins, Evolution, and Current Trends in Detective Fiction*. Eds. Barbara A. Rader and Howard G. Zettler. New York: Greenwood, 1988. 1–8.

Henseler, Christine. *Contemporary Spanish Women's Narrative and the Publishing Industry*. Urbana: University of Illinois Press, 2003.

Hermes, Joke with Cindy Stello. 'Cultural Citizenship and Crime Fiction'. *European Journal of Cultural Studies* 3, 2 (2000): 215–32.

Hogeland, Lisa Maria. *Feminism and Its Fictions. The Consciousness-Raising Novel and the Women's Liberation Movement*. Philadelphia: University of Pennsylvania Press, 1998.

Humm, Maggie. 'Feminist Detective Fiction'. *Twentieth-Century Suspense. The Thriller Comes of Age*. Ed. Clive Bloom. New York: St. Martin's Press, 1990. 237–54.

Hutchinson, John and Anthony D. Smith. 'Introduction'. *Nationalism.* Eds. John Hutchinson and Anthony D. Smith. Oxford: Oxford University Press, 1994. 3–13.

Jacobson, Stephen. 'Law and Nationalism in Nineteenth-Century Europe: The Case of Catalonia in Comparative Perspective'. *Law and History Review* 20, 2 (2002): 307–47.

Jansson, Siv. 'The Difference of Viewing: Female Detectives in Fiction and on Film'. *Sisterhoods. Across the Literature/Media Divide.* Eds. Deborah Cartmell, I. Q. Hunter, Heidi Kaye and Imelda Whelehan. London: Pluto, 1998. 149–66.

Kaplan, Cora. 'An Unsuitable Genre for a Feminist?'. *Women's Review* 8 (1986): 18–19.

Keating, Michael. *Nations against the State: The New Politics of Nationalism in Quebec, Catalonia, and Scotland.* Basingstoke: Macmillan, 1996.

—— 'Stateless Nation-Building: Quebec, Catalonia and Scotland in the Changing State System'. *Nations and Nationalities* 3, 4 (1997): 689–717.

Kelly, R. Gordon. *Mystery Fiction and Modern Life.* Jackson: University Press of Mississippi, 1998.

Kinder, Marsha. *Blood Cinema: The Reconstruction of National Identity in Spain.* Berkeley, Los Angeles, London: University of California Press, 1993.

King, Stewart. 'Role-Playing and the (De)Construction of Catalan Identities in Montserrat Roig's *L'òpera quotidiana*'. *Catalan Review* 12, 2 (1998): 37–48.

—— *Escribir la catalanidad. Lengua e identidades culturales en la narrativa contemporánea de Cataluña.* Woodbridge: Tamesis, 2005.

Klein, Kathleen Gregory. '*Habeas Corpus*: Feminism and Detective Fiction'. *Feminism in Women's Detective Fiction.* Ed. Glenwood Irons. Toronto: University of Toronto Press, 1995*a*. 171–89.

—— *The Woman Detective. Gender and Genre.* 2nd edn. Urbana: University of Illinois Press, 1995*b* [1988].

Knepper, Marty S. 'Agatha Christie – Feminist'. *The Armchair Detective* 16, 4 (1983): 398–406.

Knight, Stephen. *Form and Ideology in Crime Fiction.* London: Macmillan, 1980.

Knights, Vanessa. '¿Feminismo de la igualdad/Feminismo de la diferencia?: A Study and Bibliography of the Debate and its Implications for Contemporary Spanish Women's Narrative'. *Hispanic Research Journal* 2, 1 (2001): 27–43.

Larumbe, María Ángeles. *Una inmensa minoría. Influencia y feminismo en la Transición.* Zaragoza: Prensas Universitarias de Zaragoza, 2002.

—— *Las que dijeron no. Palabra y acción del feminismo en la Transición.* Zaragoza: Prensas Universitarias de Zaragoza, 2004.

Lawrence, Barbara. 'Female Detectives: The Feminist – Anti-Feminist Debate'. *Clues* 3, 1 (1982): 38–48.

Lehman, David. *The Perfect Murder. A Study in Detection.* Ann Arbor: University of Michigan Press, 2000.

Levine, Linda Gould. 'Feminismo y repercusiones sociales: de la Transición a la actualidad'. *La mujer en la España actual. ¿Evolución o involución?* Eds. Jacqueline Cruz and Barbara Zecchi. Barcelona: Icaria, 2004. 59–72.

Lister, Ruth. *Citizenship. Feminist Perspectives.* Basingstoke: Macmillan, 1997.

Littler, Alison. 'Marele Day's "Cold Hard Bitch": The Masculinist Imperatives of the Private-Eye-Genre'. *Journal of Narrative Technique* 21 (1991): 121–35.

Llobera, Josep. 'Catalan National Identity: The Dialectics of Past and Present'. *Critique of Anthropology* 10, 2–3 (1990): 11–28.

López, Francisca. *Mito y discurso en la novela femenina de posguerra en España.* Madrid: Pliegos, 1995.

Lorente Acosta, Miguel. *Mi marido me pega lo normal. Agresión a la mujer: realidades y mitos.* Barcelona: Ares y Mares, 2001.

Lorenzo Moledo, María del Mar. *La delincuencia femenina en Galicia. La intervención pedagógica.* La Coruña: Xunta de Galicia, 1997.

Ludmer, Josefina. 'Women Who Kill' (Part 1). *Journal of Latin American Cultural Studies* 10, 2 (2001): 157–69.

Luna, Joana and Elisenda Macià. 'L'associacionisme femení: catolicisme social, catalanisme i lleure'. *Més enllà del silenci: les dones a la història de Catalunya.* Ed. Mary Nash. Barcelona: Generalitat de Catalunya, 1988. 227–42.

Lynch, Karen. 'The 'Heterosexualisation' of Sadism and Masochism'. *Hecate* 29, 1 (2003): 34–46.

Maginn, Alison. 'Breaking the Contract in the Female Detective Novel: Lourdes Ortiz's *Picadura mortal*'. *Letras Femeninas* XXVIII, 1 (2002): 45–56.

Mandel, Ernest. *Delightful Murder. A Social History of the Crime Story.* London: Pluto, 1984.

Maresma Matas, Assumpció. *El complot dels anells.* Barcelona: La Magrana, 1988.

Margenat, Assumpta. *Escapa't d'Andorra.* Barcelona: Magrana, 1989.

—— *Wild Card.* Trans. Sheila McIntosh. Seattle: Women in Translation, 1992.

Mar-Molinero, Clare. *The Politics of Language in the Spanish-Speaking World.* London: Routledge, 2000.

Martí-Olivella, Jaume. 'L'escriptura femenina catalana: vers una nova tradició? *Catalan Review* 7, 2 (1993): 201–12.

Martín, Andreu and Verónica Vila-San-Juan. *Impunidad.* Barcelona: Planeta, 2005.

Martín Alegre, Sara. 'El caso de Petra Delicado: la mujer policía en las novelas de Alicia Giménez-Bartlett'. *Perversas y divinas. La representación de la mujer en las literaturas hispánicas: el fin de siglo y/o el fin de milenio actual.* Eds. Carme Riera, Meri Torras and Isabel Clúa. Valencia: Ediciones eXCultura, 2002. Vol 2. 415–21.

Mayans Natal, María Jesús. *Narrativa feminista española de posguerra.* Madrid: Pliegos, 1991.

McClintock, Anne. 'Family Feuds: Gender, Nationalism and the Family'. *Feminist Review* 44 (1993): 61–80.
——, Aamir Mufti and Ella Shohat (eds.). *Dangerous Liaisons. Gender, Nation, and Postcolonial Perspectives.* Minneapolis and London: University of Minnesota Press, 1997.
McGovern, Lynn. 'A 'Private I': The Birth of a Female Sleuth and the Role of Parody in Lourdes Ortiz's *Picadura mortal'. Journal of Interdisciplinary Literary Studies* 5, 2 (1993): 251–79.
McNerney, Kathleen. 'Introduction'. *On Our Own Behalf. Women's Tales from Catalonia.* Ed. and Intro. Kathleen McNerney. Lincoln and London: University of Nebraska Press, 1988. 1–23.
—— and Cristina Enríquez de Salamanca (eds.). *Double Minorities of Spain.* New York: MLA, 1994.
McRoberts, Kenneth. *Catalonia: nation building without a state.* Oxford: Oxford University Press, 2001.
Melgar-Foraster, Shaudin. '*L'hora violeta* y *Para no volver:* Dos lenguas, Barcelona y la mujer'. *Revista Canadiense de Estudios Hispánicos* XXVI, 1–2 (2001–2002): 155–65.
Mendoza, Eduardo, *La verdad sobre el caso Savolta.* Barcelona: Seix Barral, 1973.
Meyers, Marian. *News Coverage of Violence Against Women. Engendering Blame.* Thousand Oaks, London, New Delhi: Sage, 1997.
Mills, Sara, Lynne Pearce, Sue Spall and Elaine Millard. *Feminist Readings/ Feminists Reading.* Hemel Hempstead: Harvester Wheatsheaf, 1989.
Mínguez, Núria. *El crim d'una nit d'estiu.* Barcelona: Hogar del Libro, 1981.
Miura, Asunción. 'Presentación'. *Quién le puso a mi vida tanta cárcel.* Elena Canovas, Rubén Cobos and Juan Carlos Talavera. Madrid: Consejería de Servicios Sociales. Comunidad de Madrid, 2001. 9–10.
Mizejewski, Linda. *Hardboiled & High Heeled. The Woman Detective in Popular Culture.* London and New York: Routledge, 2004.
Molinaro, Nina L. 'Writing the Wrong Rites?: Rape and Women's Detective Fiction in Spain'. *Letras Femeninas* XXVII, 1 (2002): 100–17.
Möller-Soler, Maria-Lourdes. 'La mujer en la pre- y postguerra civil española en las obras teatrales de Carme Montoriol y de Maria Aurèlia Capmany'. *Estreno* 12, 1 (1986): 6–8.
El Mundo. 'Piden su indulto. Miles de personas acompañan a «Tani» a Alcalá-Meco'. (25. 10. 00): http://www.el-mundo.es/2000/10/25/madrid/25N0007.html.
—— 'La parricida de Melilla tenía planes de boda con su amante'. (23. 09. 05): 22.
Munt, Sally. *Murder by the book? Feminism and the crime novel.* London: Routledge, 1994.
Nash, Mary. 'Política, condició social i mobilització femenina: les dones a la Segona República i la Guerra Civil'. *Més enllà del silenci: les dones a la història de Catalunya.* Ed. Mary Nash. Barcelona: Generalitat de Catalunya, 1988. 241–64.

Navajas, Gonzalo. 1994. 'El pasado utópico en *La veu melodiosa* de Montserrat Roig'. *Revista Hispánica Moderna* XLVII, 2 (1994): 210–20.

—— *Más allá de la posmodernidad. Estética de la nueva novela y cine españoles.* Barcelona: UEB, 1996.

Nichols, Geraldine Cleary. 'Exile, Gender, and Mercè Rodoreda'. *MLN* 101, 2 (1986): 405–17.

—— *Escribir, espacio propio: Laforet, Matute, Moix, Tusquets, Riera y Roig por sí mismas.* Minneapolis: Institute for the Study of Ideologies and Literature, 1989.

—— *Des/cifrar la diferencia. Narrativa femenina de la España contemporánea.* Madrid: Siglo Veintiuno, 1992.

—— 'Ni una, ni 'grande', ni liberada: la narrativa de mujer en la España democrática'. *Del franquismo a la posmodernidad. Cultura española 1975–1990.* Ed. José B. Monleón. Madrid: Akal, 1995. 197–217.

Nogueira, Charo. 'Un estudio vincula los malos tratos a mujeres en España con la cultura patriarchal'. *El País* (11. 07. 02): 31.

Oakley, Ann. *Housewife.* London: Allen Lane, 1974.

—— *The Sociology of Housework.* Oxford: Blackwell, 1985.

O'Donnell, Hugh. 'Recounting the Nation: The Domestic Catalan *Telenovela*'. *Cultura Popular. Studies in Spanish and Latin American Popular Culture.* Eds. Shelley Godsland and Anne M. White. Oxford: Peter Lang, 2002. 243–61.

Olesti, Isabel. *El marit invisible.* Barcelona: Columna, 1999.

Oliver, Maria-Antònia. 'On ets, Mònica?' *Negre i consentida.* Ofèlia Dracs. Barcelona: Laia, 1983. 119–47.

—— 'Where Are You, Monica?' *A Woman's Eye.* Ed. Sara Paretsky. New York: Delacorte Press, 1991. 370–99.

—— *Estudi en lila.* 6th edn. Barcelona: La Magrana, 1991 [1985].

—— *Study in Lilac.* Trans. Kathleen McNerney. London: Pandora, 1987.

—— *Antípodes.* 5th edn. Barcelona: La Magrana, 1993 [1987].

—— *Antipodes.* Trans. Kathleen McNerney. Seattle: Seal Press, 1989.

—— *El sol que fa l'ànec.* Barcelona: La Magrana, 1994.

—— *Blue Roses for a Dead . . . Lady?* Trans. Kathleen McNerney. Intro. Patricia Hart. New Orleans: University Press of the South, 1998.

Ortiz, Lourdes. *Picadura mortal.* Madrid: Sedmay, 1979.

Özkırımlı, Umut. *Theories of Nationalism. A Critical Introduction.* Basingstoke: Macmillan, 2000.

Paglia, Camille. *Sex, Art and American Culture: Essays.* London: Penguin, 1993.

El País. 'Las denuncias por acoso moral se han cuadruplicado en un año'. (10. 11. 02): np.

—— 'Medio millón de españoles sufre acoso moral en el trabajo'. (28. 10. 03): np.

—— 'Los obispos relacionan la violencia doméstica con la "revolución sexual"'. (03. 02. 04): np.

—— 'Los obispos quieren llevar a la escuela su doctrina sobre sexo y violencia doméstica'. (04. 02. 04): 27.

—— 'Un dirigente episcopal vincula el divorcio con la violencia doméstica'. (23. 04. 04): np.

—— 'El registro central de maltratadores "ficha" a 90.000 hombres en dos años'. (03. 09. 05): 26.

—— 'La "envenenadora de Melilla" actuó en pleno uso de sus facultades'. (23. 09. 05): 29.

—— 'La fiscal eleva la pena para la "envenenadora de Melilla" a 84 años'. (24. 09. 05): 25.

El País Semanal. 'Asesinadas por ser mujeres'. (04. 04. 04): 45–48.

Palmer, Jerry. *Thrillers. Genesis and Structure of a Popular Genre.* London: Edward Arnold, 1978.

Palmer, Óscar. 'Entrevista: Alicia Giménez-Bartlett'. *Más libros* (verano 1999): np.

Palmer, Paulina. 'The Lesbian Thriller: Transgressive Investigations'. *Criminal Proceedings. The Contemporary American Crime Novel.* Ed. Peter Messent. London: Pluto, 1997. 87–110.

Pardo Bazán, Emilia. *Cuentos policiacos.* Sel. y pról. Danilo Manera. Madrid: Bercimuel, 2001.

Paredes Núñez, Juan (ed.). *La novela policiaca española.* Granada: Universidad de Granada, 1989.

Paretsky, Sara. 'What do Women Really Want?: An Interview with V.I.'s Creator'. *Professional Communicator* 10, 3 (1990): 12–13.

Pérez, Genaro J. 'Lo factual, facticio y feminista en *Mujer de preso* y *La chivata* de Teresa Pàmies'. *Letras Femeninas* XXIV, 1–2 (1998): 139–56.

—— *Ortodoxia y heterodoxia de la novela policíaca hispana: variaciones sobre el género negro.* Newark: Juan de la Cuesta, 2002.

Pérez, Janet. *Contemporary Women Writers of Spain.* Boston: Twayne, 1988.

Pérez Abellán, Francisco. *Ellas matan mejor. 50 crímenes cometidos por mujeres.* Madrid: Espasa Calpe, 2000.

—— *Mi marido, mi asesino. Cincuenta casos reales.* Barcelona: Martínez Roca, 2002.

Pettman, Jan Jindy. *Worlding Women: A Feminist International Politics.* London: Routledge, 1996.

Pi-Sunyer, Oriol. 'The maintenance of Ethnic Identity in Catalonia'. *The Limits of Integration: Ethnicity and Nationalism in Modern Europe.* Ed. Oriol Pi-Sunyer. University of Massachusetts, Research Reports no. 9, 1971.

Piña, Begoña. 'Julia Navarro. Con la Biblia hemos topado'. *Qué Leer* 97 (marzo 2005): 62.

Piris, Cristina. 'Guaitant el nou segle'. *Quin feminisme per al segle XXI?* Coord. Pilar Blasco. Valencia: Esquerra Unida del País Valencià, 2000. 69–77.

Plain, Gill. *Twentieth-Century Crime Fiction. Gender, Sexuality and the Body.* Edinburgh: Edinburgh University Press, 2001.

Pollino Piedras, Francisco Antonio and María del Pilar Vela Ferrero. *Delincuencia, mujer y prisión en Valladolid. Análisis social y posibles alternativas de tratamiento.* Valladolid: Ayuntamiento de Valladolid, 1999.

Pottecher, Beatriz. *Ciertos tonos del negro*. Barcelona: Lumen, 1985.

Pykett, Lyn. 'Investigating Women: The Female Sleuth after Feminism'. *Watching the Detectives. Essays on Crime Fiction.* Eds. Ian A. Bell and Graham Daldry. Basingstoke: Macmillan, 1990. 48–67.

Ramond, Michèle. '¿Qué fue de la Diosa-Madre?' *Imágenes de mujeres, images de femmes.* Eds. Bernard Fouques and Antonio Martínez González. Caen: Universidad de Caen, 1998. 45–54.

Reddy, Maureen T. *Sisters in Crime. Feminism and the Crime Novel.* New York: Continuum, 1988.

Reichert, Tom and Charlene Melcher. '*Film Noir*, Feminism, and the Femme Fatale: The Hyper-Sexed Reality of *Basic Instinct*'. *Mediated Women. Representations in Popular Culture.* Ed. Marian Meyers. Creskill: Hampton, 1999. 287–304.

Resina, Joan Ramon. 'The Link in Consciousness: Time and Community in Rodoreda's *La Plaça del Diamant*'. *Catalan Review* 2, 2 (1987): 225–46.

—— 'Detective Formula and Parodic Reflexivity: *Crim*'. *The Garden Across the Border. Mercè Rodoreda's Fiction.* Eds. Kathleen McNerney and Nancy Vosburg. Selinsgrove: Susquehanna University Press, 1994. 119–34.

—— *El cadáver en la cocina. La novela criminal en la cultura del desencanto.* Barcelona: Anthropos, 1997.

Riera, Ignasi. *Los catalanes de Franco.* Barcelona: Plaza y Janés, 1999.

Riera, Josep Maria and Elena Valenciano. *Las mujeres de los 90. El largo trayecto de las jóvenes hacia su emancipación.* Madrid: Morata, 1991.

Rivera, Milagros. *Nombrar el mundo en femenino. Pensamiento de las mujeres y teoría feminista.* Barcelona: Icaria, 1994*a*.

—— 'Feminismo de la diferencia. Partir de sí'. *El Viejo Topo* 73 (1994*b*): 31–5.

—— *El fraude de la igualdad. Los grandes desafíos del feminismo hoy.* Barcelona: Planeta, 1997.

Rodgers, Eamonn. 'Autonomous Communities'. *Encyclopaedia of Contemporary Spanish Culture.* Ed. Eamonn Rodgers. London: Routledge, 1999. 38–9.

Rodoreda, Mercè. *Crim.* Barcelona: Edicions de la Rosa dels Vents, 1936.

Rodríguez, Jesús. 'La vergüenza del maltratador'. *El País Semanal* 1436 (04. 04. 04): 38–44.

Roiphe, Katie. *The Morning After: Sex, Fear, and Feminism.* London: Hamish Hamilton, 1994.

Roldán Barbero, Horacio. 'La mujer como víctima de delitos. La influencia del pensamiento feminista en el derecho penal y la criminología'. *Perspectivas sociales y jurídicas de la mujer. del presente hacia el futuro.* Eds. María José Porro Herrera and María Dolores Adam Muñoz. Córdoba: Universidad de Córdoba, 2000. 165–89.

Rosal, Juan del. *Crimen y criminal en la novela policíaca.* Madrid: Reus, 1947.

Rubio Castro, Ana. 'El feminismo de la diferencia: los argumentos de una igualdad compleja'. *Revista de Estudios Políticos* 70 (1990): 185–207.

Ruiz, Eduardo. 'De la transgresión histórica en *La verdad sobre el caso Savolta* de Eduardo Mendoza'. *Eduardo Mendoza. A New Look.* Eds. Jeffrey Oxford and David Knutson. New York: Peter Lang, 2002. 147–58.

Sáez-Angulo, Julia. *¡Es tan fácil matar!* San Fernando de Henares: Editorial Bitácora, 1991.

Salabert, Juana. 'Lenguaje de corazones dobles'. *¿Quién mató a Harry?* Coord. Elena Butragueño and Javier Goñi. Barcelona: Plaza y Janés, 2000. 41–58.

Sanroma Aldea, Ángela. 'La violencia de género'. *La mujer como víctima: aspectos jurídicos y criminológicos.* Eds. Ana Cristina Rodríguez Yagüe and Silvia Valmaña Ochaíta. Cuenca: Universidad de Castilla La Mancha, 2000. 13–21.

Scanlon, Geraldine M. *La polémica feminista en la España contemporánea (1868–1974).* Madrid: Siglo Veintiuno, 1976.

Scott-Clark, Catherine and Adrian Levy. *The Amber Room: The Untold Story of the Greatest Hoax of the Twentieth Century.* London: Atlantic, 2004.

Sendón de León, Victoria. *Sobre diosas, amazonas y vestales. Utopías para un feminismo radical.* Madrid: Zero, 1981.

—— 'El feminismo visto por sus protagonistas'. *El feminismo en España. Dos siglos de historia.* Comp. Pilar Folguera. Madrid: Pablo Iglesias, 1988. 141–6.

SESM. 'El movimiento feminista en España. De 1960 a 1980'. *La mujer española: de la tradición a la modernidad.* Eds. Concha Borreguero et al. Madrid: Tecnos, 1986. 29–40.

Shafir, Gershon. *Immigrants and Nationalists. Ethnic Conflict and Accommodation in Catalonia, the Basque Country, Latvia, and Estonia.* Albany: SUNY Press, 1995.

Shaw, Margaret. 'Conceptualizing violence by women'. *Gender and Crime.* Eds. R. E. Dobash, R. P. Dobash and L. Noaks. Cardiff: University of Wales Press, 1995. 115–31.

Shuker-Haines, Timothy and Martha M. Umphrey. 'Gender (De)Mystified: Resistance and Recuperation in Hard-Boiled Female Detective Fiction'. *The Detective in American Fiction, Film, and Television.* Eds. Jerome H. Delamater and Ruth Prigozy. Westport, Conn: Greenwood Press, 1998. 71–82.

Simó, Isabel-Clara. *Una ombra fosca, com un núvol de tempesta.* Barcelona: Àrea, 1991.

—— *A Corpse of One's Own.* Trans. Patricia Hart. New York: Peter Lang, 1993.

Slung, Michele. 'Let's Hear It for Agatha Christie: A Feminist Appreciation'. *The Sleuth and the Scholar. Origins, Evolution, and Current Trends in Detective Fiction.* Eds. Barbara A. Rader and Howard G. Zettler. New York: Greenwood, 1988. 63–8.

Smith, Ángel and Clare Mar-Molinero. 'The Myths and Realities of Nation-Building in the Iberian Peninsula'. *Nationalism and the Nation in the Iberian Peninsula. Competing and Conflicting Identities.* Eds. Clare Mar-Molinero and Ángel Smith. Oxford: Berg, 1996.

Smith, Anthony D. *Nationalism. Theory, Ideology, History*. Cambridge: Polity, 2001.

Soler Onís, Yolanda. *Malpaís*. Santander: Ayuntamiento de Santander/ DVD Ediciones, Los Cinco Elementos, 2003.

Sommers, Christina Hoff. *Who Stole Feminism? How Women have Betrayed Women*. New York: Touchstone, 1995 [1994].

Spencer, Philip and Howard Wollman. *Nationalism. A Critical Introduction*. London: Sage, 2002.

Spires, Robert C. 'Lourdes Ortiz: Mapping the Course of Postfrancoist Fiction'. *Women Writers of Contemporary Spain. Exiles in the Homeland*. Ed. Joan L. Brown. Newark: University of Delaware Press, 1991. 198–215.

Spitzmesser, Ana Maria. 'Women's Writing in Postmodern Spain. Is There a Canon?' *Writing Women*. Ed. Alastair Hurst. Melbourne: Antípodas Monographic (La Trobe University), 2002. 77–87.

Stewart, Melissa A. 'From Ofèlia Dracs to Oliver and Fuster: Self-Reflexive Games in Catalan Detective Narrative'. *Crítica Hispánica* XXIV (2002): 181–92.

Stewart, Miranda. *The Spanish Language Today*. London: Routledge, 1999.

Stroud, Matthew D. *Fatal Union: A Pluralistic Approach to the Spanish Wife-Murder Comedias*. Lewisburg: Bucknell University Press; London: Associated University Presses, 1990.

Súñer, Maite. *Maltratadas*. Barcelona: Plaza y Janés, 2002.

Symons, Julian. *Bloody Murder. From the Detective Story to the Crime Novel: A History*. London: Faber and Faber, 1972.

Talbot, Lynn K. 'The Politics of a Female Detective Novel: Lourdes Ortiz's *Picadura mortal*'. *Romance Notes* XXXV, 2 (1994): 163–9.

Tébar, Juan. 'Novela criminal española de la transición'. *Ínsula* 464–5 (1985): 4.

Termes, Josep. *Les arrels populars del catalanisme*. Barcelona: Empúries, 1999.

Thompson, Jon. *Fiction, Crime, and Empire. Clues to Modernity and Postmodernism*. Urbana: University of Illinois Press, 1993.

Thompson-Casado, Kathleen. 'Petra Delicado: A Suitable Detective for a Feminist?' *Letras Femeninas* XXVII, 1 (2002): 71–83.

—— 'On the Case of the Spanish Female Sleuth'. *Reading the Popular in Contemporary Spanish Texts*. Eds. Shelley Godsland and Nickianne Moody. Newark: University of Delaware Press, 2004. 136–49.

Todorov, Tzvetan. 'The Typology of Detective Fiction'. *The Poetics of Prose*. Foreword Jonathan Culler. Trans. Richard Howard. Oxford: Blackwell, 1977 [1966]. 42–52.

Tomc, Sandra. 'Questing Women: The Feminist Mystery after Feminism'. *Feminism in Women's Detective Fiction*. Ed. Glenwood Irons. Toronto: University of Toronto Press, 1995. 46–63.

Tremlett, Giles. 'The View from Spain'. The *Guardian*. The *Editor* supplement (13. 07. 02): 5.

—— 'Catalans' goal divides Spain. Football pride fuels drive for autonomy'. *The Observer* (30. 04. 06): http://football. guardian.co.uk/News_Story/0,,%201764694,00.html.

Tsuchiya, Akiko. 'Gender, Sexuality, and the Literary Market in Spain at the End of the Millenium'. *Women's Narrative and Film in Twentieth-Century Spain*. Eds. Ofelia Ferrán and Kathleen M. Glenn. New York: Routledge, 2002. 238–55.

Tyras, Georges. 'Novela negra española: encuentros del tercer milenio (con Giménez Bartlett, Silva, Abasolo y Sánchez Soler)'. *Iberoamericana* II, 7 (2002): 97–110.

Ugalde, Mercedes. 'Notas para una historiografía sobre nación y diferencia sexual'. *ARENAL* 3, 2 (1996): 217–56.

Urioste, Carmen de. 'Mujer y narrativa: escritoras/escrituras al final del milenio'. *La mujer en la España actual. ¿Evolución o involución?* Eds. Jacqueline Cruz and Barbara Zecchi. Barcelona: Icaria, 2004. 197–217.

Valiente, Celia. 'Sexual Harassment in the Workplace. Equality Policies in Post-Authoritarian Spain'. *Politics of Sexuality. Identity, Gender, Citizenship*. Eds. Terrell Carver and Véronique Mottier. London: Routledge, 1998. 169–79.

Vallvey, Ángela. *La ciudad del Diablo*. Barcelona: Destino, 2005.

Vanacker, Sabine. 'V. I. Warshawski, Kinsey Millhone and Kay Scarpeta: Creating a Feminist Detective Hero'. *Criminal Proceedings. The Contemporary American Crime Novel*. Ed. Peter Messent. London: Pluto, 1997. 62–86.

Vázquez Montalbán, Manuel and Jaume Fuster. *Diàlegs a Barcelona*. Barcelona: Ajuntament de Barcelona/Laia, 1985.

Vázquez de Parga, Salvador. *La novela policiaca en España*. Barcelona: Ronsel, 1993.

—— 'El género policíaco'. *La novela popular en España*. Eds. Fernando Martínez de la Hidalga et al. Madrid: Robel, 2000*a*. 85–96.

—— *Héroes y enamoradas. La novela popular española*. Barcelona: Glénat, 2000*b*.

Veraldi, Gabriel. *La novela de espionaje*. Trans. Marcos Lara. Mexico City: Fondo de Cultura Económica, 1986.

Vosburg, Nancy. 'Genre Bending: Maria-Antònia Oliver's Catalan Sleuth'. *Letras Femeninas* XXVII, 1 (2002): 57–70.

Walton, Priscilla L. and Manina Jones. *Detective Agency. Women Rewriting the Hard-Boiled Tradition*. Berkeley: University of California Press, 1999.

Warner, Marina. *Monuments and Maidens. The Allegory of the Female Form*. London: Weidenfeld and Nicolson, 1985.

Watson, Colin. *Snobbery with Violence. Crime Stories and their Audience*. London: Eyre and Spottiswoode, 1971.

Werbner, Pnina and Nira Yuval-Davis. 'Introduction. Women and the New Discourse of Citizenship'. *Women, Citizenship and Difference*. Eds. Nira Yuval-Davis and Pnina Werbner. London and New York: Zed Books, 1999. 1–38.

West, Lois. 'Introduction'. *Feminist Nationalism*. Ed. Lois West. London and New York: Routledge, 1997. xi–xxxvi.

Whelehan, Imelda. *Modern Feminist Thought. From the Second Wave to 'Post-Feminism'*. Edinburgh: Edinburgh University Press, 1995.

Wilford, Rick. 'Women, Ethnicity and Nationalism. Surveying the Ground'. *Women, Ethnicity and Nationalism. The Politics of Transition.* Eds. Rick Wilford and Robert L. Miller. London and New York: Routledge, 1998. 1–22.

Wolf, Naomi. *Fire with Fire: The New Female Power and How to Use It.* New York: Fawcett Columbine, 1994 [1993].

Woolard, Kathryn. *Double Talk: Bilingualism and the Politics of Ethnicity in Catalonia.* Stanford: Stanford University Press, 1989.

Young, Alison. *Imagining Crime. Textual Outlaws and Criminal Conversations.* London: Sage, 1996.

Zatlin, Phyllis. 'Detective Fiction and the Novels of Mayoral'. *Monographic Review/Revista Monográfica* 3, 1–2 (1987): 279–87.

Žižek, Slavoj. *Looking Awry. An Introduction to Jacques Lacan through Popular Culture.* Cambridge, Mass: MIT Press, 1991.

Index